# STREET KIDS, STREET DRUGS, STREET CRIME

## AN EXAMINATION OF DRUG USE AND SERIOUS DELINQUENCY IN MIAMI

# CONTEMPORARY ISSUES IN CRIME AND JUSTICE SERIES

Roy Roberg, San Jose State University
Series Editor

# STREET KIDS, STREET DRUGS, STREET CRIME

## AN EXAMINATION OF DRUG USE AND SERIOUS DELINQUENCY IN MIAMI

James A. Inciardi
Ruth Horowitz
Anne E. Pottieger
*University of Delaware*

**Wadsworth Publishing Company**
Belmont, California
*A Division of Wadsworth, Inc.*

Consulting Editor: Roy R. Roberg

*Sponsoring Editor:* Cynthia C. Stormer
*Editorial Associate:* Cathleen S. Collins
*Production Coordinator:* Fiorella Ljunggren
*Production:* Cecile Joyner, The Cooper Company
*Manuscript Editor:* Micky Lawler
*Permissions Editor:* Carline Haga
*Interior Design:* John Edeen
*Cover Design:* Vernon T. Boes
*Cover Illustration:* Harry Briggs
*Typesetting:* Scratchgravel Publishing Services
*Printing and Binding:* Malloy Lithographing, Inc.

3   4   5   6   7   8   9   10—96   95   94   93

**Library of Congress Cataloging-in-Publication Data**

Inciardi, James A.
    Street kids, street drugs, street crime : an examination of drug
use and serious delinquency in Miami / James A. Inciardi, Ruth
Horowitz, Anne E. Pottieger.
    p.   cm.
    Includes bibliographical references and index.
    ISBN 0-534-19242-4
    1. Juvenile delinquency—Florida—Miami—Case studies.   2. Drug
abuse—Florida—Miami—Case studies.   3. Juvenile delinquents—
Florida—Miami—Attitudes.   I. Horowitz, Ruth, [date].
II. Pottieger, Anne E.   III. Title.
HV9016.M45153   1992
364.3'6'09759381—dc20

                                                    92-5753
                                                    CIP

# ABOUT THE AUTHORS

**James A. Inciardi** (Ph.D., New York University) is Director of the Center for Drug and Alcohol Studies at the University of Delaware, Professor in the Department of Sociology and Criminal Justice at Delaware, Adjunct Professor in the Comprehensive Drug Research Center at the University of Miami School of Medicine, and a member of the South Florida AIDS Research Consortium. Dr. Inciardi has extensive research, clinical, field, teaching, and law enforcement experience in substance abuse and criminal justice and has published some two dozen books and more than a hundred articles and chapters in the areas of substance abuse, criminology, criminal justice, history, folklore, social policy, AIDS, medicine, and law.

**Ruth Horowitz** (Ph.D., University of Chicago) is Associate Professor in the Department of Sociology at the University of Delaware and Director of the graduate programs in Sociology and Criminology. Her book *Honor and the American Dream: Culture and Identity in a Chicano Community* (Rutgers University Press, 1983) received honorable mention for the 1983 C. Wright Mills Award. She has published a number of articles on gangs and teen mothers.

**Anne E. Pottieger** (Ph.D., University of Delaware) is a senior Scientist in the Center for Drug and Alcohol Studies at the University of Delaware and Visiting Assistant Professor in the Division of Criminal Justice at the University of Delaware. Dr. Pottieger has been Project Director and Co-Principal Investigator on a series of grants funded by the National Institute on Drug Abuse for research on the relationships between drug use and crime.

# FOREWORD

The Contemporary Issues in Crime and Justice Series introduces important topics that until now have been neglected or inadequately covered to students and professionals in criminal justice/criminology and related fields, including law, psychology, public administration, social work, and sociology. The volumes cover philosophical and theoretical issues and analyze the most recent research findings and their implications for practice. Consequently, each volume will stimulate further thinking and debate on the issues it covers, in addition to providing direction for policy formulation and implementation.

In their study of *Street Kids*, Inciardi, Pottieger, and Horowitz have made a significant contribution to the study of juvenile delinquency. More specifically, they have provided us with some essential baseline information regarding serious delinquency among juveniles on the streets, a topic that is currently not well understood but is growing in importance as the number of adolescents committing repeated, serious criminal offenses continues to increase.

To this end, the researchers conducted on-street interviews of some 600 active serious delinquents in 20 neighborhoods within the Miami/Dade County (Florida) metropolitan area. Serious delinquency was defined as major and/or chronic criminal behavior; over 429,000 criminal acts, of which more than 18,000 were major felonies, were committed by those interviewed in the previous 12 months! The major focus of the study was on the relationship between criminal behavior and drug involvement. The findings are both significant and alarming, as *all* of the youth interviewed had extensive histories of multiple drug use, with identifiable patterns of onset and progression. The availability and use of crack cocaine were particularly widespread, contributing to early and violent criminal activities. Surprisingly, little variation was found to exist between drug use and crime involvement with respect to age, gender, and race/ethnicity; the link, however, between serious criminality and extensive drug use was undeniable.

The book also explores the relationship between AIDS and drug use, especially of crack cocaine. Again, the findings are disturbing, as it appears that the increased use of drugs by juveniles on the street may be a contributing factor to the transmission of HIV infection. It is further apparent that educational programs relating to the risks for HIV infection are only a small part of the solution. The results of this critical work extend the general understanding of adolescents enmeshed in street life, serious crime, and drug abuse. Furthermore, these findings point the way for major policy developments and future research. Both scholars and policymakers involved in juvenile delinquency should pay careful attention to the implications of this landmark investigation.

*Roy Roberg*

# PREFACE

As is the case with most research projects, this study of serious delinquency has a history. I guess you can say it began with a phone call from Dr. Michael Backenheimer in early 1984. At the time, Mike was my project officer on a drugs/crime grant funded by the National Institute on Drug Abuse, and he was asking me to participate in an upcoming panel on juvenile crime. Although I had one paper on the topic to my credit (on delinquency in Iraq, of all things),[1] I was no expert on juvenile issues. In fact, I was only barely acquainted with the whole field of delinquency. But when the project officer at your primary funding agency asks you to participate in something, you try your best.

When I arrived at this little "panel" on April 17, 1984, I found out that I was to sit at the head table (a "raised" head table on a platform, under lights and video cameras) and was scheduled to be the discussant of a paper about to be presented by the notable delinquency researchers Delbert Elliott and David Huizinga. After finding Del Elliott and asking for a copy of the paper I had never received, I was presented with a report that should have been measured in pounds, not page numbers.[2]

I managed not only to read much of the paper but even to make a few intelligent comments, the most significant of which had to do with general lack of data on "serious delinquents." In fact, in listening to delinquency researchers throughout the two-day conference, it appeared to me that "street research" on delinquents hadn't been done for quite some time. After the conference I checked the literature and, *lo*, with the exception of a few very small studies, street research *hadn't* targeted delinquents for decades.

Such were the roots of the current project. Anne Pottieger and I prepared and submitted a grant application to the National Institute on

---

[1]Chambers, Carl D., and James A. Inciardi. 1971. "Deviant Behavior in the Middle East: A Study of Delinquency in Iraq." *Criminology*, 9:291–315.

[2]Elliott, Delbert S., and David Huizinga. 1984. "The Relationship between Delinquent Behavior and ADM Problem Behaviors." Paper presented at the ADAMHA/OJJDP "State of the Art" Research Conference on Juvenile Offenders with Serious Alcohol, Drug Abuse, and Mental Health Problems. Bethesda, MD, April 17–18.

Drug Abuse, and the four-year effort was funded in late 1985.[3] Ruth Horowitz joined our small research team in 1987 as our resident "delinquency expert." Miami had been selected for the research site because I had been conducting street research there since the early 1970s. When you do drug research in the same area over a lengthy period, you develop good contacts—with drug users, dealers, and traffickers; with drug counselors and treatment personnel; with police and other criminal justice authorities; and with the arms merchants, insurgents, mercenaries, executioners, groupies, and hangers-on who populate the street worlds of drug use and crime. This level of access, combined with South Florida's locus in cocaine-trafficking networks and Dade County's high rates of drug use and crime, made Miami an ideal place for a study of drug use and serious delinquency.

The primary aim of our research project—and this book—was to describe the kinds of drug use and crime that *serious* delinquents engage in, *on the street, today.* Some of what we found turned out to be phenomena never dreamed of the last time this kind of study was done: frequent cocaine use by adolescents, behaviors that put very young people at risk of death by AIDS, and chronic, extensive involvement by teenagers in for-profit crime. Because of the obvious social importance of these problems, we wanted to make the study and its findings understandable to a general audience (including, but certainly not limited to, students in juvenile delinquency courses), not just technical specialists. The book, therefore, includes several features aimed at increasing reader comprehension: discussions of earlier theory and research on delinquency and how our findings relate to them, explanations of how our research was done and what its methodological features mean for the applicability of the findings, direct quotes from some of the youths interviewed for the study to illustrate the behaviors being described, and a glossary that defines key theoretical and methodological terms used in the book and in delinquency studies in general.

## Acknowledgments

Although Anne, Ruth, and I are listed as the authors of this work, without the cooperation of many people the overall study in general, and this book in particular, would not have been possible. First, thanks must go to our project officers at the National Institute on Drug Abuse—Drs. Michael Backenheimer, Beatrice Rouse, and Mario De La Rosa. Several interviewers

[3]This research was supported by PHS Grant #RO1-DAO1827, Drug Use and Serious Delinquency, from the National Institute on Drug Abuse. The conclusions and opinions expressed are those of the authors.

assisted me on the streets of Miami: in particular, Brian Russe, Jody Rosen, and Paul Nemeth. My special thanks go out to them, and to the many street informants who provided access and completed interviews. I wish to express our gratitude also to the reviewers of the manuscript for their many helpful comments and suggestions. They are Kathleen J. Block of the University of Baltimore, Holly A. Dershem of Dawson Community College, Gregory S. Kowalski of Auburn University, and Thomas Phelps of California State University, Sacramento. For their assistance with manuscript preparation, thanks must be extended to Nancy Quillen and Jane Reynolds. Finally, I'd like to acknowledge sponsoring editor Cindy Stormer for her patience.

*James A. Inciardi*

# CONTENTS

C H A P T E R   4
## STUDYING SERIOUS DELINQUENCY
## ON THE STREET   50

C H A P T E R   5
## TEENAGE COKE HEADS, BANDITS,
## AND HUSTLERS   73

C H A P T E R   6
## STREET KIDS AND CRACK COCAINE   97

# LIST OF TABLES

# STREET KIDS, STREET DRUGS, STREET CRIME

## AN EXAMINATION OF DRUG USE AND SERIOUS DELINQUENCY IN MIAMI

# CHAPTER 1

# THE CURRENT YOUTH CRIME CRISIS

In the mid-1980s, six decades' worth of scientific research on delinquency proved dismayingly useless in explaining the latest youth crisis: crack-related crime. City newspapers across the country were reporting on 12-year-old drug dealers, sometimes as homicide victims shot for not turning over receipts to their connections. Hospitals were delivering unprecedented numbers of cocaine-addicted babies—many to adolescent mothers—and family courts were overloaded with grandmothers attempting to obtain custody of infants born to their crack-addicted daughters who were far too enmeshed in crack use and prostitution to assume parental roles. Urban and even suburban neighborhoods were being terrorized by the violence occurring near crack houses and open-air drug markets. Families were being evicted from public housing because they were unable to stop their teenagers' drug involvement before it resulted in arrest. School boards and state legislatures were discussing students' possession of the telephone-paging beepers reputed to be standard equipment for drug dealers. The already overloaded American criminal justice system was sent reeling by an increase in drug-related arrests, particularly of first-time offenders and especially of youths and women. Many community leaders were describing the crisis as an entire generation of inner-city youth "gone to hell."

Delinquency researchers were unable to describe—let alone explain—this phenomenon. The most obvious reason for this inability was that crack use exemplifies the rapidity with which drug fads can appear, spread, and cause completely unanticipated problems. But a more basic problem for delinquency researchers was that they were out of touch with "the street." As a result, their studies were lacking in three ways: (1) the few field studies undertaken in the prior twenty years had been small projects, mostly studies of particular gangs; (2) the large-sample surveys had not located enough serious delinquents in their school and household samples for separate analysis; and (3) the existing research on drugs/crime relationships was almost entirely about adult heroin addicts. Analysis of adolescent crack-related crime was thus left to journalists and politicians, for the simple reason that delinquency researchers had no data on it.

In response to this situation, a new study was designed to conduct on-street interviews with some 600 **serious delinquents**—youths under the age of 18 involved in major and/or chronic criminal behavior[1]—with particular attention to the relationship between their crimes and their drug involvement. Most of this book is a report of findings from this new study. First, however, three topics must be discussed to set the context for the project: the relationships between drug use and crime, reviewed in Chapter 3; existing explanations for teenage crime, discussed in Chapter 2; and, in the balance of this opening chapter, information about how serious a problem youth crime actually is.

That is, to what extent is there a real crisis in youth crime today? Are there statistics to back up the impressions given by mass media reports? How many youths are actually involved in serious crime? Does this number represent some large recent increase? Isn't the current situation likely to be temporary, with no long-term impact?

---

[1]Throughout this text, key terms are set in boldface and defined at their first appearance. The Glossary at the back of this volume is a compilation of these definitions.

Direct answers to such questions are simply not available. Indirect evidence, however, suggests that there is indeed a crisis, since the number of youths involved is proving to be large and is placing a severe strain on available resources for dealing with youth crime. Further, more general social factors suggest that the problem will continue for some time to come. Consider the evidence.

# THE EXTENT OF
# SERIOUS YOUTH CRIME

Only one study has ever provided an adequate national-level estimate of American youth crime: the 1976 **National Youth Survey**. Its data came from a national household probability sample of 1,725 youths who were interviewed once a year from 1977 through 1981 and a sixth time in 1984; in each case the interviews focused on offenses committed during the prior twelve months. Because the sample was representative of the total 11–17-year-old population as established by the U.S. Census, its findings for 1976 can be generalized to American youth as a whole.

The questions about criminal behavior were considerably more comprehensive than any used before. The offense categories were like those in official arrest statistics, and the survey asked for past-year total frequencies ("How many times did you . . . ?"). For analysis, the National Youth Survey defined "serious delinquency" as having committed, in the last year, at least three serious offenses (felony assault, robbery, motor vehicle theft, burglary, or a $50+ theft). For 1976, of the 1,719 youths aged 11–17 classified by delinquency type, 8.6% (146 youths) were categorized as serious delinquents (Elliott and Huizinga 1984, p. 26; also see Dunford and Elliott 1984; Elliott and Huizinga 1983; Elliott, Huizinga, and Ageton 1985; Elliott, Huizinga, and Menard 1989).

The 8.6% figure suggests a large youth crime problem—for the one year of 1976 a numerical estimate of 1 to 3 million youths involved in frequent, serious delinquency (Elliott and Huizinga 1984, p. 23). The seriousness of adolescent crime is further indicated by consideration of not only its **prevalence**—the number of criminal offenders—but also its **incidence**—the number of crime occurrences. Although only three serious crimes in the prior year were sufficient to classify youths as serious delinquents, individuals in this category actually averaged 4.6 felony assaults, 5.1 felony thefts, 3.2 robberies, 10 total serious crimes, and 118 total offenses (Elliott, Huizinga, and Menard 1989, p. 52).

These findings probably underestimated some aspects of serious delinquency and overestimated others. The underestimate comes partly from the fact that, although this survey was far superior to prior large-sample research on adolescent crime, it was a household survey rather than a street study. Consequently, it necessarily missed those youths so enmeshed in an active street life as to be in their parents' homes only rarely, as well as those living on their own in makeshift or transient circumstances. It also omitted youths removed from their homes to correctional institutions or residential drug treatment facilities.

Furthermore, the restriction of "serious delinquency" to major crimes against persons and property excludes youngsters committing high numbers of offenses such as drug sales and prostitution. These legally less serious crimes can be more damaging to the youth's own life in terms of both physical safety and potential immersion in a criminal lifestyle. On the other hand, this omission may be quite small, because it appears that almost all such offenders also commit at least three "serious" crimes. In the 1976 National Youth Survey, serious delinquents committed 82% of all such "illegal services" reported for the entire sample (Elliott, Huizinga, and Menard 1989, p. 54).

These various underestimates for the prevalence (and especially the incidence) of serious delinquency may be somewhat balanced out by an overestimate: the generosity of the study's definitions for "serious" offenses. Thus, if the definitional level were raised from three serious crimes in a year to ten, for example, but the sample also included delinquents not in conventional households plus those committing high numbers of only lesser crimes, the prevalence rate might be just a bit lower than the 8.6% reported.

Since the 1976 National Youth Survey, the only source of national-level crime statistics covering the entire youth population has been the arrest statistics in the *Uniform Crime Reports (UCR)*. This is a nationwide compilation of crime and arrest data from local police departments, compiled each year by the Federal Bureau of Investigation (FBI). These statistics are reported in two categories. **Part I offenses** (also referred to as **Index offenses**, because they are used to construct the national Crime Index) are the most serious crimes against both persons (homicide, forcible rape, aggravated assault, and robbery) and property (burglary, motor vehicle theft, arson, and larceny/theft). **Part II offenses** include lesser crimes against persons or property: other assaults (those not involving weapons or injury), forgery, fraud, embezzlement, stolen goods offenses, and vandalism. However, most Part II categories are **public order offenses**—violations of laws designed to protect general public safety and moral standards, as opposed to property or persons; these crimes involve alcohol and other drugs, prostitution, gambling, possession of weapons, and a wide range of minor nuisance behaviors such as loitering and disorderly conduct.

The *UCR* statistics, like the National Youth Survey, suggest a high incidence of youth crime. In 1990 alone, almost 1.8 million arrests were made among persons under age 18—including more than 650,000 arrests for Index offenses. The latter figure means that 28% of all arrests for the most serious crimes were of persons age 17 and under (hereafter, "youths"); offenders age 18 and 19 add another 11% to the total (Federal Bureau of Investigation 1991, p. 184). These percentages are even more impressive when one notes that, in the National Youth Survey, only 24% of the 1976–1978 *chronic* serious delinquents—those identified as serious delinquents for two or more consecutive years—were *arrested* for even one of their offenses during this time period. Similarly, only 22% of youths who committed twenty or more Index offenses in 1976 or 1978 were arrested, and only one of them was arrested for an Index offense (Dunford and Elliott 1984). However, analyses of arrest trend data suggest relatively little change in overall rates of youth Index crime since the 1976 National Youth Survey was done (Cook and Laub 1986; Osgood et al. 1989; Strasburg 1984). That is, if 11–17-year-olds were surveyed today, these analyses indicate no reason to expect a significantly different estimate.

# JUVENILE JUSTICE CRISIS INDICATORS

To suggest that the 1976 National Youth Survey remains adequate as an estimate of youth Index crime, however, is not the same as saying there is no evidence of a new crisis in serious delinquency. Even arrest trends, looked at somewhat more specifically, imply that there is indeed a new problem. The five-year arrest trends in the most recent *Uniform Crime Reports* coincide with the first five years following the initial popularity of crack use: 1986–1990 (Federal Bureau of Investigation 1991, pp. 180–181). This information shows three trends of particular relevance to the subject of crack use and youth crime.

The most obvious is the marked increase in youth arrests for violence-related behaviors between 1986 and 1990. As shown in Table 1.1, arrests of both males and females under age 18 increased for homicide, robbery, aggravated assault, and total violent Index offenses, as well as for the three Part II violence-related offenses of other assaults, weapons offenses, and disorderly conduct.

**TABLE 1.1**
**Persons under Age 18 Arrested for Violence-Related Offenses, 1986–1990**

| Offense | Males | | | Females | | |
|---|---|---|---|---|---|---|
| | 1986 | 1990 | Percent Change | 1986 | 1990 | Percent Change |
| Homicide | 1,054 | 2,060 | +95 | 72 | 109 | +51 |
| Forcible rape | 3,884 | 4,024 | +4 | 74 | 64 | −14 |
| Robbery | 17,424 | 21,147 | +21 | 1,146 | 1,739 | +52 |
| Aggravated assault | 25,341 | 37,915 | +50 | 4,571 | 6,698 | +47 |
| Part I violence* | 47,703 | 65,146 | +37 | 5,863 | 8,610 | +47 |
| Other assaults | 57,461 | 81,366 | +42 | 17,029 | 24,635 | +45 |
| Weapons offenses | 20,304 | 26,435 | +30 | 1,340 | 1,662 | +24 |
| Disorderly conduct | 53,536 | 62,385 | +17 | 12,954 | 16,280 | +26 |

*Part I violence is all violent Index crimes—the sum of the preceding four crime types. The last three offense types are Part II crimes.

SOURCE: Table 30 (p. 181), Federal Bureau of Investigation, 1991, *Uniform Crime Reports: Crime in the United States—1990*. Washington, DC: FBI.

The second arrest indicator of interest is five-year increases in youth arrests for stolen goods offenses—25% for males and 30% for females. This Part II category is rarely singled out for attention in discussions of serious crime, but it is the most common theft-related Part II arrest among teenagers, and persons under age 18 accounted for 26% of all stolen goods arrests in 1990. The connection to serious delinquency is that this offense is a common youth crime only in high-crime urban neighborhoods. Thus, unlike shoplifting or other petty theft, it is rare among middle-class suburban teenagers. It requires either criminal contacts (to purchase stolen property) or criminal-minded enterprise (to trade or sell) and as such is by far most likely as a youth offense among adolescents most at risk of, or already involved in, serious delinquency.

Third, youth arrests for drug law violations over the 1986–1990 period, in spite of law enforcement shifts in focus from users to traffickers and dealers, decreased only slightly (2%). An especially worrisome aspect of this problem is the extent to which young teens are involved. A Gannett News Service analysis of FBI data shows that ten times as many youths age 15 and under were arrested on drug charges in 1988 as in 1984; further, the relatively minor charge of possessing marijuana dropped from 72% to 41% of drug charges for this age group while the much more serious charge of selling cocaine or opiates increased from 2% to 21% (Wilmington [Delaware] *News Journal*, December 20, 1989, p. A4).

These three increases in arrests are of particular interest in that they are compatible with what would be expected if current youth crime problems were reflecting serious drug involvement, especially crack use. The increase in drug-related arrests reflects this directly. But in addition, as is discussed in some detail in Chapter 3, a drug/crime link would predict (1) an increase in violence-related offenses, because of both drug-market involvement and physiological factors related to cocaine use; and (2) more stolen goods offenses, because in urban poverty areas they are such an easy means of financing drug use, even for very young offenders.

A further significance of these arrest increases is that they are contributing to the already enormous problems of the American correctional system, which clearly *is* in crisis. In 1989, for the first time in American history, there were a million people locked up in prisons and jails, not counting temporary holding facilities, drunk tanks, or juvenile facilities. By the end of 1990, this figure had increased by another 8% for prisons (to 771,243 inmates) and 2.5% for jails (405,320 inmates); state prisons were at least 15% over their maximum capacity, federal prisons were more than 50% over capacity, and 142 local jurisdictions with large jail populations had at least one jail under court order to reduce crowding (U.S. Department of Justice 1991a, 1991b).

This crush has also affected juvenile facilities, in large part because of increased legal punitiveness toward juveniles by both state legislators and courts (Hamparian et al. 1982; Shoemaker 1988). For example, Philadelphia's youth detention center, designed for 105 youths, held 146 near the end of 1989 and had recorded some 4,963 admissions during the year (Goodman 1989). In nearby Delaware, more than 40 youths were locked by twos and threes into single cells smaller than horse stalls in a county pretrial facility designed to hold 19; plans to move some of them to the state-run youth facility were halted because the latter was over its own capacity due to a surge in youth drug convictions (Pope 1989). This pattern can be seen all over the country; e.g., some 9,000 juveniles have been incarcerated by the California Youth Authority in facilities designed to hold 5,800, with hundreds of youths sleeping on floormats in Los Angeles County detention centers already filled well beyond capacity (Steinhart 1988).

Much of the reason for overcrowding in juvenile detention facilities, it should be noted, is political—stemming from legislators and judges attempting to deal with public perceptions of too much leniency in the juvenile justice system, plus increased difficulties in state financing of all sorts of public services and facilities, including youth detention centers. That is, the overcrowding problem is not evidence of some sort of new youth crime wave. It is, however, evidence of severe inadequacy in responding to youth crime, since it has decreased the ability of the justice system even to process and hold serious delinquents—let alone provide the educational, health, and social services many of them need.

# THE CHILD
# WELFARE CRISIS

Large numbers of serious delinquents and severely strained resources for dealing with them indicate the existence of a significant youth crime problem. That this problem is not likely to disappear soon is suggested by still another, and more general, difficulty in American society: a multifaceted crisis in "child welfare"—a term referring to the health and well-being of children and adolescents. Much of this crisis stems from two relatively new types of poverty, but there are also a multitude of other problems decreasing the chance that American youth will emerge from adolescence as healthy, contributing members of society.

The most enormous child welfare problem stems from the economic crises being experienced by inner-city communities (e.g., Duster 1987; Gibbs 1988; Joe 1987; Wilson 1987). Long-term shifts in the American economy raised typical educational requirements for employment and moved jobs from cities to suburbs, without any corresponding shift in the ability of the urban poor to qualify for employment or even get transportation to it. Furthermore, the few inner-city residents who do get good jobs move to more desirable housing as soon as possible, in large part because poverty areas are almost always high-crime-rate areas as well. This leaves behind neighborhoods in which young people have few adult role models or job-location contacts for successful employment but many youth role models for dropping out of school and participating in street life. Inner-city poverty is an old problem, but what is new—and what suggests crisis—is the possibility that the current generation of inner-city residents has become a permanent **underclass**: people with little chance to ever escape poverty. They have been locked out of the normal occupational structure of American society; whereas previous generations of urban poor held the least desirable jobs in society, this new generation has little hope of any employment.

The impact of this situation on young people is already apparent in distressingly high rates for both black adolescent unemployment (32% in 1988, compared to 13% for whites) and black children living in poverty (46% in 1987, compared to 16% for whites) (U.S. Bureau of the Census 1989). Most of these young people—like most white suburban middle-class children, as is discussed in Chapter 2—commit crimes during adolescence. But whereas most teenagers terminate illegal behavior as they move into conventional adult roles, a permanent underclass structure would by definition block entry into such roles for inner-city youth. Young men are imperiled by such a situation at an especially early age, since what minimal public support exists for the poor is aimed at women and their children, leaving young men to fend for themselves. In short, the possibility of a permanent underclass is equivalent to the possibility of a permanent major street-crime problem.

A second relatively new type of poverty (besides the solidification of an underclass) also puts children in jeopardy. This involves the growing number of children who were not born into poverty but are being forced into it, with their mothers, following parental divorce. This poverty stems from low wages for most predominantly female jobs, high percentages of men failing to pay child support, and inadequate public assistance even for emergencies like a child's illness (see Hewlett 1986; Sidel 1986). The consequences for these children include all the traditional risks of poverty, including poorer health, parents too exhausted from the struggle for economic survival to supervise them properly, poorer chances of finishing school, and low probabilities of economic success as adults.

Another prominent aspect of the child welfare crisis is the number of neglected, abused, and abandoned children. The National Committee for Prevention of Child Abuse found that, between 1980 and 1985, thirty states reported child maltreatment increases of *over 50%* and that, in 1986, at least 1,300 children died from abuse or neglect (Forer 1988). Most studies find higher rates of child maltreatment among poor than among affluent families, probably because deprivation of necessities (neglect) is the most common type of child maltreatment (see Garbarino 1989). This problem connects directly to juvenile crime, since abuse has been reported in the histories of large percentages of both incarcerated youths (Dembo, Dertke, et al. 1987; Garbarino 1989) and young prostitutes, male as well as female (Weisberg 1985). Parental violence during childhood has also been linked to subsequent violent behavior among both youths and adults, as well as to theft, vandalism, and drug involvement for children and adolescents (Hotaling, Strauss, and Lincoln 1989).

Another consequence of increased child abuse and neglect is an increase in foster-care placement—23% between 1985 and 1988 according to a congressional report (House Select Committee on Children, Youth and Families, Dec. 12, 1989, as reported by Cimons 1989). The aim of foster-home placement is to protect endangered children, but foster care has often been criticized as too poorly paid and supervised to guarantee even minimal care; many people who undertake it are thus poor or close to poor themselves, with no better way to secure an income (e.g., Forer 1988).

Even where poverty is clearly not an issue, child welfare remains problematic. Weithorn (1988) provides a dramatic example: a 450% increase in national adolescent admissions to private psychiatric hospitals between 1980 and 1984. She found that much of this increase was due to the institutionalization of "troublesome" (as opposed to seriously disturbed) youths, motivated by well-intentioned but utterly frustrated parents. The therapeutic consequences of such institutionalizations are commonly more negative than positive, sometimes to the point of being severely traumatic experiences for the adolescents involved. Economically, the problem here is underfunding of community-based (out-patient) programs while for-profit hospital corporations have multiplied, prospered, and successfully advertised.

The runaway problem is another aspect of the child welfare crisis that is especially closely linked to youth crime. A high percentage of run-aways are trying to escape from abusive homes or from placement outside the home (Garbarino 1989; Kufeldt and Nimmo 1987). Arrests of runaways increased 17% between 1984 and 1988 (Federal Bureau of Investigation 1989, p. 174), and estimates of the total number of youths involved run as high as a million each year (Boyer and James 1982; Nye and Edelbrock 1980). Community efforts to help these youngsters are scarce, and most runaways rely at least partly on crime to survive—usually petty theft, pros-titution, and drug sales (Boyer and James 1982; Edelbrock 1980; Kufeldt and Nimmo 1987; Nye 1980; Weisberg 1985).

## POSTSCRIPT

The evidence just reviewed suggests that about 8% of American youths age 12–17—some 2 million adolescents—are involved in repeated serious crimi-nal offenses. This high prevalence rate for serious delinquency is not par-ticularly new, but the latest arrest data indicate recent shifts of a troubling nature, particularly increases suggesting more violence and more serious drug involvement by young teens. To the extent that serious youth crime today is in fact related to serious drug use, these numbers and trends do suggest a crisis (a full explanation of *why* appears in Chapter 3).

More certainly, there is a crisis in the nation's capacity to deal with troubled adolescents. First, public demand for more arrests and convictions has recently cycled more young offenders into the juvenile justice system, leading to severe overcrowding of juvenile correctional facilities and a sense of desperation. Second, there is also a crisis in child welfare in this country: numerous minority children are now growing up in what may be an entrenched underclass position; even more youths are forced into pov-erty after family breakups; cases of child neglect and abuse have increased; there are critical deficiencies in community response to troubled young-sters; and large numbers of runaways are likely to need crime just to sur-vive. These assorted problems related to the child welfare crisis make it very likely that the current youth crime problem will continue well into the 1990s.

# CHAPTER 2

# DELINQUENCY RESEARCH AND THEORY

Prior delinquency research contains many ideas and findings that are helpful in understanding elements of the current youth crime crisis. One major purpose of this chapter, therefore, is to define concepts and theories that will be useful in analyzing findings from the new study; another is to discuss results and methodological problems of prior studies that will help explain the new study's sample selection and other procedures (discussed in Chapter 4). This overview is organized chronologically and focuses on research rather than on theory per se, so that it can also show how delinquency research, which began with street studies of serious youth crime, could end up so far out of touch with such studies.

## THE CHICAGO SCHOOL AND SOCIAL DISORGANIZATION

The first studies of American youth crime to combine both theory and empirical research were done by a group of sociologists often referred to as "the Chicago school," because their unique approach to social research was that taught at the University of Chicago from about 1915 into the 1940s. Their emphasis was on field research describing the various social worlds of deviants and outcasts found within the complex environment of the rapidly changing Chicago area.

The image of the delinquent presented by the Chicago school is exemplified in this description from Frederic M. Thrasher's well-known study of 1,313 gangs in Chicago during the 1920s:

Edmond Werner, fifteen, self-styled leader of the roving Northwest Side gang which carries the cognomen of the "Belmonts"—and pockets of darnicks [throwing stones]—prefaced his story of the gang fighting between the Belmonts and the Elstons, which Saturday resulted in the death of Julius Flosi, eleven, with this bitter statement today.

He told me of the innumerable battles of fists and bricks which have been staged for the possession of the lonesome bit of railroad trackage at California and Elston avenues, in the last two years, and describes how, when the two gangs realized the impotency of bare knucks [knuckles] and ragged stones, each turned to firearms.

In the show-down scrap Saturday between Werner's Belmonts and the Elstons, Flosi was killed by a bullet from a 22-caliber rifle. He was an Elston. (Thrasher 1927, p. 180)

These gangs are fairly typical of the hundreds Thrasher studied, although some more closely resembled rough and tumble play groups, few had guns, and some were more deliberately vicious or more involved in major property offenses. But this greatly varied collection of small to medium-sized youth groups had in common both their operating locale and the social background of their members. Located in a broad semicircular zone surrounding the central business district, juvenile gangs were almost entirely made up of the sons of European immigrants struggling to support their families in crowded, inner-city neighborhoods.

These same neighborhoods were identified by Clifford Shaw and Henry McKay (1942) as those with the highest percentages of boys arrested, referred to juvenile court, and committed to correctional institutions. Earlier Chicago-school researchers had called this central city area the "zone of transition," because it was the area of first settlement for new immigrants with little money and no place else to live. So many people sought work in the rapidly industrializing city that Census records show a 17-fold increase in the population of Chicago between 1850 and 1880, and another doubling by 1890. Further, both the 1890 and the 1900 Census found that more than three-fourths of the city's population was made up of foreign-born people and their children.

As families got enough money to move out, they left these crowded, broken-down neighborhoods for better places to live. But while they were still there, the crowding, lack of money, and constantly changing population contributed to a situation the Chicago school termed **social disorganization: a breakdown in the ability of families, schools, and other community-based groups and organizations to control deviant behavior**. Parental attention to economic survival and the sheer number of children in these crowded neighborhoods made supervision of youngsters difficult. Many boys were left to the influences of the streets, learning criminal values and behaviors from older youths and from gangs already existing in the area. However, as ethnic groups moved out toward the periphery of the city, into more stable, better organized communities, their rates of delinquency dropped and the next ethnic group to arrive became the next high-crime-rate group. Thus, Irish and German gangs around 1900 were replaced by Polish and Italian gangs by 1920; by 1930 some gangs were composed of the sons of black immigrants from rural areas of the South. But in all time periods the same neighborhoods were the problem areas, and youth crime took the same basic forms.

Social disorganization was also a key theme in the first major study of delinquent girls, another contribution of the Chicago school. In *The Unadjusted Girl* (1923), W. I. Thomas described rapid urbanization, immigration, and residential instability as leading to a breakdown in traditional restraints on female behavior. Small-town ideals of the mother and wife roles were no longer enforced by community expectations, gossip, and support. Girls growing up without these controls consequently received inadequate training in socially approved ways of expressing what Thomas saw as a natural female instinct toward giving and needing love; for this reason, Thomas suggested, female delinquency took the form of sexual promiscuity and prostitution. The view of female criminality as semibiological and sexuality oriented persisted in the social science literature well into the 1960s, with very little further empirical study of female delinquency compared to the amount of work done on males (see, e.g., Klein 1973; Mann 1984, pp. 55–112; Smart 1976).

Overall, the most general contribution of the Chicago school to understanding delinquency was the social disorganization perspective on the origins and persistence of youth crime. The primary emphasis of this perspective was on the difficulties parents had in transmitting conventional values to their children due to economic problems and inadequate community support. But an equally vital part of the explanation for the most serious kinds of youth crime was that juvenile and adult gangs were teaching criminal values to boys growing up in these neighborhoods. Thus, part of the "social *disorganization*" was conflict between conventional and criminal values due to the *organization* of local criminal activities. Later sociologists developed all of these ideas more fully.

The images of delinquency presented by the Chicago school influenced researchers for several decades: the female delinquent was essentially a troubled girl involved in sexual misbehavior; serious delinquency was a male behavior; and the male delinquent was a poor or working-class boy from the inner city who committed serious crime as a member of a close-knit gang. Most delinquency research and theory therefore continued to focus on gang delinquency, and the standard research methodology was the fieldwork techniques pioneered by the Chicago school.

## GANG STUDIES
## AND SOCIAL CLASS

The gang studies of the 1940s through the 1960s were fairly consistent in their description of who delinquents were and what they did. The dominant image was that of a tough group of lower-class boys involved in a variety of assault-related and property crimes and in repeated contact with the law (e.g., Cloward and Ohlin 1960; Cohen 1955; Klein 1971; Miller 1958; Short and Strodtbeck 1965; Whyte 1943). Most researchers collected their data by going to the streets and spending large amounts of time with gang members, although supplemental questionnaires were sometimes used (e.g., Short and Strodtbeck 1965).

Although these researchers agreed that serious delinquency was a lower-class phenomenon, they argued about exactly how class and crime were related. The most common view was some variety of **strain theory**: the idea that delinquency results from frustrated needs or wants. This "strain" toward delinquency is strongest for youngsters in poverty areas, it was argued, because poor youth are as oriented as middle-class youth toward the American dream of economic success, but their social class position makes it difficult for them to achieve this goal. This mismatch between culturally defined goals and socially structured means of achieving those goals was discussed earlier by Merton (1938) as one cause of "anomie," a breakdown or confusion in a society's shared standards for acceptable behavior. In a sense anomie is a more persistent and widespread form of social disorganization than the kind described by the Chicago school.

Delinquency researchers during this time period documented a variety of responses to growing up poor in a success-oriented culture. William F. Whyte (1943), in a classic study of a slum neighborhood, found that some youths ("college boys") focused on overcoming obstacles and achieving success through education and other legitimate routes, whereas others ("corner boys") gained access to the criminal enterprises already existing in the neighborhood, obtaining both income and some local status by joining in these illegal activities.

Albert K. Cohen (1955, pp. 128–130) pointed out that most corner boys adjust to the idea of becoming a conventional working-class citizen, not wishing either to be a college boy or to be involved in behaviors that would alienate them from parents and teachers. Delinquency, Cohen argued, is a third option; the delinquent is distinct from the corner boy because he engages not only in law breaking but in flagrant violation of conventional adult standards of behavior. Delinquency can be traced to the problems poor and working-class boys experience in the middle-class-oriented school system, which sometimes makes them reject not just conventional educational goals but a wide range of middle-class values. Conse-

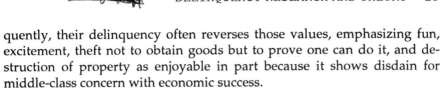

quently, their delinquency often reverses those values, emphasizing fun, excitement, theft not to obtain goods but to prove one can do it, and destruction of property as enjoyable in part because it shows disdain for middle-class concern with economic success.

Still other responses to poverty, as noted by Richard Cloward and Lloyd Ohlin (1960), are dependent on opportunities for illegitimate as well as legitimate means of getting money or status. These researchers argued that economically oriented crime by youths is thus only one form of delinquency; it is most likely in neighborhoods where adult criminal enterprises are well established and boys can be gradually brought into these already existing activities. Where such illegitimate economic opportunities are not available, delinquency is more likely to be characterized by gang wars over turf (territory) and by a value system emphasizing toughness, courage, and similar qualities that impart gang status, not money. In still other neighborhoods—typically the most totally disorganized ones—delinquent youths may abandon any achievement efforts, escaping to a "retreatist" world of heroin addiction. In all three variations, Cloward and Ohlin noted, delinquent youths from poverty areas are oriented toward achieving success or status, but not the middle-class version of it; instead, boys entering criminal gangs want big money and a flashy image, conflict-gang members want the esteem of their peers, and the addicts just want escape.

Walter Miller (1958) took still another approach to the social-class issue by arguing that, in poverty areas, all youth—not just serious delinquents—learn a set of "lower-class focal concerns" that permit or even encourage a certain amount of illegal behavior. Boys growing up in female-headed households tend to exaggerate some of these focal concerns, such as trouble and toughness, in trying to assert their masculinity. Delinquents, then, are simply corner boys who engage in these behaviors more frequently than most and happen to be selected out for police attention. Other delinquency theorists rejected much of Miller's theory, pointing out that the mass media and public education ensure that lower-class and middle-class cultures share a great many values and that serious youth crimes, such as burglary, robbery, or gang killings, violate the values of lower-class as well as middle-class people (e.g., Cloward and Ohlin 1960, pp. 68–71). But Miller's emphasis on class culture, like Cloward and Ohlin's descriptions of gang subcultures, helped to correct some erroneous impressions left by the term *social disorganization* in describing urban poverty areas. These neighborhoods are not failures at teaching values to their children; on the contrary, some delinquency is attributable to their *success* in transmitting local values and traditions.

These issues continued to be debated through the 1960s. Whereas James F. Short and Fred L. Strodtbeck (1965) argued that poverty creates socially disabled male youths who feel comfortable only with their fellow gang members, Malcolm W. Klein's (1971) participant observation study began to shift the theoretical orientation of delinquency research to the reactions of middle-class institutions to the poor. He argued that delinquency, particularly in gangs, develops among the poor in part because society treats poor youths like criminals. Klein's study thus provides some important conceptual links between the class-oriented gang studies and labeling theory, which came into prominence in the 1960s. This perspective argues that being labeled deviant can cause further deviance by affecting a person's self-concept, so that societal reactions to initial misbehaviors are more important in defining deviance than are rule-breaking behaviors themselves.

Several books written in the early 1960s revived interest in this idea, so that soon thereafter researchers began to investigate the effect of juvenile justice system processing on subsequent attitudes, self-concepts, and criminal behaviors of youths labeled delinquent (see, e.g., Shoemaker 1984, pp. 180–198). This research in turn fueled interest in how much delinquency there really was—the focus of the self-report surveys discussed next—and whether those formally labeled were representative of all delinquents. In addition to the new interest in labeling and self-report methodology, a number of social and political changes at this time made field research more difficult and dangerous than ever before (see Bookin-Weiner and Horowitz 1983); thus only a few small gang studies were done after the 1960s.

# SELF-REPORT STUDIES AND "GARDEN-VARIETY" DELINQUENCY

During the 1940s several sociologists experimented with the novel idea of studying delinquency by simply asking ordinary young people about their own past behavior. By the early 1960s, more rigorous methods were being used in this new **self-report** research, and a classic study by James F. Short and F. Ivan Nye (1958) had inspired a host of other efforts that confirmed their general findings. What these studies reported was a surprising amount of "hidden delinquency"—many more delinquent youths and much more illegal behavior than had been implied by official arrest data. Further, categories of young people who rarely appeared in arrest statistics were found to be involved in delinquent acts—girls, rural youths, whites from middle-class suburbs, grade-school children. By the mid-1970s such an extensive series of self-report studies had been done that the predominant image of the delinquent had shifted from that of a male inner-city gang member to that of a classless, placeless, ethnicless, genderless youth—the ubiquitous delinquent.

The most serious delinquents described in these studies are exemplified by Case 026 of a study in Flint, Michigan, done by Martin Gold

(1966, p. 37). A description of every offense committed by this boy in the nine months beginning May 1961 is as follows:

- one instance of trespassing with a friend (playing around in a farmer's hay loft awhile);
- six petty thefts with one stolen goods offense (two hubcaps, later sold; the net from a basketball hoop, later given away; some beer and small equipment from an unattended motorboat, the beer consumed and the other items split among the participants; two tires out of car trunks, for use by one of the other boys involved; two cases of soda pop, some consumed immediately and the rest discarded; shoplifting some small items from stores in a shopping center);
- two fights (pulling a knife on a boy who had taken his notebook and, with some other white boys, a fight with some black boys); and
- participation in two successive Saturday night drinking parties (liquor at a friend's house when the friend's parents were not at home and then beer, bought by an older boy, in a car parked behind a school).

This fairly long list of offenses is composed of ten minor crimes and three alcohol-use occasions, over a nine-month time period, and yet this boy had considerably more crime involvement than most youths described by self-report researchers. Even the fact that Gold could identify more serious offenders was unusual because of the limited crime questions typical of these studies, especially the earliest ones. Some minor criminal offenses, such as petty theft and fighting, were included, but most questions concerned **status offenses**: behaviors that have been made illegal because they violate the standards of behavior expected of children or youths, such as running away, being truant, staying out late, using alcohol, engaging in sexual behavior, and disobeying parents. These offenses are crimes only for **juveniles**— persons below the legal age of adulthood, most commonly age 18.

More problematically, crime frequency questions were generally lifetime indicators, asking if a youth "ever" had done something rather than how often (let alone how often in a specific recent time interval). The sampling procedures also restricted the number of serious offenders included; most of these studies were done in schools located in small cities (or small towns), whereas serious delinquents are most commonly dropouts or truants, living in larger cities and especially in the largest ones. In short, although these studies showed the existence of a great deal of hidden delinquency, they were not able to describe all delinquents or all delinquency patterns. Instead, what they studied was **garden-variety delinquency**: minor law violations, status offenses, and other misbehaviors that are extremely common during adolescence.

Later self-report studies (e.g., Gold 1970; Hirschi 1969; Johnson 1979) used more sophisticated methodologies and large random samples, especially as computer-assisted analysis became more common. A **random sample** is one in which every potential member of the sample has an equal chance of being included in a study; findings from a correctly drawn random sample can be used to make accurate generalizations about the much larger total population from which the sample was drawn. Random-sample survey methodology remains highly attractive to many researchers because the resulting data are amenable to powerful new statistical techniques, as well as being much less dangerous to collect and considerably less expensive per respondent than the data from street research. Thus, the great majority of delinquency studies in the 1960s and 1970s entailed large-scale questionnaire research on high school students or surveys of youth in the household population (see Hindelang, Hirschi, and Weis 1981, pp. 15–24).

But even with expanded questions and improved sampling techniques, most random-sample surveys remained appropriate to the study of only "garden-variety" rather than "serious" delinquency, for several reasons. First, although cities became the predominant research locale, school studies remained the most common sample type. This focus misses most serious delinquency because (1) both youth crime and predictors of youth crime are strongly correlated with dropping out of school, (2) dropout rates in large cities are commonly around 50% and approach 70% in some neighborhoods, and (3) delinquents who are enrolled in school have significantly higher truancy rates than other students (Fagan and Pabon 1990; Hindelang, Hirschi, and Weis 1981, p. 37; Horowitz 1983, p. 44; Kandel 1975). When the National Institute on Drug Abuse has attempted to survey entire grade cohorts on a national basis, 15–20% of each cohort must be omitted as dropouts, and 20% of the remainder do not complete the questionnaire, most often because of absence from class (Miller 1981).

Another factor that keeps serious delinquents out of random-sample studies is that both school and household surveys generally include few if any true inner-city areas and few "underclass" youth as indicated by parents receiving welfare or at least being unemployed (R. Johnson 1980; Thornberry and Farnworth 1982). Studies with better sample-selection procedures—most notably the National Youth Survey (e.g., Elliott and Huizinga 1983)—show clearly that *serious* delinquency is more common among lower-class youths than among their more affluent peers.

Finally, limited data to indicate serious crime involvement continued to confine most random-sample surveys to garden-variety delinquency. For example, Travis Hirschi's (1969) study contained over 400 questions, but only six dealt with delinquent acts that were not status offenses, and his response categories could not distinguish two lifetime offenses from 200. Similarly, Michael J. Hindelang, Travis Hirschi, and Joseph G. Weis (1981) administered an extensive questionnaire four different ways in order to test principles of self-report methodology; although these variations have made the study very important, its complete delinquency data findings are of limited utility because they were reported using "ever-lifetime" crime data ("Did you ever . . . ?") rather than the previous-year frequency counts also collected.

In spite of these limitations, random-sample self-report surveys have contributed to the study of serious delinquency in two ways. First, continued methodological improvements finally permitted an adequate estimate of the national prevalence of serious delinquency in the National Youth Survey, as previously discussed. Several other surveys have provided similarly reliable data at a more regional level—for example, in New Jersey, the Rutgers Health and Human Development Project (e.g., White, Pandina, and LaGrange 1987).

Second, the findings of self-report studies led to new theoretical efforts to explain delinquency. The repeated finding that delinquency occurs in all social classes required new explanations having little to do with strain theory, class values, or gang formation; further, new theories were necessary to explain why so many young people commit delinquent acts. Three kinds of answers were formulated out of the random-sample surveys, all of them revisions of earlier work: control theory, social learning theory, and attempts at integrated theory.

**Control theory** focuses on the personal and social factors that tend to *prevent* delinquency. Hirschi (1969) used self-report data to support his new revision of control theory, a version that has remained very influential. He defined four different ways in which people form bonds to conventional society: (1) attachments to other people—caring about their opinions and expectations; (2) commitment to conformity through investments of time, energy, past achievements, reputation, etc.; (3) involvement in conventional activities, which thus limits time for (or even thought of) deviance; and (4) belief in the legitimacy of conventional values. The fairly large number of research studies based on control theory have been especially successful in documenting the impact on delinquency of family relationships and—even more so—school experiences (see, e.g., Hirschi 1969; Shoemaker 1984, pp. 167–176).

**Social learning theory,** a second perspective, emphasizes the ways in which deviance is learned in the process of interacting with other people, just as conformity is. One element involved is **differential association:** different degrees of interaction, for particular individuals, with groups having favorable versus unfavorable attitudes toward conformity. This concept was first developed in the 1930s by Edwin H. Sutherland (1939), a sociologist from the Chicago school. The other primary element in this theory was borrowed in the 1960s from behaviorism, a psychological theory based on studies of how learning is affected by rewards and punishments. Ronald L. Akers and his associates (e.g., Akers 1977; Akers et al. 1979; Burgess and Akers 1966) combined differential association concepts with the idea of **differential social reinforcement:** different degrees of social rewards and costs (e.g., verbal expression of approval or disapproval) as a consequence of particular behaviors. Although Akers described social learning theory as compatible with the "social bonding" elements of Hirschi's control theory, most delinquency researchers (including Hirschi) have seen them as competing explanations, which has led to many empirical comparisons (for reviews, see, e.g., Akers and Cochran 1985; Elliott, Huizinga, and Ageton 1985, pp. 33–63). The results most commonly indicate that social learning of deviance in peer-group settings is a critically important factor in delinquency, although researchers disagree on whether it is important enough to totally outweigh the significance of the family and school factors emphasized by control theory. Lack of suitable data has prevented tests of the relative importance of these factors as causes of serious delinquency.

Finally, since the 1970s increasing attention has been devoted to theoretical integration: combining two, or all three, of the major perspectives on delinquency—strain theory, control theory, and social learning theory. Most of these efforts to integrate theory have used empirical methods rather than theoretical logic, performing complex statistical analyses of self-report data from large random samples of adolescents (e.g., Elliott, Huizinga, and Ageton 1985; Elliott, Huizinga, and Menard 1989, pp. 137–168; Johnson 1979; White, Pandina, and LaGrange 1987). The results of these studies are necessarily more helpful in understanding garden-variety delinquency than serious youth crime, since the samples consist of young people still in school or at least residing at home. Thus, some common findings are probably not applicable to serious delinquency—most notably the often-reported conclusion that strain/social-class variables contribute little or nothing to an overall, integrated explanation of delinquency. On the other hand, the largest household survey studies of this type have been able to locate small subsamples of serious delinquents, permitting comparative tests of garden-variety delinquency models on both serious and nonserious delinquents. These tests are discussed in the next chapter, since they concern drug/crime as well as serious/nonserious comparisons.

# RENEWED CONCERN WITH SERIOUS OFFENDERS

Whereas the dominant image of the delinquent in the early 1970s was based on random-sample self-report data, a new study based on official records renewed research interest in serious offenders: *Delinquency in a Birth Cohort*, by Marvin E. Wolfgang, Robert M. Figlio, and Thorsten Sellin (1972). The study sample was the entire cohort of 9,945 boys born in 1945 who lived in Philadelphia from at least their tenth through eighteenth birthdays. Police arrested 35% of these boys before they were 18; of those 3,475 arrestees, 627—6% of the total cohort—were "chronic" offenders (five or more arrests), who accounted for 52% of *all* arrests for the cohort. A later analysis of the same data showed that this chronic-offender group was also responsible for 70% of all cohort arrests for violent Index offenses (Hamparian et al. 1978, p. 6).

Further, a follow-up study showed that these same chronic juvenile offenders were the youths most likely to become chronic adult offenders (five or more adult arrests). When the original cohort was age 30, arrest data were obtained for a representative 10% subsample of 975 men. Results indicated that, of the 630 men never arrested as juveniles, only 3% became chronic adult offenders and 82% still had never been arrested; among the 73 chronic juvenile offenders, however, 45% were chronic adult offenders and 78% had at least one adult arrest (Wolfgang, Thornberry, and Figlio 1987, pp. 33-34).

The Philadelphia cohort project inspired several new studies of serious delinquents identified by the juvenile justice system. Many were analyses of official records kept by police, courts, or detention centers (e.g., Hamparian et al. 1978; Sorrells 1977; Strasburg 1978), but a few were inter- view studies of institutionalized offenders (e.g., Fagan, Hansen, and Jang 1983; Hartstone and Hansen 1984).

Both methodological approaches are limited. The most basic prob- lem is that they include only youths enmeshed in the justice system, al- though even *chronic* delinquents are not very likely to be arrested (Dunford and Elliott 1984). In addition, official records are problematic as a sole data source because they contain so little information; even such basic facts as numbers and types of crimes committed are lacking, since both may be considerably more extensive than indicated by a youth's arrest record. Fur- thermore, official records typically include little if any information about a delinquent's family and educational background, let alone attitudes, noncrime problems, or interpersonal relationships. Studies of institutional- ized offenders are especially troublesome, because, even more so than for arrested delinquents, it is hard to guess how many differences there are between those included in the sample and other serious delinquents. In addition, most institutionalized samples are small and have been selected to focus specifically on violent offenders.

However, the value of these studies is that they describe youths who clearly are involved in serious crime. This research has been suffi- ciently influential that, starting with Wolfgang et al.'s birth-cohort study, the image of the delinquent has shifted again, this time to that of an urban, poor, often minority male likely to have been arrested and possibly incar- cerated, often for a violent offense. Violence and dangerousness are themes repeated throughout these studies, even in the book titles: e.g., *The Violent Few: A Study of Dangerous Juvenile Offenders* (Hamparian et al. 1978) and *Violent Delinquents* (Strasburg 1978).

In "Kids Who Kill," James M. Sorrells (1977, pp. 312–313) provides an illustration of this new focus:

Eddie, fifteen, had been in trouble quite a bit, mostly for a variety of
thefts. He was attached to a particular girl, but they kept their relationship
hidden from their parents and their peers. Learning that she was seeing
another boy, he took his rifle to her house, called to her bedroom window,
and confronted her. When she confirmed his suspicions, he shot and
killed her, saying, "If I can't have you, nobody else is going to."

Eddie was one of the 31 institutionalized juveniles whose records
Sorrells studied; all were charged with homicide or attempted homicide.
This sample is too small to provide firm support for Sorrell's conclusion
that most homicide-involved youths come from unstable, violent, or argu-
mentative families and are influenced by violence in the media. However,
two of his findings—both factors that are hinted at in the portrait of
Eddie—are echoed in several other studies: (1) negative findings on psychiatric impairment and (2) an association between violence and chronicity in
the overall offense patterns of serious delinquents.

The possibility of serious mental illness as an explanation for
youth violence is raised by the very act of homicide by a fifteen-year-old
boy. But Sorrells concluded that, in general, the youngsters in his sample
were "neither disturbed in a psychiatric sense nor insane in a legal sense"
(p. 316). Similar findings were reported by Paul A. Strasburg (1978, pp.
68–69) in an analysis of court records in the New York metropolitan area
for 510 youths charged with a criminal offense (excluding individuals with
status offenses only). Of the 143 delinquents for whom psychiatric
diagnoses were available, two—1.4%—were diagnosed as psychotic and
another 9.8% were classified as having a less serious disorder variously
termed antisocial personality, psychopathology, or sociopathology. Thus,
89% of even those youths for whom psychiatric evaluation was deemed
appropriate were not found to be seriously disturbed. Since Strasburg's
total sample included 510 youths, this means that the sixteen judged
psychotic or sociopathic represented only 3% of the total, all of whom had
displayed criminal behavior serious enough to get them to the stage of a
juvenile or family court petition.

Similar conclusions were reached in an entirely different manner in
a birth-cohort study of arrest records for youths born between 1956 and
1960 who were arrested for a violent crime in Columbus, Ohio. Donna M.
Hamparian, Richard L. Schuster, Simon Dinitz, and John P. Conrad (1978)
examined repeated severe violence in the 1956–1958 cohort, which was old
enough by the end of data collection so that their juvenile arrest record was
complete; of these 811 youths, only 22—2.7%—were arrested for more than
one aggravated offense in which physical harm was threatened or afflicted.
Such a small percentage, these researchers argue, contradicts the view of
the violent delinquent as "the young monster," an obviously disturbed
youth whose predatory violence constitutes a clear danger to society and
suggests membership in some uniquely vile subspecies of humanity (pp.
130–131).

The latter approach to evaluating psychiatric impairment overlaps with the second topic common to many of these studies: offense patterns for violent delinquents. Sorrells noted that Eddie had been in trouble before he shot his girlfriend, mostly for theft. Prior trouble made Eddie typical; of the 31 homicide-involved youths in this study, 81% had at least one previous arrest and 61% had three or more. This finding corroborates the Philadelphia cohort data showing that a very small percentage of arrested youths accounted for the majority of all arrests for the cohort.

The general conclusion of a strong association between *violent* and *chronic* youth crime is reported by numerous studies (e.g., Fagan, Hansen, and Jang 1983; Hamparian et al. 1978; Hartstone and Hansen 1984; Strasburg 1978; Wolfgang, Figlio, and Sellin 1972). Relatedly, these studies report that violent youths do not specialize in violence; rather, many of their offenses (or arrests) involve property crimes or lesser offenses. Several investigators also comment on the relatively low level of seriousness of even those offenses labeled violent, stressing the extremely small number of chronically violent youths (e.g., Hamparian et al. 1978, p. 128; Strasburg 1978, pp. 5, 78).

As therefore might be expected, violence is not predictable in the careers of chronic delinquents; it might first appear almost anywhere within a delinquent's arrest history—early, middle, or late. Furthermore, if arrests are rated for offense seriousness, the trend toward increasing seriousness over a juvenile's arrest history is extremely slight (Hamparian et al. 1978; Strasburg 1978; Wolfgang, Figlio, and Sellin 1972). In short, arrest histories suggest that the distinctive element about violent delinquency patterns is not the timing of when violence first occurs, or a trend toward increasing violence, or even the total amount of violence; rather, it is the chronicity of the career in terms of length and number of *total* offenses committed.

Finally, another topic reported by most of the new studies is the sociodemographic distribution of serious delinquents. They find that, in their juvenile-justice-based samples (compared to the general youth population), there is a clear overrepresentation of males, blacks, and lower-class youths (e.g., Hamparian et al. 1978; Hartstone and Hansen 1984; Strasburg 1978; Wolfgang, Figlio, and Sellin 1972). However, more detailed analysis shows a more complex situation. For example, Wolfgang, Figlio, and Sellin (1972) emphasized that, within the Philadelphia cohort, nonwhites and lower-class youths were more likely to be both chronic offenders and serious offenders. But it can be argued that (1) race and class showed too strong an overlap to make a clear analytic separation; (2) race and class differences were not so much consistently strong or impressive as they were consistently more predictive of arrest frequency and seriousness than other variables in the study; and (3) the finding of more severe juvenile court dispositions for nonwhite and lower-class boys (controlling for seriousness and prior record) suggests a pattern of discrimination that may explain the arrest variations in the first place.

Later large studies of justice system records placed more emphasis on the complexity of the relationship between delinquency and either race or social class, noting that the existence of such relationships was highly dependent on geographical location (Hamparian et al. 1978, p. 40; Strasburg 1978, pp. 55–56). The Columbus arrest study found extremely slight differences by race in both number and type of violent offenses (Hamparian et al. 1978, pp. 54, 82). Moreover, Strasburg (1978, pp. 62–63) reported a slight tendency for youths from welfare families to have arrests for *fewer* and *less serious* offenses; he also saw less serious and less violent offenses among lower-class than among middle-class whites (but not blacks or Hispanics).

Gender findings, it might be noted, are more consistent. Although commonly excluded from serious delinquency samples (e.g., Hartstone and Hansen 1984; Wolfgang, Figlio, and Sellin 1972), girls have been included in other studies. In both the Columbus study and the New York area court petition cases, girls accounted for about one-sixth of all arrests for violent offenses, although compared to boys they were more likely to be first offenders and much less likely to have five or more arrests (Hamparian et al. 1978, pp. 44, 53; Strasburg 1978, p. 47). Interestingly, Strasburg reported no significant gender difference for his court sample in having ever been charged with a violent crime, although girls' violent offenses tended to be less serious than those by boys.

Overall, two primary contributions have been made by these various studies of serious delinquents identified by the juvenile justice system. First, they describe offense patterns for those youths involved in the justice system to a serious degree (i.e., either officially recorded as violent offenders or else into the system up to the court petition or incarceration stage). The patterns described—diversity rather than specialization, chronicity/violence overlap, lack of clear escalation over a juvenile career—are especially interesting in that they contradict some common expectations. However, it is possible that such patterns typify only officially identified serious delinquents. Worse, the described patterns might be at least partially a function of using arrests to characterize offenses. This suggests the need for a street study of serious delinquents to see whether such patterns typify offenders who are still active in the community.

The second important contribution of these studies has been the stimulus for new theory and research provided by their near-unanimous identification of inner-city youths—especially minority males—as the primary group involved in serious delinquency. As noted, these studies were not able to do much beyond making this characterization. The obvious need for explanation, however, has inspired several different kinds of new research on serious delinquency.

One approach is a kind of systematized and updated social disorganization perspective emphasizing the ways in which crime can result from such factors as population density, residential instability, housing dilapidation, and the cultural diversity of urban areas—characteristics of places, not of individuals (see, e.g., Bursik 1988; Reiss and Tonry 1986; Stark 1987). Most of this research has used police or court statistics to indicate crime, census-tract data to measure neighborhood characteristics, and complex statistical analysis to analyze crime/community relationships. Thus, it is especially weak for describing offense types that may indicate chronic criminal involvement but that have very low probabilities of arrest. On the other hand, when official statistics are combined with supplemental self-report data, some particularly powerful analyses of neighborhood factors can result, suggesting that such studies may provide new theoretical breakthroughs in the future (see Bursik 1988).

A second approach has been studies of normal adolescents in urban poverty areas. These have generally been random-sample cohort studies (e.g., Brunswick and Messeri 1985; Dembo et al. 1981; Dembo and Shern 1982), although a major on-the-street descriptive project comparing several cities has also been done (Williams and Kornblum 1985). These studies focus on the response of youths in such areas to their obviously high-risk situation. As a result, they provide far more information about the great majority of teens whose delinquency never surpasses the garden-variety stage than about serious delinquents.

A third kind of recent research related to urban youth crime has been gang studies, a topic that had been almost abandoned by the mid-1970s (Miller 1975). Most of this work is only peripherally concerned with youth crime as such, focusing instead on the internal structure and history of gangs and their relationship to the neighborhoods in which they exist (e.g., Hagedorn 1988; Horowitz 1983; Joe and Robinson 1980; Moore 1978). However, the involvement of gangs and semigang "crew" organizations in drug sales has also been studied (e.g., Fagan 1989; Mieczkowski 1986; Williams 1989); this research is discussed in Chapter 3.

Fourth and finally, a project led by Jeffrey Fagan, which was started in 1980 to develop prevention and treatment programs, has produced a number of descriptions of violent male adolescents interviewed in institutions as well as comparisons between these violent youths and two comparison samples from high-risk neighborhoods: students and dropouts, including females as well as males (e.g., Fagan, Hansen, and Jang 1983; Fagan, Piper, and Moore 1986; Fagan and Wexler 1987; Hartstone and Hansen 1984). The project has also conducted separate studies of the student and dropout subsamples (e.g., Fagan and Pabon 1990; Fagan, Weis, and Cheng 1990). Their results generally support an integrated theoretical approach of the type first formulated for random-sample surveys, but with special attention to the impact of problems that are especially common in urban poverty areas (dropping out of school, experiencing crime as a victim, and using drugs). However, this project is not an on-street study of serious delinquency, since its focus has been on prevention among high-risk youth and treatment for a highly specialized subsample of serious delinquents (chronically violent institutionalized males).

On the whole, it is significant that, throughout the renewed attention to serious youth crime, delinquency research methodology has remained oriented away from the hazards of street studies and toward the large-sample statistical analyses that came into prominence with the garden-variety delinquency studies. Much of this methodology employs large data sets drawn from official juvenile justice records; most of the rest uses random-sample approaches to study youth who are at high risk for—but not actually involved in—serious delinquency. Although such studies are helpful in theorizing about the causes of youth crime, they provide only limited information about serious delinquents active in the community today.

## POSTSCRIPT

The social science images of delinquency reviewed in this chapter are not entirely compatible with the description of the current youth crime crisis provided in Chapter 1. Especially in comparison to older views of delinquency, serious youth crime today is perhaps unique in the degree to which it is simultaneously (1) reflected in high numbers of arrests, (2) apparently drug related, and (3) committed by individual youths rather than being a gang phenomenon.

Social scientists were caught unprepared for these apparent shifts in serious delinquency, in large part because of two changes in social science itself by the 1980s: (1) the decline of field research as a major methodological approach and (2) an emphasis on data susceptible to computer methodologies, such as official-record databases or large, random-sample surveys. These approaches led to sophisticated analyses of garden-variety delinquents and youths in the juvenile justice system—but they also left researchers unable to describe, let alone explain, serious crime by youths still at large in the community. It was for these reasons that the new study described in this book undertook on-street interviews with some 600 active serious delinquents.

Two recent developments in delinquency research are especially helpful in analyzing these new data. First, the long tradition of approaching conflicting theories in a competitive comparison mode is gradually being replaced by efforts to integrate various theories in a pieces-of-the-puzzle approach. Thus far this work has focused on explaining garden-variety delinquency, because the popular methodologies make it very difficult to obtain samples of serious delinquents. The new sample provides an opportunity to apply an integrated approach to serious youth crime. Second, renewed interest in serious delinquency has resulted in several recent studies with relevant samples for comparison to the new data—youth at high risk of drug and crime involvement, arrested or institutionalized offenders, the National Youth Survey serious delinquent subsample, and the three-sample study (students, dropouts, and institutionalized violent offenders) by Fagan and his associates. Findings from these other studies provide both initial hypotheses and helpful comparisons for the new study.

Finally, it should be noted that drug topics have been discussed only briefly thus far, with at least three questions left hanging. The most basic is the significance of a drug connection for serious delinquency today, as suggested by both media reports of crack-related youth crime and youth arrest trends. This connection will be the major topic of Chapter 3. A second topic left hanging is also addressed in Chapter 3: research findings on the applicability of garden-variety delinquency explanations to serious delinquency, a question that includes trivial/serious contrasts for drug use as well as crime. The topic of transition to serious delinquency also relates to the third issue: the relevance of drug dealing (and other non-Index offenses) to *serious* delinquency, which has always been defined in terms of Index crimes. This empirical question about what serious delinquency looks like on the street today will be discussed at some length in Chapter 5 and subsequent chapters.

# CHAPTER 3

# Drugs/Crime Connections

Considering the vastness of the research literature on the connections between drug use and crime, astonishingly little is known about the impact of drug use on serious youth crime. There are three primary reasons for this information gap. One is that almost all drug/crime research has focused on heroin addicts, and entry into a full-scale heroin lifestyle most commonly begins only at age 18 or later (see, e.g., Gandossy et al. 1980; Nurco 1979). The second is that, as discussed in the last chapter, recent studies of serious delinquency have relied heavily on data from the criminal justice system, and one of the many kinds of information not found in official records is drug use histories and patterns. Third, the drug most heavily implicated in serious delinquency is not heroin but cocaine, especially cheap and ultrapotent cocaine, whose widespread availability is a relatively recent phenomenon; hence, studies of its impact on crime are just now beginning to appear.

Nonetheless, sufficient drug/crime research does exist to indicate that drug use can be a critically important factor in the illegal behavior of seriously crime-involved youths. This chapter explains why, reviewing the two primary sources of information about drug/crime connections: (1) studies of drug use in relation to garden-variety delinquency and (2) analyses of drug/crime relationships among serious offenders. First, however, the logically prior question is explored: how extensive is drug use among youth today?

# YOUTH DRUG ABUSE

The early self-report studies of delinquency rarely asked about illicit drug use. On the few occasions that they did, they found very few users. For example, the Short-Nye study did not include drug use in its final delinquency scale (Nye 1958) because having committed even one drug-law violation, ever, was reported by only 2.2% of small-city male students and by only 1% or fewer of girls and small-town boys (Short and Nye 1958). Only with the advent of the drug revolution of the late 1960s did illicit drugs—marijuana, pills, and hallucinogens—become widely available even to middle-class youth (see Inciardi 1986, pp. 1–47; Mandel and Feldman 1986; National Commission 1973).

But this transformation in American culture was not followed very rapidly by modifications in social science procedures for studying illegal behavior among adolescents. Drug questions remained rare in delinquency research throughout the 1970s. For example, the widely cited attempt at theoretical integration by Richard Johnson (1979) did not contain a single drug use item in its questionnaire. Most delinquency studies that did include drug items asked only about lifetime use ("Have you *ever* tried . . . ?"), which resulted in some high rates being reported. For example, Hindelang, Hirschi, and Weis found (1981, pp. 225–226) that over 70% of every group in their 1978–1979 sample—blacks and whites, males and females—had tried marijuana; and for the most drug-experienced group, white males, there were surprisingly high rates of lifetime involvement in drug sales (41.5%) as well as in the use of prescription depressants and stimulants (22.4%), cocaine (21.6%), and hallucinogens (16.9%). These figures, however, do not distinguish a single marijuana sale from a cocaine-dealing business or current daily use from brief experimentation two years previously.

More recent delinquency studies have typically included drug use and have asked more meaningful questions about it. But their primary contribution has been to demonstrate that a major difficulty in studying serious drug/crime problems among adolescents is the relative rarity of their joint occurrence. The National Youth Survey, as discussed in Chapter 1, defined "serious delinquency" as the commission of three or more Index offenses in the previous year. The study also included comprehensive drug use questions and defined the most serious drug use category as use, in the previous year, of alcohol *and* marijuana *and* any other drug at least four times each. These definitions reflect considerably more serious crime and drug use behaviors than could have been identified in earlier delinquency studies, although it should be noted that they tap a minimum level for "seriousness." But even at these levels, serious drug or crime involvement was rare. In 1976, of the 1,719 youths ages 11–17 interviewed, only 8.6% (146 youths) were classified as seriously delinquent and a mere 3.4% (58 youths) were multiple illicit drug users; the intersection of the two categories—serious delinquents involved in multiple illicit drug use—accounted for 1.4% of the sample (23 youths), too few cases to analyze separately (Elliott and Huizinga 1984, pp. 26, 37).

Unlike the estimate for serious crime, this figure for serious drug involvement among youth is probably too low as a current estimate, even if the definitional minimum were raised and even though general drug use prevalence rates among youth appear to have gradually declined since the beginning of the 1980s. There are six factors that make the estimate appear low: (1) annual surveys of high school seniors, (2) smaller, more specialized surveys conducted in the 1980s, (3) the National Youth Survey's limited definition of serious drug use, (4) changes in drug availability and popularity since 1976, (5) age trends for illicit drug use, and (6) American experience with treating adolescent drug problems.

A few years after the 1976 National Youth Survey, annual surveys of high school seniors began documenting a decline in serious illicit drug use, particularly the use of pills but also marijuana use, especially daily marijuana use (University of Michigan 1991). By 1986 even cocaine use began to decline. The latest survey, conducted in 1990, indicates that only 2.2% of high school seniors used marijuana on a daily basis in the prior 30 days, and 3.7% used alcohol this frequently. However, there were also indications of problems. In the previous month, 17.2% had used an illicit drug and 57.1% had used alcohol. A third of the participants admitted having five or more drinks in a row at least once in the prior two weeks. Further, during the past year, 32.5% of seniors had at least experimented with some illicit drug—including 27% with marijuana and 5.3% with cocaine (University of Michigan 1991). As George M. Beschner (1985) has noted, such statistics from high school seniors are especially troubling because they show a relatively high degree of drug involvement among youths who have attained at least this level of education. The recent overall drops in marijuana and cocaine use documented in these surveys suggest that preventive education may be working among the most successful adolescents (see Inciardi and McBride 1989). But if drug involvement is somewhat common among high school seniors, the potential problems among dropouts appear frightening, particularly in inner-city neighborhoods where street-corner crack dealers are ubiquitous.

Second, some evidence of these potential problems is provided by smaller, more specialized surveys. For example, among inner-city youth in six cities interviewed in 1985 by Fagan and his associates, illicit drug use in the previous year was reported by 30% of students but 54% of dropouts; use of cocaine, heroin, or PCP was reported by 12% of the students but 31% of the dropouts (Fagan and Pabon 1990, calculated from Table 3). It should be noted that this study shows, in addition to the very high rates for dropouts, markedly higher rates for inner-city *students* than are reflected in the national high school senior survey.

Third, restricting the definition of "serious" drug use to *only* use of multiple substances excludes heavy use of a single drug. Prior studies suggest that numerous problems, including criminal behavior, can result from heavy use by adolescents of either alcohol (e.g., Clayton 1981; White and LaBouvie 1989) or marijuana (e.g., Dembo, Washburn et al. 1987; Hendin et al. 1981). Since alcohol and marijuana are the two most commonly used drugs, even small percentages of heavy use would greatly increase the estimate of total serious drug use among adolescents.

Fourth, several changes in drug availability and popularity have occurred since the 1976 National Youth Survey. In 1976 almost all of the "other drug" category (i.e., drugs other than alcohol and marijuana) consisted of pills—prescription-type depressants and stimulants. Today, "other drug" is much more likely to mean cocaine. The considerably greater addiction potential of cocaine (discussed later in this chapter) means that youth drug use beyond alcohol and marijuana will be even more problematic. It has also been argued that marijuana, the most commonly used illicit substance, is considerably stronger today than it was in the mid-1970s (see Inciardi and McBride 1989; Lipkin 1991; Schwartz, Gruenwald, and Klitzner 1988; Wu et al. 1988; *Drug Enforcement Report*, June 8, 1989, pp. 1-2; *New York Times*, October 10, 1991, pp. A1, B4).[1]

Fifth, another change since 1976 is that age at first illicit drug use has continued to drop. This age decrease has been documented for any and all illicit drugs, including heroin and cocaine (Gandossy et al. 1980; O'Donnell et al. 1976; Washton 1987). Further, this trend has been occurring for the general youth population since the late 1960s (Green 1979; Kandel 1981) and for heroin/crime offenders since the 1950s (Greenberg and Adler 1974). This factor all by itself suggests that there may be more drug use within the total youth population now than in 1976. The young age in the National Youth Survey (from 17 all the way down to 11) is thus a major reason for the finding of serious drug use problems in only 3.4% of the sample. Further elaboration on this point is provided by a more limited study also done in 1976 in a junior high school in the South Bronx, New York. Although this was an inner-city, high-poverty-rate area, with a primarily Puerto Rican (44%) and black (40%) sample, only 6% had ever even tried drugs other than alcohol, tobacco, and marijuana (Dembo et al. 1986).

Sixth and finally, although there are no current data on adolescent admissions to drug treatment facilities—partly because there are so few treatment programs set up to handle adolescents (Beschner 1985; Shapiro 1985)—data from the Drug Abuse Warning Network (DAWN) offer some insights. DAWN monitors drug-related admissions to major hospital emergency rooms across the nation. Of the 249,349 drug emergencies reported during 1989, 13.2% involved persons under age 20 (National Institute on Drug Abuse 1990, p. 106). One expert—the former head of the Treatment Research Branch for the National Institute on Drug Abuse—has estimated

---

[1]However, the opposite argument has also been made; see Mikuriya and Aldrich (1988).

that possibly as many as 5% of all youth age 14–18 have such serious drug-related problems that they need treatment (Beschner 1985, p. 2).

To summarize, several different kinds of indicators suggest that large numbers of American youths are seriously involved in drug use, just as Chapter 1 indicated a substantial problem with serious youth crime. The fact that prior delinquency studies have located very few of these youths is a result not of an insignificant problem but, rather, of a methodological limitation. To estimate the prevalence of serious drug/crime problems, random-sample surveys of normal populations must be used. But within realistic economic limitations, the results of such a study cannot be used to study serious drug/crime problems because too few cases will be found. Interviewing 1,719 youths to locate 23 who are seriously involved in both crime and drugs (as in the 1976 National Youth Survey) is obviously not cost efficient. This problem is not confined to the study of delinquency. A representative national survey of men age 20–30 (a high heroin-usage-rate group) in 1974–1975 found only 46 current heroin users among 2,510 men interviewed (O'Donnell et al. 1976, p. 46). Alternative ways of studying serious drug/crime problems are discussed in Chapter 3.

# Drug Use and Garden-Variety Delinquency

The garden-variety delinquency studies described in Chapter 2 have produced most of the existing research on drug use among adolescents. Their findings about the drug/crime relationship will be discussed from two perspectives: (1) common-cause "deviance syndrome" theory and (2) analyses of the progression from garden-variety delinquency to serious adolescent criminal involvement.

## Common-Cause "Deviance Syndrome" Theory

Most random-sample delinquency studies that include drug use treat it as just one more form of illegal behavior, so that drug/crime interrelationships are rarely explored. They also provide relatively little information about drug use itself, since (1) questions are largely confined to alcohol and marijuana use, (2) items on current usage frequency are rarely included, and (3) drug use measures are severely limited—e.g., no use versus any use in the previous three months (Thompson, Smith-DiJulio, and Matthews 1982) or a 0-to-4 range, indicating no use to ten or more uses lifetime (Johnson, Marcos, and Bahr 1987).

But even with such weak measures, this literature as a wh[ole is] quite consistent in showing a general level association between crime and drug use—i.e., for both trivial and more serious delinquency, and both licit and illicit drugs. Consequently, the drug/crime relationship for adolescents is most often described as a matter of drug use and crime being components of a general **deviance syndrome**: a larger behavioral pattern involving deviant, rebellious, and socially problematic activities (Braucht 1980; Elliott and Ageton 1976; Jessor and Jessor 1977; Johnston, O'Malley, and Eveland 1978; Robins 1966). For example, Donovan and Jessor (1985) identify the underlying problem as "unconventionality" in both personality (e.g., a high value on independence and a tolerance of deviance) and social environment (e.g., low parental control and more models and opportunities for deviant behavior).

Efforts to explain the origin of this syndrome using general delinquency theories have often taken a competitive rather than an integrative approach. The most uniform finding of these studies is that peers have a much stronger influence on drug use than parents do (Elliott, Huizinga, and Ageton 1985; Johnson, Marcos, and Bahr 1987; Kandel, Kessler, and Margulies 1978). However, most research attempting to examine both peer/learning and social control factors in the same study finds, as one might expect, that both kinds of variables contribute to an overall explanation of deviance (Fagan, Piper, and Moore 1986; Johnson 1979; Massey and Krohn 1986; Matsueda 1982; Thompson, Smith-DiJulio, and Matthews 1982; White, Pandina, and LaGrange 1987).

A commonly discussed implication of these studies is that the drug/crime relationship among youth—at least those involved in garden-variety delinquency—is "spurious." That is, for most youths, drug use and delinquency are associated not because of a causal relationship in either direction but, rather, because both derive from common causes such as deviant peers, poor relationships with parents, and normal adolescent tendencies to experiment briefly with a wide range of behaviors. This viewpoint has its critics (e.g., Clayton 1981; Newcomb and Bentler 1988, pp. 114–115), but it appears to be growing in popularity (Fagan, Weis, and Cheng 1990; Watters, Reinarman, and Fagan 1985; White, Pandina, and LaGrange 1987).

Even if this deviance syndrome theory is correct about garden-variety drug/delinquency relationships, however, this does not mean that it can be extended to the topic of serious youth drug/crime involvement. Logically, such an extension would require a different kind of sample and different sorts of measures, so that more serious drug/crime behaviors could be located and described. Further, there is some empirical evidence of a different drug/crime relationship existing for serious versus garden-variety delinquents in two youth studies large enough to include at least moderately serious delinquents.

Helene Raskin White, Robert J. Pandina, and Randy L. LaGrange (1987) took their data from a household survey of New Jersey adolescents in which 441 males and 441 females were interviewed twice: first at age 12, 15, or 18 (in 1979–1981) and again three years later. Like many other researchers, they found several variables from both control theory and social learning theory to be related to both drug use and delinquency. But they were also interested in testing whether a "common cause" association—i.e., both drug use and delinquency relating in the same way to the same set of variables—could be found for serious drug use and serious delinquency. For their tests they used the re-interview data (hence 15-, 18-, and 21-year-olds—somewhat beyond the "youth" category of 12–17) on only the males, since so few females were in the "serious" categories. Serious delinquency was defined as either three or more Index offenses in the past three years or institutionalization, probation, or parole during that time. The serious drug use indicators included not only usage rates but also perceived adverse consequences of drug and alcohol use.

The results of the New Jersey study indicated that (1) psychological variables commonly used to explain youthful deviant behavior were significantly related only to serious drug use (particularly serious alcohol use), not to serious delinquency; (2) serious versus trivial involvement was best differentiated by somewhat different factors for drug use and delinquency; and (3) although most serious delinquents were also serious drug users, only one-third of the serious drug users were serious delinquents. White and her associates concluded that there may be an additional set of predictors not used in prior delinquency research that distinguish youth who will become seriously delinquent (and seriously drug involved) from those who will become substance abusers with little or no criminal involvement. Overall, they concluded that the "common cause" explanation of the drug/crime link for youth applies appreciably less well to serious than to garden-variety drug/crime behaviors.

A similar conclusion came from an analysis of the National Youth Survey data (Elliott, Huizinga, and Ageton 1985). Complex statistical procedures were used to build mathematical predictions for changes over time in drug/crime behaviors, and the same variables (from strain, control, and social learning theory) were found related in similar ways for general delinquency, serious delinquency, marijuana use, and hard-drug use. But the equations gave considerably better predictions for general delinquency and marijuana use than for serious crime and hard-drug use. Further, in equations to estimate *future* delinquency and drug use, one of the two best predictors was *current* delinquency and drug use—by definition, a weightier factor for serious than for garden-variety offenders. Once again, this leads directly to the question of how initially trivial delinquent behaviors progress, for a small percentage of adolescents, to serious drug/crime involvement.

## Progression beyond
## Garden-Variety Delinquency

*all other drugs on top*

Within the "deviance syndrome" of garden-variety delinquency, researchers have discovered strong tendencies toward a consistent sequence of events. Minor forms of delinquency apparently precede at least use of hard liquor and illicit drugs in this sequence, according to several intensive reviews of the literature (Elliott and Ageton 1976; Greenberg and Adler 1974; Kandel 1980), as well as more recent longitudinal studies of random samples (Elliott, Huizinga, and Menard 1989, pp. 169–190; Johnston, O'Malley, and Eveland 1978; Kandel, Simcha-Fagan, and Davies 1986). This does not mean that all youths involved in minor delinquency proceed to illicit drug use—only that the delinquency-to-drugs transition is much more common than the reverse.

Further details about drug use and delinquency transitions are clearest when each factor is taken separately, since they have only rarely been studied together (Kandel 1988). Studies of drug-type transitions are particularly numerous and especially consistent in their findings. Longitudinal and cross-sectional studies of both males and females in both adolescent and young adult populations portray the same four stages: (1) beer or wine, (2) hard liquor, (3) marijuana, and (4) other illicit substances—most commonly prescription drugs (see Kandel 1988). Further, these stages are cumulative: marijuana users continue to use alcohol; users of other illicit drugs still use both marijuana and alcohol. Again, this does not mean that youths in any given stage invariably proceed to the next one—only that a different ordering to the stages is clearly the exception.

In further contrast to the common-cause thesis of "deviance syndrome" theory, these studies also report that different types of social and behavioral factors are related to each stage. Specifically, (1) minor forms of delinquency predict use of hard liquor, (2) peer influences and youths' beliefs and values predict marijuana use, and (3) other illicit drug use is best predicted by parental influences, especially the quality of the parent/child relationship, although peer influences also remain important (Kandel, Kessler, and Margulies 1978). The least-well-understood aspect of these drug-type transitions is the role of usage frequency. It has been suggested, for example, that the transition from marijuana to other illicit drugs may be stimulated by the development of problem drinking (Donovan and Jessor 1983), as well as by more extensive use of marijuana (Kandel, Kessler, and Margulies 1978).

For delinquency a variety of different schemes have been proposed, and the idea of sequential stages is more controversial (see Kandel 1988). This is not surprising, since delinquency has only rarely been studied with follow-up interviews, and even classification of delinquency into degrees of seriousness is difficult for the many studies that could identify only nonserious behaviors. Further problems for conceptualizing delinquency stages are that most delinquency *theories* simply ignore developmental issues and that most delinquency *studies* either have little age-range variation or neglect analysis of age if they do have such data (LaGrange and White 1985; Thornberry 1987).

Again, the best available data are those of the National Youth Survey, since it was a longitudinal design with a good range of delinquency seriousness indicators. Delbert S. Elliott, David Huizinga, and Scott Menard (1989, pp. 127–130) report that data from the first five years of the National Youth Survey show a clear tendency toward progressive stages, with youths going from (1) nonoffenders to (2) exploratory delinquents, (3) nonserious delinquents, and (4) serious delinquents. From one year to the next, there was an 84% probability that a nonoffender would remain a nonoffender, but those who did become involved in delinquency were twice as likely to move to the adjacent "exploratory" category as to the next, "nonserious," type, and they almost never moved all the way to the "serious" category. Exploratory offenders, in turn, were likeliest to return to nonoffender status (a 47% probability) or to remain in the exploratory category (31%); but if they did become more delinquent, they were almost three times likelier to move to the adjacent, "nonserious," category than to "serious" delinquency. Serious offenders were quite likely (a 40% probability) to remain in that category from one year to the next. An additional status of "serious delinquent career" was defined for serious offenders who remained in that category for two or more consecutive years. Serious delinquents had a 47% chance of entering this status at some later point, compared to 4% of nonserious offenders and 2% of exploratory delinquents (Elliott and Huizinga 1984, p. 68). It should be noted that these percentages show clearly that the primary trend is for garden-variety delinquency to either remain trivial or fade away completely. However, those few delinquents who are serious offenders tend to *progress* through less serious stages first, rather than starting out as serious delinquents; further, they are the least likely to terminate criminal involvement by the time they are young adults.

The idea of progressive stages in delinquency is also supported by the repeated finding that the particular offense of drug dealing plays a significant role in increased drug/crime involvement among adolescents (Anglin and Speckart 1986; Carpenter et al. 1988, p. 44; Clayton and Voss 1981; Johnson 1973; Single and Kandel 1978). More specifically, these studies found that marijuana use is not uncommonly financed by marijuana sales—first "just to friends" and then more broadly. The contacts required to purchase sufficient marijuana for resale involve relationships with people who typically use illicit drugs other than marijuana; such contacts increase the likelihood of both use and sales of these other drugs. In a worst-case situation, the seriousness of the use/sales involvement escalates all the way to a street-addict lifestyle.

The idea of escalation is also implicit in the finding from the National Youth Survey that the proportion of serious delinquents who were serious (polydrug) drug users steadily increased over the course of the study: from 16% at the first survey (1976, age 11–17) to 49% by the fifth year (1980, age 15–21), to 70% by the time of the 1983 follow-up (Elliott, Huizinga, and Menard 1989, p. 69). In fact, by 1983 *all* serious offenders were using at least alcohol, and 92% were using illicit drugs. Because of declining delinquency rates as the sample got older, the crime/illicit drug convergence did not work the other way too: over time, *fewer* drug users were also crime involved (p. 70).

On the other hand, this reverse influence does appear in the construction of mathematical risk models for "chronic problems," defined as classification in the most serious drug or crime category for two or more years (pp. 181–187). Specifically, chronic polydrug use was predicted almost as well by prior serious delinquency as by prior polydrug use. Predictions of chronic serious delinquency were considerably stronger and simpler: prior serious delinquency was about twice as important as prior polydrug use, but the effect was apparently additive. Elliott, Huizinga, and Menard thus conclude (1989, p. 190) that the apparent effect of drug use on delinquency is to reduce the probability of dropping out of delinquent involvement over time.

At first glance, these assorted progressive-stage findings appear to contradict the common-cause deviance syndrome theory of how drug use and delinquency are related. In a deviance syndrome, sequence is a matter of happenstance and opportunity. The progressive-sequence studies, in contrast, suggest that delinquency and drug use influence each other, tend to occur in an orderly progression, and are influenced by different rather than common factors at each stage. But because these progressive stages tend to be cumulative, youths who progress further will share some traits and influences with those at earlier stages; hence, to a certain extent, different stages of drug and crime involvement also share some common causes (see Kandel 1988). In this sense, progressive-sequence studies do not so much contradict deviance syndrome theory as provide more detail about why and how both common causes and stage-specific factors affect drug use and delinquency. This kind of integrated view of their relationship has been confirmed statistically (Osgood et al. 1988), in what Kandel (1988), the most prominent drug-sequence researcher, calls a breakthrough study.

Finally, another key factor in progression beyond garden-variety delinquency is age at initiation. For crime, illicit drug use, and a variety of other deviant behaviors, younger offenders have a greater probability (and rapidity) of advancement to further degrees of involvement (Blumstein et al. 1986; Chaiken and Chaiken 1982; Clayton and Voss 1981, pp. 117–128; Petersilia, Greenwood, and Lavin 1978; Robins 1966; Wolfgang, Thornberry, and Figlio 1987). More specifically, the youths who are at greatest risk of persisting in drug/crime involvement are those who begin such behaviors at an earlier age than is typical for their peers. The specific age defining this "younger" involvement therefore varies with the specific behavior (e.g., marijuana use versus burglary), the type of sample (e.g., household versus prison), and the time variables identifying respondent age and study year (since, as discussed above, average age at initiation has tended to decrease for younger cohorts). Carpenter and her associates suggest (1988, p. 11) that, today, age 13 might be an appropriate specification for "precocious" serious crime (burglary, robbery, felony theft) or "precocious" use of drugs other than alcohol and marijuana.

In summary, although the great majority of youths involved in garden-variety delinquency never progress to serious crime, a few—perhaps 8%—become seriously delinquent at some point during adolescence. The majority of even these youths terminate criminal behavior by the time they are young adults. However, adolescents making the transition to serious crime also commonly progress to serious drug use, which increases the probability of their persisting into chronic serious criminal involvement.

# Drug/Crime Relationships for Serious Offenders

Most of what is known about drug/crime relationships among serious offenders comes from research on the classic heroin/crime interactive cycle: crime finances use; use encourages more use; more use encourages more crime (see Austin and Lettieri 1976; Gandossy et al. 1980; Inciardi 1992, pp. 135–172; McBride and McCoy 1982; Research Triangle Institute 1976; Weissman 1978). Four key elements of this cycle are discussed below, with special emphasis on their connections to cocaine (as well as heroin) and their applicability to serious delinquents (as well as adult criminals). The first two topics discussed—addiction and the need for crime to pay for it—are the most commonly recognized elements of street-addict life. The causal importance of these factors for addict careers, however, has been overemphasized compared to that of the third factor discussed: crime and drug use as two conditions of a preferred lifestyle and subculture. Finally, the significance of being high on drugs while committing crime is discussed.

## Addiction

A basic element in the classic drug/crime cycle is **addiction**. Today the most commonly accepted definition of addiction entails three characteristics: chronic use, plus compulsion, plus resulting problems (see, e.g.,

Lingeman 1974; Nelson et al. 1982; Smith 1986). Repeated use leads to a compulsion to use again, forming a behavior pattern of chronic repeated use such that the user—now an addict—*cannot* stop using even after the drug use produces severe or repeated adverse consequences, physically, psychologically, and/or socially. The driving force behind an addictive behavior pattern is either physical or psychological dependence—most commonly both, but with one predominating.

**Physical dependence** is a state in which a drug has been used in sufficient quantity over sufficient time that the user's body has changed to accommodate the presence of the drug and now requires that presence to function normally. This condition develops especially rapidly with narcotic analgesics (morphine, heroin, and other opiates) and other strong central nervous system depressants (prescription sedatives); with such drugs, stopping use can cause physical illness or even death. However, by the 1980s, scientists had documented proof that physical dependence is possible for almost every recreational drug in existence, including not only milder depressants like alcohol and minor tranquilizers but also marijuana, cocaine, prescription stimulants, and many hallucinogens (see Cohen 1988; Grinspoon and Bakalar 1985; Institute of Medicine 1982).

The term **psychological dependence** (sometimes also called "habituation") refers to a craving for the pleasurable mental effects of a drug and a strong preference for those effects over a normal state of consciousness. Although it is medically less dangerous than physical dependence, psychological drug dependence is much more difficult to combat, even with professional treatment. Most experts agree that, even though an addictive behavior pattern can be overcome, the underlying psychological dependence can never be "cured" (Carroll et al. 1987; Cohen 1985, pp. 21–31; Smith 1986; Weiss and Mirin 1987, pp. 147–148). Drugs vary in their potential for psychological dependence, depending on the type and degree of pleasure they provide. The experience of both treatment programs and laboratory studies suggests that the single most psychologically addictive drug ever known is cocaine (Arif 1987, pp. 19–20; Cohen 1987, 1988, p. 64; Erickson et al. 1987, p. 79; Extein and Dackis 1987).

Once addiction has begun, it contributes to the classic interactive drug/crime cycle in two ways. First, by definition, obtaining and using drugs are intensely compulsive preoccupations for the addict. Surprisingly little else in the addict's life is permitted to interfere with this obsession, including loved ones, legal or moral obligations, physical health, the threat of jail, or the risk of death. Among heroin addicts this kind of total drug focus might seem to be at least partially a function of the addict's typically impoverished socioeconomic circumstances. But the irrelevance of status, education, stable job histories, or other resources is demonstrated by the fact that middle-class people addicted to alcohol or cocaine exhibit the same degree of drug obsession.

Second (again by definition), use—and anything that facilitates use—leads to more use. At the very least this means solidifying an addictive behavior pattern, making it even more difficult to stop. More commonly it means a worse addiction pattern, due to increasing tolerance or withdrawal rebound problems. **Tolerance** is a particular problem for heroin users, although it also occurs, more slowly, for cocaine. As the body adjusts to a drug, more of the drug is needed to obtain the same effect. **Withdrawal rebound** problems, on the other hand, are especially likely to increase a cocaine addiction, although they also occur for addiction to narcotics such as heroin. If drug intake stops suddenly, the opposite drug effects begin to occur: instead of sedation from depressant drugs, there will be restlessness and agitation; instead of stimulation from cocaine or amphetamines, there will be severe depression (see Cohen 1988, p. 61).

Use leading to more use takes on a special force in the case of cocaine. Both the pleasure of use and the depth of the "crash" afterward are extreme; also, compared to other major recreational drugs, cocaine's whole cycle—from use to "high" to "crash"—is very rapid. Whereas four doses of heroin can maintain an addict all day, an all-day high on cocaine requires multiple uses per *hour* or less (and for *crack* cocaine, use every few minutes), typically repeated until the supply is gone. Such frequent reuse, which simply cannot occur with other drugs, makes addiction highly likely. As Sidney Cohen has commented (1987, p. 6), this process of extreme high, extreme crash, and extreme rapidity is so compelling that, if a sinister master chemist set out to design a maximally addictive drug, it would act like cocaine.

However, it should be noted that not all users of addictive drugs become addicts. Many heroin users remain occasional users for years, others give up heroin relatively easily when their surroundings change, and most people who have tried heroin have not continued into heavy use (see Nelson et al. 1982, p. 5; Zinberg 1984). The low quality of the heroin available most of the time in the majority of locales (Goldman 1981; Stephens 1987, p. 18) probably helps account for the significant minority of heroin users who use it on a sporadic basis, commonly only on weekends—a pattern known as "chipping" or "chippying." Less-than-daily use has been reported for over one-third of all heroin users, not only in street studies (Brunswick and Messeri 1985; Inciardi 1986, p. 124; Johnson et al. 1985, p. 30) but also in treatment samples (Collins, Hubbard, and Rachal 1985; McCarthy and Hirschel 1984). On the other hand, less-than-daily heroin use does not certify the absence of heroin addiction, since the physiological need can be met with prescription opiates, methadone diverted from clinics, and, to a certain extent, even nonopiate depressants such as alcohol and tranquilizers or sedatives (see Bernard 1983).

Chipping may occur with cocaine as well, but it is probably much less likely than with heroin, for several reasons. First, as previously implied, cocaine appears to produce psychological dependence more rapidly than heroin produces physiological dependence. Second, the cocaine available for street purchase is typically much more potent than is street heroin— anywhere from 10–90% for *powder* cocaine (Weiss and Mirin 1987, p. 37) and in the 5–40% range for *crack* cocaine (Inciardi 1987), as opposed to 3– 7% for heroin (Stephens 1987, p. 18).

Third, newly popular methods of administration—notably intravenous injection, freebasing, and crack smoking—increase the addictiveness of cocaine. Whereas the euphoric effects of snorting arrive gradually within three to fifteen minutes and may last up to an hour, these newer techniques have a massive impact in a matter of seconds and then end within twenty, ten, or even five minutes (Weiss and Mirin 1987, pp. 15–22). The rapidity of this cycle, the strength of the initial impact ("the rush"), and the complementary depth of the post-use crash make these routes even more rapidly addicting than snorting (Inciardi 1992, pp. 127–128).

Fourth, cocaine sales, particularly crack sales, appear to be much more common and public in many more neighborhoods than was ever the case for heroin sales, even at the height of the worst heroin epidemic. Thus, maintaining a nonaddictive cocaine use pattern is considerably more difficult than chipping heroin, especially for residents of neighborhoods where street crack sales appear to be ubiquitous.

Finally, although a variety of (cheaper) alternatives will satisfy the need for heroin, there is no comparable substitution possible for cocaine. The stimulant high produced by amphetamines and related drugs— whether in pill, intravenous, or smokable form—is neither as intense nor as pleasurable as that from cocaine.

## The Need for Crime to Pay for Drugs

A second basic element in the classic drug/crime interactive cycle is use not merely of an addictive drug but specifically of one that is too expensive to finance without resorting to crime. This specification eliminates any addiction that can be financed through ordinary legal income, even for working-class users and in most instances even for very young users: notably, alcohol, pills, and marijuana. In short, it means that the classic interactive drug/crime cycle applies in its complete form to only two drugs: heroin and cocaine.

This restriction explains the finding by several studies that, in their youth samples, drug use did not increase crime. In a recent study in New York State, most youths reported paying for their drugs out of money received from their parents for movies, lunch, and records—but the drugs in question were marijuana, alcohol, and pills (Carpenter et al. 1988, p. 220). On the other hand, the same study found that the youths involved in the largest numbers and most risky types of thefts were the heavier drug users (p. 84) and that regular drug dealers not only tended to be heavier drug users but also tended to increase their usage after they started to deal (pp. 39–59).

The best known of the studies arguing that drug use does not increase crime is the Youth in Transition cohort study (Johnston, O'Malley, and Eveland 1978), which followed drug and delinquency changes for the same youths over a seven-year period. The majority of the youths who dropped out of this study over the years were precisely those most likely to enter a crime/drug lifestyle: ones who were urban, poor, from single-parent families, and from high-delinquency neighborhoods and ones who were the more serious delinquents at the start. However, these researchers stressed that (1) delinquency preceded drug use in the lives of drug-using delinquents, (2) they found no evidence of *nonaddictive* drug use increasing criminality, and (3) generalizations to addictive use cannot be made from their study precisely because addicts were not represented in their sample.

Turning to the matter of just how much expense is involved in addictive drug use, the best evidence comes from a detailed economic study of adult heroin users in Harlem, New York City, from 1980 to 1982 (Johnson et al. 1985). About 70% of the 201 users interviewed were using heroin regularly (3–5 days per week) or daily (6–7 days); average heroin usage for these groups was three or four $10 bags a day. Eliminating days when no heroin was used, annual heroin costs thus ran from $6,431 ("regular" use) to $13,189 ("daily"). Even for a middle-class professional this expense, although not prohibitive, could be a budgetary strain. But it is well beyond the normal legal income of the much more typical heroin user—an impoverished high school dropout with, at most, a minimum-wage job—even considering the many noncriminal means of securing necessities, and the noncash means of securing drugs, typical of addicts (see Goldstein 1981; Johnson et al. 1985). Thus, the Harlem economic study found a fairly direct relationship between the size of a heroin user's habit and the amount, and seriousness, of crimes committed by the user. Similarly strong evidence of this drug/crime causal link is provided by several long-term analyses of addict careers that show much more crime for any given addict during periods of daily as opposed to lesser use (e.g., Anglin and Speckart 1986; Ball et al. 1981; McGlothlin, Anglin, and Wilson 1978).

A cocaine addiction might appear, at first glance, to be considerably cheaper than a heroin habit, particularly for cocaine in the form of crack. Half of a $5 piece of crack (a "nickel rock") can be enough to get at least a new user high. Compared to heroin, there is less physiological need for regularly spaced use of the drug throughout the entire day. Thus, a minimal crack habit might run something like $35 to $50 a week—manageable even for many teenagers. But the peculiarities of cocaine discussed earlier present two problems with this picture. One is the extreme addictiveness of crack, which makes it unlikely that a small crack habit will stay small for very long. The other is the extremely short-term duration of a cocaine high, permitting use of large numbers of doses per day. Together these factors make cocaine much more expensive than heroin for a heavy addictive use pattern.

Some specifics have been provided by the 1985 National Survey of callers to the 800-COCAINE Hotline (Washton 1987). The study found that persons experiencing enough trouble with cocaine to call the Hotline were spending an average of $535 per week on their habits, which is more than twice the weekly cost for the *daily* Harlem heroin users. Even adolescents—1% of callers in 1983 but 7% in 1985—were averaging $95 per week on cocaine in 1985. The same analysis (Washton 1987) also reports that, compared to 1983, average cost per gram and hence expense per week had decreased by 1985, but average grams used per week increased (from 6.5 to 7.2), even though fewer callers had annual incomes over $25,000 (27% rather than 40%).

Finally, an exception to the classic heroin/crime interaction pattern should be noted. Studies of heroin users often describe female addicts who do *not* need to commit crime to finance their heroin use because boyfriends or husbands provide it for them (see Bowker 1977; Ferrence and Whitehead 1980; Rosenbaum 1981, pp. 30–31). This seems likely with cocaine as well. However, Marsha Rosenbaum (1981), in a detailed study of female heroin users, found that these kinds of relationships are unstable, with drug use being a common cause of arguments leading to breakup of the relationship (pp. 88–92). Moreover, this source of drugs tends to be common only early in a woman's heroin career, so that it merely delays rather than prevents her entry into fulltime street crime (p. 55). In the case of cocaine, men again tend to control women's initial access (Morningstar and Chitwood 1987), but instability in the relationships appears even likelier because (1) cocaine's higher addiction potential means more expense will probably be involved, and (2) although heroin generally permits its users to feel and act "normal," cocaine use is much more likely to lead to personality changes, particularly increased aggressiveness (Estroff 1987; Weiss and Mirin 1987, pp. 49–52).

## Street-Addict Lifestyle and Subculture

The third basic element in the classic drug/crime cycle is by far the most important: the fact that drug use and crime are intertwined definitional characteristics of a preferred lifestyle and subculture—that of the street addict. Numerous studies of this world document that it provides heroin users with a clear identity, a role they can fulfill, activities and expected behaviors they enjoy, and the opportunity for social status among their peers (Agar 1973; Chein et al. 1964; Feldman 1968; Gould et al. 1974;

Hanson et al. 1985; Preble and Casey 1969; Rosenbaum 1981; Sutter 1966; Waldorf 1973). In the street-addict lifestyle, the most significant relationship of heroin use and crime is the most general one: both are major requirements for successfully participating in that subculture and, hence, for reaping its satisfactions and rewards.

It is important to realize that commitment to a lifestyle is considerably more important than heroin addiction per se in explaining either drug use or crime among street addicts. Thus, unwillingness to enter the street-addict lifestyle—to the point of developing rituals and values incompatible with this world, as well as keeping nonuser friends—is one way in which occasional heroin users resist addiction (Zinberg 1984, pp. 77–81). Conversely, commitment to the street-addict lifestyle is a primary reason why heroin addicts generally resist methadone-maintenance programs; being a clinic patient can satisfy a heroin habit, but it would restrict too many other elements of the addict's lifestyle. Studies of street addicts who do abandon heroin thus indicate that, for them, the rewards of the lifestyle have been surpassed by its problems (see Stephens 1985).

Within this way of life, crime is more than simply a means of getting drugs, in part because of the intensely interactive nature of the drug/crime relationship. Most obviously, expensive addictive drug use—a need for a drug combined with no legal means of financing that need—can motivate crime. Less obviously, criminal patterns may result in more, or less, drug use. An addict who initiates a criminal enterprise to finance drug use may be willing (or able) to go only so far in the effort, thereby restricting drug intake to a level possible within that crime profit level. On the other hand, a criminal activity may prove much more profitable than ever anticipated, decreasing the user's need to care how much income is being spent for drug expenses and hence increasing usage levels. Drug use can also affect crime directly by making risky or otherwise difficult offenses psychologically easier—e.g., theft (Inciardi and Russe 1977), prostitution (James 1976), or assault (see Goldstein 1985).

Still another kind of drug/crime interaction results from what Paul J. Goldstein (1985) has called "systemic violence," which has come to characterize street drug sales in recent years. Buyers as well as dealers are at risk of assault, robbery, and death just by participating in the drug market, because fear of getting cheated during the sale is such a major concern that arguments escalate to violence quite easily (McBride 1981).

Over time, any single heroin addict experiences many of these drug/crime interactions, leading to a sometimes chaotic existence. Anything that changes one factor—drug use or crime—will have an impact on the other. The social and psychological consequences of this chaos amount to further dedication to the street-addict lifestyle: contacts with other people are increasingly limited to other addicts; values are altered as needed to fit behaviors; crime is accepted as not just a means of obtaining drugs but as part of the addict's self-concept; and conventional people and conventional values are defined as square—pathetically out of touch with what's really important and enjoyable (see Akerstrom 1985; Johnson 1973; Stephens 1985).

These values and attitudes have been identified among serious juvenile offenders as well as among adult street addicts. The most commonly reported attitude is that of crime as a source of fun and excitement. This hallmark of street-addict subculture (see Stephens 1985) is also prominent in the attitudes of serious delinquents (Carpenter et al. 1988, pp. 34–35; Cusson 1983, pp. 33–42; Katz 1988; Williams and Kornblum 1985, pp. 53–55). Among addicts a hedonistic value set is also related to materialism, conspicuous consumption, and other hallmarks of "the fast life" (see, e.g., Binderman, Wepman, and Neman 1975; Rosenbaum 1981, pp. 41–43; Stephens 1985). Again, adolescents share these values since, for them, the single most common motivation for theft has been reported to be a consumeristic mentality—a perceived "need" to obtain fashionable clothes, expensive jewelry, stereo equipment, etc., in order to be popular with peers (Carpenter et al. 1988, pp. 61–85). Youth in impoverished neighborhoods discover especially rapidly that crime is a more accessible, easier, and faster way of attaining such desires than is legal employment (Williams and Kornblum 1985, pp. 49–59).

However, although seriously drug/crime-involved youths may acquire many of the values of the street-addict subculture, they are not yet living in it. That world is almost entirely an adult subculture, in which even the most active adolescent street hustlers are excluded from mainstream participation (see English and Stephens 1975). The primary exception is that teens engaged in frequent drug sales are often supplied by an adult dealer (Carpenter et al. 1988, pp. 47–49; Chaiken and Johnson 1988; Williams and Kornblum 1985, pp. 11–12). Still, their customers are most often other youths, including the many who themselves sell drugs but only occasionally and only to friends, so that they do not regard themselves as dealers (Carpenter et al. 1988, pp. 41–42). Most adolescent drug dealers thus spend the majority of their time with other youths, in normal adolescent social settings, rather than in the environment of a street-addict subculture. However, some friendship groups become so focused on drug use as a major activity that they become the nucleus of a local *youth* drug subculture that can be instrumental in not only popularizing drug use but also escalating other illegal behaviors in its members (see Feldman 1977; B. Johnson 1980).

In inner-city areas, on the other hand, youth drug dealing may operate through more firmly organized gang or semigang "crew" organizations (Fagan 1989; Mieczkowski 1986; Williams 1989; Williams and Kornblum 1985, pp. 73–82). Such groups may vary considerably from mass media portraits of them. Notably, these young dealers may use very little of the drug they are selling (or, for heroin, none at all) in order to maintain the alertness and caution needed in this increasingly violent occupation.

Further, in many gangs drug use and crime are related only in the same ways typically found for nongang youth; that is, most sales are to support the seller's own use rather than a business as such, the drug focus is on use in a social context (gang or not), and crimes other than dealing may or may not be present (Fagan 1989).

The occurrence of violence in gang or crew drug sales also varies greatly. In some instances the response to threat is simply to take flight and avoid violence (Mieczkowski 1986), and most cases of drug-gang violence are less related to protection or expansion of drug markets than to the traditional gang concern with protecting "turf"—the area defined as the gang's territory (Fagan 1989). Finally, these studies find that most drug gangs and crews gradually disintegrate as members get older, with only a very few developing into adult criminal organizations.

## Crime Committed under the Influence of Drugs

A final aspect of drug/crime relationships requiring discussion is the role of "being under the influence" of a drug while committing crime. This kind of behavior would be expected among street addicts, since they are strongly involved in both crime and drug use. Thus, not surprisingly, the 1986 Survey of Inmates of State Correctional Facilities (Innes 1988) found that, of all prisoners sentenced for robbery, burglary, larceny, or a drug offense, half were daily drug users and about 40% reported being under the influence of an illegal drug at the time they committed the crime for which they were incarcerated. That cocaine is increasingly likely to be involved is suggested by a comparison of 1984 and 1986 urinalysis tests of arrested persons in New York City (Wish 1987): in both years about 30% of all arrestees showed positive tests for heroin and other opiates, but the September/October 1986 finding of 83% positives for cocaine was almost double the 1984 figure of 42%. The cocaine increase was especially sharp for the age 16–20 arrestees: from 28% to 71%.

Delinquency studies have also asked youths whether they were under the influence of drugs, including alcohol, when they committed crimes. Hartstone and Hansen (1984) interviewed 114 boys institutionalized for a violent offense who also had a prior adjudication for a felony. Half (50%) reported that use of either alcohol (29%) or other drugs (33%) contributed to their violent behaviors; as these figures indicate, some reporting one also reported the other. In addition, 41% said that they had used alcohol (17%) or other drugs (34%) immediately prior to the violent offense for which they were institutionalized. In a study of less seriously crime-involved youths, far fewer reported drug/alcohol use immediately prior to crime and most denied any causal connections—but the exceptions were particularly likely to involve aggressive behaviors (Carpenter et al. 1988, pp. 30–37).

The National Youth Survey also asked these kinds of questions in 1979 (when the sample was age 14–21) and 1983 (age 18–24). Results showed more reports of substance use prior to assaults than prior to other serious crimes, but a much greater implication of alcohol than of other drugs in assaults. However, polydrug users were almost always likelier than marijuana/alcohol users, who in turn were likelier than alcohol-only users, to report some substance use prior to serious offenses (Elliott, Huizinga, and Menard 1989, pp. 172–175).

It should be repeated, however, that these kinds of findings can be expected in samples for which both drug use and crime are routine behaviors. As the National Youth Survey researchers warn, reports of use immediately prior to crime cannot be taken as reports of use *causing* crime, because (1) use immediately before *non*criminal activities might be even more common, and (2) anticipation of committing a crime may have caused the substance use. Both of these logical possibilities imply the reverse causality direction (Elliott, Huizinga, and Menard 1989, p. 174).

Another interpretation of drug effects on adolescent crime is provided by a study of youths brought for intake to a Florida detention center in 1985 (Dembo, Washburn, et al. 1987). These researchers found over twice as many *nondrug* felony referrals to juvenile court among youths who tested positive for marijuana as among those testing negative for it. They also found that more frequent self-reported lifetime marijuana use was associated with more frequent use of many other drugs. However, rather than interpreting these findings as indicators of youths being "under the influence" during crimes, these authors suggest that the primary significance of frequent marijuana use among youth is to indicate *commitment to a lifestyle* that also results in repeated involvement in serious crime.

In addition, being constantly high may indicate the presence of chronic **problem drug use**—that is, drug use resulting in severe and repeated adverse consequences: social conflicts, behavioral failures, emotional or psychological difficulties, or physical impairment. It has been suggested for both adults (James 1976; Weitzel and Blount 1982) and adolescents (Williams and Kornblum 1985, p. 55) that offenders with drug/alcohol problems are those most likely to be arrested, because their chronic intoxication reduces their ability to function as criminals.

Finally, problem drug use itself may contribute to criminality, especially—although not only—to violence. In a comparison of three samples of boys from poor urban neighborhoods, Jeffrey Fagan, Elizabeth Piper, and Melinda Moore (1986) found that drinking problems were associated with property and violent crimes for both students and dropouts, whereas drug problems showed such associations for students as well as for institutionalized violent offenders. Another youth study (Carpenter et al. 1988, pp. 87–101) found that the most serious violence occurred among the heaviest drug users; this violence included not only drug-market and gang violence but also instances of racial antagonism, revenge, and protection of image or honor. According to the researchers, all these manifestations of violence shared the common motivational theme of "protectionism"—protecting image, status, possessions, and so forth. But another interpretation is that such behaviors are evidence of emotional overresponse, proneness to social conflict, and the generally dysfunctional behavior typical of problem drug use.

# POSTSCRIPT

The primary purpose of this chapter has been to review what is known about drug/crime relationships, especially for serious youth crime. It indicates that drug use may be a critical factor in the move from trivial to serious delinquency, increasing the chances that those few youths completing the transition will stay involved in serious crime. Research on serious adult drug/crime offenders shows that a great variety of different kinds of drug/crime relationships operate—often simultaneously—for any given offender. The most general and most important of these relationships is that both drug use and crime are definitional characteristics of a preferred lifestyle. The few studies that have been conducted on drug/crime relationships among serious adolescent offenders report many of the same values, problems, and drug/crime dynamics as found in adult street-addict subcultures. The primary difference is the surrounding social context: the adults are almost completely immersed in their street subculture, whereas the delinquents are in youth environments—sometimes gangs, but more often the normal adolescent round of school, family, and peer-group social activities.

This review also indicates why cocaine is the drug of primary concern in examining drug/crime relationships among adolescents today. It is a powerful drug widely available at a cheap price per dose, but its extreme addictiveness can rapidly increase the need for more money.

Finally, this chapter also identifies several areas where existing information is especially weak, to the point of being entirely too sketchy to provide hypotheses for a study of serious delinquents still at large in the community. This means that, rather than being guided by hypotheses, the new study described in the following chapters had to be essentially exploratory in nature. Four general issues were chosen to serve as orienting questions for the project—questions that defined both the research subject matter and at least some of the methods the study would need to use.

The most important orienting question is the simplest: what patterns of drug use and crime exist among serious nongang delinquents at large in the urban community? What variations, offense rates, and drug/crime relationships would be displayed given not several dozen but several hundred youths, all *clearly* rather than *at least minimally* involved in major and/or chronic criminal activity?

The second orienting question does return to hypotheses. Specifically: of what utility are concepts and hypotheses from traditional delinquency theory when applied to such a sample rather than to garden-variety delinquents? Do variations in parents' socioeconomic status, or social controls from school and family, or differences in the deviance of peers, help explain variations in their drug/crime involvement?

The third question concerns the role of cocaine—especially *crack* cocaine—in serious delinquency today. What specifically is that role? For example, is cocaine more strongly linked than are other drugs to violent crimes? To more crime-to-pay-drug-expenses? Are seriously delinquent youths as involved in the crack business as media reports suggest?

Fourth and finally, as an aspect of all the preceding questions, what variations are there among serious delinquents of different sociodemographic backgrounds? Analysis by age group and consideration of seriously delinquent girls are two areas in which particularly little prior work exists. Questions of ethnic variations have received more attention, but they need work in a sample with large numbers of serious offenders.

Consideration of these questions, with data from the new street study, begins in Chapter 5. First, however, Chapter 4 describes where and how this new study was done.

# STUDYING SERIOUS DELINQUENCY ON THE STREET

A street study of serious delinquency requires a series of decisions: WHAT should be included as *serious* delinquency? WHERE can serious delinquents be found in sufficient numbers to study? WHO should be included in terms of gender, age, and race/ethnicity? And HOW can such a study be done? Fortunately, prior research efforts provide a great deal of information on which to base most of these decisions. Each topic in this chapter will be discussed in terms of prior research findings, the goals and problems particular to the new study, the decisions that were made, and results from 611 systematic interviews conducted between December 1985 and November 1987, with continuing field contacts through the end of 1991.

## WHAT: DEFINING SERIOUS DELINQUENCY

"Serious delinquency" was defined at the outset of this book as major and/or chronic youth crime. At a general level, this brief definition summarizes what prior research has studied as serious delinquency. Greater specification is complicated, however, because both "major" and "chronic" have been given a wide variety of definitions. Further, most studies emphasize "major" to the virtual exclusion of "chronic," and thus some aspects of crime frequency in defining serious delinquency have only rarely been considered.

## Major Crime and
## Serious Delinquency

Some analyses of serious delinquency discuss only violent Index crimes: homicide, aggravated assault, forcible rape, and robbery (Zimring 1977). However, most empirical studies include both these violent Index crimes and the most severe Index crimes against property: burglary and motor vehicle theft (and often arson, a fairly recent addition to the Index). Beyond this brief list of the *most* serious offenses, studies vary greatly in what they define as major crimes.

One common definitional tactic is to use the well-known crime seriousness scale developed by Sellin and Wolfgang (1964), or (more often) some variation on it. This kind of scale determines the seriousness of a crime based primarily on damage done—the degree of physical harm suffered by a victim and the monetary value of property stolen or damaged. Whether the crime is an Index offense is given much less emphasis in rating seriousness. Thus, non-Index property crimes such as fraud or vandalism may be defined in a severity scale as serious crime. This approach gives a concrete definition to "seriousness," but it is very difficult to use because the necessary details are hard to obtain. Information on the victim's medical condition, or on the results of property assessments, is only rarely included in official records. Such details are especially difficult to obtain in self-reported crime data because (1) offenders themselves may not have this information and (2) even if they do, accurate recall can be highly problematic, especially for high-frequency offenders.

Another possible tactic is to include any felony (as opposed to misdemeanor) as a serious offense. Generally, a **felony** is a crime punishable by death or incarceration in a state or federal prison; the maximum penalty for a **misdemeanor** is incarceration, typically for less than a year, in a local jail. Defining felonies as major crimes results in many property offenses being labeled as serious crime, most commonly at a lower monetary minimum than with a severity-scale approach; in addition, public order offenses such as selling drugs or carrying a concealed deadly weapon are felonies in many jurisdictions. The problems with this approach stem from the fact that the distinction between a felony and a misdemeanor varies, sometimes considerably, from one state to another. As a result, what most studies actually do is identify some felonies as "major crimes" but not others, resulting in an ultimately arbitrary selection, especially for public order offenses. This can present problems for comparability among studies. Further, as for the severity-scale studies, the necessary details may be difficult to obtain in a self-report study, especially since the same act may be defined as either a felony or a misdemeanor depending on police or court discretion or on whether the legislature has chosen to revise the law recently (see Lindquist 1988). In short, although a felony/misdemeanor distinction might appear to be a straight-forward way of defining major/minor crime, it is actually quite complex.

A considerably simpler approach is that taken by the National Youth Survey: defining Index crimes, because they are the most serious offenses identified in the *Uniform Crime Reports*, to be "serious crimes," excluding only thefts of $50 or less. This has the advantage of using a small number of offenses and readily obtainable data, since most Index crime categories are fairly general rather than highly specified. Further, most Index offenses in this scheme are felonies, with only the smaller larcenies likely to be misdemeanors. It is in the area of potentially minor theft of-fenses where the crime-frequency, or chronicity, dimension enters. The Na-tional Youth Survey required *at least three* Index offenses in the prior year for their "serious delinquent" category. Although this cutoff point is ulti-mately arbitrary, the relative success of this definition is suggested by the finding that the 12–17-year-olds so classified by their 1976 crimes actually averaged ten Index crimes and 118 total offenses (Elliott, Huizinga, and Menard 1989, p. 52). Later studies have adopted the same scheme—notably the New Jersey study described in Chapter 3 (White, Pandina, and LaGrange 1987).

Other studies have set a higher minimum frequency on major crimes to define serious delinquency and have used a less apparently arbi-trary means to do so. For example, Stephen A. Cernkovich, Peggy C. Giordano, and Meredith D. Pugh (1985) selected a random sample of 914 persons age 12 to 19 in a large Midwestern metropolitan area in 1982. They defined "major" crimes as robbery, aggravated assault, motor vehicle theft, burglary, felony theft, and drug sales (other than marijuana). The cutoff definition for high-frequency ("chronic") major offenses was determined by calculating the median number of major crimes committed in the previ-ous year by adolescents who had committed *any* such offenses (i.e., exclud-ing those who committed none); the number arrived at in this fashion was five. The 5+ cutoff to define chronic delinquency is most well known as the definition employed by the Philadelphia cohort arrest study (Wolfgang, Figlio, and Sellin 1972). However, in this latter study the definition was not comparable because it identified lifetime juvenile arrests as opposed to prior-year major offenses actually committed.

## Minor Crime and Serious Delinquency

One uniformity among these various schemes is that none of them consider such low-profit misdemeanors as prostitution and stolen goods offenses, even though such crimes generate sufficient income to support both the offender and his or her drug habit. The obvious part of the rationale for this exclusion is that such offenses are not "major" crimes in the sense of being *legally* serious offenses. A less obvious factor is that these crimes are not necessarily serious *at the frequency levels* generally taken as cutoff points for "chronic" serious delinquency—e.g., 3+ or 5+ offenses. But what about such offenses at a much higher frequency?

One of the few studies to address this topic at all is the previously mentioned Midwest-city survey by Cernkovich, Giordano, and Pugh (1985). They found that, of adolescents involved in major offenses, 100% also committed minor offenses and 68% did so at a high frequency. Thus, the "assumption that seriousness of offense is more salient than frequency of offense" (p. 712) led these researchers to ignore low/high minor-offenses frequencies and to consider only major offenses in defining serious delinquency. One problem with this assumption is that the low/high categories were determined (as for major offenses) by the median for offenders only; the minimum for high-frequency minor offenses was thus only 48, not very high. A more important problem is that many of the minor offenses considered were of a type best labeled "trivial misbehaviors"—status offenses (running away, being truant, lying about age, having sexual intercourse), misbehaviors with no legal status (cheating on tests), and public order offenses centering on drug use (public drunkenness, disorderly conduct, drug use, alcohol use). Other minor offenses were, in contrast, minor *crimes*—assault-related behaviors (simple assault, incidents of throwing things at cars or people) and the two potentially profit-making crimes of petty theft and prostitution. It can be argued that a youth with 48 occasions of the trivial misbehaviors listed above is "troubled" and perhaps "potentially delinquent," but it seems clear that such a youth is *not* seriously crime involved. This is not so clear for a youth who has committed 48 of the minor crimes listed, especially those likely to result in financial gain.

Another reason why non-Index for-profit crimes like prostitution and stolen goods offenses may be regarded as minor is that the base reference is to the legal code defining *adult* crimes. It does seem obvious that, of street crimes committed by adults, these offenses are almost in a nuisance category compared to such serious activities as robbery and burglary. But, for an adolescent, a minor but high-frequency profit-making crime can serve as an entrance to an entire way of life: an independent income, with much less time and effort expended than in some legal job that probably pays only the minimum wage. Particular minor offenses present additional problems: the high profits of cocaine sales make legal wages for even professional jobs look paltry; dealing in drugs or stolen goods requires personal contacts that may lead to relationships with established criminals; and prostitution can damage a youth's capacity for healthy interpersonal relationships as well as present a substantial risk for contracting sexually transmitted diseases, including AIDS. Further, any repeated street crime, however minor, entails repeated time on the street—time to learn how the adult street world operates, time to become known to future crime partners and bosses, time to be victimized by bigger, older offenders. In short, at high-frequency levels, youth crime need not entail an Index offense or even a felony to constitute serious crime involvement.

## Definition for the New Study

Before proceeding to the definition used for the new study, it should be noted that another uniformity in prior studies is that serious delinquency almost always has been defined *after* data collection. This kind of timing permits use of the data distributions as one basis for determining crime type or degree definitions. For the new study, however, a specific definition was needed *before* data collection, to determine eligibility for a sample to consist of *only* serious delinquents. This meant that the minimum-level cutoff would be necessarily arbitrary, although the problem of questionable cases could be resolved fairly easily by setting a minimum level high enough to eliminate them.

Considering all of the preceding, the decision made for this study was to specify eligibility under either of two rules: within the prior year, *either (1) 10 or more Index crimes or (2) 100 or more lesser profit-making crimes.* The 10 and 100 figures were chosen because they are nice round numbers that are significantly larger than those commonly used in defining serious, major, or chronic crime levels. Index crimes were categorized as robbery, assault (including homicide and rape), burglary, motor vehicle theft, and larceny. Lesser profit-making crimes included drug-business offenses (selling, steering, smuggling, manufacturing, etc.), prostitution, procuring, stolen goods offenses (trading or selling, but not merely buying), confidence games, and "bad paper" offenses (forged or kited checks, use of stolen credit cards, etc.).

The part of this plan most vulnerable to criticism is its inclusion in the Index crime category of all larcenies and all assaults. Defined in this way, (1) "larceny" includes petty/misdemeanor thefts as well as grand/ felony thefts, and (2) "assault" includes possible non-Index "simple" and "other" assaults as well as the Index crimes of aggravated assault, homicide, and forcible rape. The primary rationale for this decision was the desire to minimize the amount of detail interviewers had to record while maximizing the probability of accurate recall by respondents. For larceny, rather than asking about dollar values, interviewers collected information about larceny *types* committed: shoplifting, thefts from vehicles, pickpocketing, prostitutes' thefts from clients, and other sneak thefts (most often from family members or employers). Questions for assault were placed after those for all other crimes, and the assault categories were used solely for memory-jogging purposes. For analysis, all categories were combined into a single "assault" measure: (1) assaults in conjunction with any of the other crimes committed (e.g., fighting a security guard while shoplifting or a customer while selling drugs), (2) gang or other group fights, and then (3) any other assault (including any volunteered information about homicide or rape, since we did not ask specifically about these categories). For both larceny and assault, the details *not* asked about—value of goods stolen, degree of physical harm done—represent instances for which reliable reports are very difficult to obtain. The larceny-type details recorded, on the other hand, help make the larceny total itself *more* reliable.

Further, now that the new study has been completed, it is possible to determine empirically whether the larceny and assault categories did actually cause sample-selection problems. The results of this analysis, as shown in Table 4.1, indicate that neither category was very important. Even if both larceny and assaults are totally removed from all eligibility considerations, 95.6% of the sample (584 of the 611 cases) remain eligible by the other criteria—49.8% because they committed 10+ other Index

**TABLE 4.1**

**Eligibility Types as Nonoverlapping Categories (Showing Overlap within Each Eligibility Type)\***

| Eligibility Type and Specific Offenses | Number of Cases Eligible | Mean Crimes | |
|---|---|---|---|
| | | Type | Total |
| **Type A.  Major Index crimes** (Criterion: 10+) | 304 | 56.3 | 29.1 |
| Robbery | 193 | 19.5 | 10.3 |
| Burglary | 197 | 32.5 | 16.5 |
| Motor vehicle theft | 66 | 4.3 | 2.3 |
| **Type B.  Non-Index for-profit** (Criterion: 100+) | 280 | 594.3 | 578.5 |
| Drug-business offenses | 254 | 426.6 | 420.9 |
| Prostitution, procuring | 50 | 107.4 | 72.0 |
| Stolen goods offenses | 67 | 57.2 | 77.9 |
| Other non-Index for-profit | 1 | 3.1 | 7.8 |
| **Type C.  Mixed/total crimes** (Criterion: 100+) | 13 | 151.5 | 702.4 |
| Assault | 0 | 0.8 | 1.2 |
| Larceny | 9 | 103.0 | 93.0 |
| Larceny, assault, and non-Index | 13 | 150.3 | 672.7 |
| **Type D. Remainder** (see text) | 14 | | |

\*For example, of the 304 youths eligible because they committed 10+ major Index crimes, 193 were eligible solely because they did 10+ robberies, although some were also eligible due to the number of other major Index crimes they committed. Mean number of robberies done was 19.5 for (all of) the 304 youths in Type A and 10.3 for the total 611 respondents.

crimes (robberies, burglaries, or motor vehicle thefts) and an additional 45.8% because they committed 100+ non-Index for-profit crimes. Treating larceny as a non-Index for-profit crime adds 13 more cases eligible under the "100+ lesser offenses" rule, for a total of 97.7% eligible without considering larceny or assault as an Index offense.

For the 14 remaining cases, assaults were irrelevant because none of these respondents reported any such crime. One male did not meet any of the stated criteria but was interviewed, appropriately, because his major activity was dealing cocaine "in weight"; in the prior twelve months, he sold at least a pound on 85 occasions; his other 13 offenses during that time included 10 prostitution offenses plus a theft from one of those clients. This leaves only 13 cases (2.1% of the total sample) eligible solely because larcenies were treated as Index crimes. Of this small number of youths, furthermore, 7 reported at least 50 larcenies and another 5 youths committed 17–40 larcenies as part of their 23–40 total Index crimes (and their 50–80 total profit-making crimes). It can be argued that these crime figures are at least equal to the three $50 larcenies defining the minimum for "serious" delinquency in the National Youth Survey. This leaves only one youth who was included at the minimum level of 8 larcenies plus 2 burglaries totaling 10 Index crimes; even he had 70 other profit-making offenses—20 drug sales and 50 stolen goods offenses.

Finally, it might also be noted that Table 4.1 reflects a markedly more crime-involved group than the "serious delinquent" subsample for the National Youth Survey. Means for the latter reflected 118 total offenses and 10 Index crimes, whereas the new study located youths who reported an average of 702 total offenses and 29 Index crimes even without considering assault and larceny. More details about specific offenses and crime totals are included in subsequent chapters.

# WHERE: STUDY LOCATIONS

Where to find serious delinquents in sufficient numbers to study is one of the easiest social science questions to answer: the worst neighborhoods of the biggest cities. Even during the years when delinquency research was so strongly focused on garden-variety delinquency that serious youth crime was ignored, the following was true:

> Social scientists somehow still knew better than to stroll the streets at night in certain parts of town or even to park there. And despite the fact that countless surveys showed that kids from upper- and lower-income families scored the same on delinquency batteries, even social scientists knew that the parts of town that scared them were not upper-income neighborhoods. (Stark 1987, p. 894)

Evidence on the locations of high-crime areas is unusually consistent for social science data. At the most general level, both drug use and crime show a relationship to urban residence. Heroin use in particular is almost entirely an urban problem, but use of all other recreational drugs except tobacco and alcohol also varies directly with city size (Johnston, O'Malley, and Bachman 1987; O'Donnell et al. 1976). Official crime statistics show a similarly strong relationship to city size (see, e.g., FBI 1991), and studies of delinquents in particular also indicate more serious offenses among urban than rural delinquents (e.g., Elliott, Huizinga, and Menard 1989, pp. 46–48; Fagan, Piper, and Moore 1986; Gold and Reimer 1975; Lyerly and Skipper 1981).

At a more specific level, serious delinquency clearly occurs disproportionately in city areas characterized by poverty, little education, low occupational skills, poor housing, overcrowding, and transience (Baldwin 1979; Inciardi 1986, pp. 160–162; Laub and Hindelang 1981; Rutter and Giller 1984, pp. 202–210; Sampson 1986). Further, these same neighborhoods with high crime and delinquency rates have been shown to be those with the highest prevalence of narcotics use (Gandossy et al. 1980, pp. 24–26; McBride and McCoy 1981).

## Sampling Considerations

Within large urban areas, a sample of serious delinquents can be selected in a variety of ways. Every possible approach necessarily has limitations, so the choices must be guided by what is least problematic given the purpose of the study. The three main questions involve (1) the number of neighborhoods and/or cities, (2) the sample-selection technique, and (3) the specific geographic locale(s).

The number of possible locations for sample selection ranges, logically, from one neighborhood to a nationwide sample of all major cities. Generally, delinquency studies have chosen either one metropolitan area (e.g., Carpenter et al. 1988; Hirschi 1969) or some three to six different cities (e.g., Fagan and Pabon 1990; Short and Nye 1958; Williams and Kornblum 1985). A multiple-cities approach is often preferable in order to generalize beyond the specific sample, but whether this is possible depends on the purpose of the study. For the new delinquency study, the concern with drug/crime relationships required consideration of what multiple cities might mean for data on drug use as well as crime. The problem is that illicit drug use is perhaps more subject to local variations than is any other form of deviant behavior. Specifically, cities may vary greatly in local drug-preference fads, supply circumstances, law enforcement styles and moods, and even local norms for age at first use. Splitting a given number of cases over multiple cities could thus reduce effective sample size dramatically because proper analysis would require analytic controls for city. At the time this new study was planned, a particular concern was the recent rise in youth cocaine use. Cities varied enormously in both the availability of cocaine (especially crack) and the degree to which it was favored by young adolescents in particular.

Thus, altogether, the best choice appeared to be *a single metropolitan area with a known high availability level of cocaine, but with multiple neighborhoods within that area* to permit some analysis of geographic contrasts. Such analysis is possible because drug availability varies markedly among neighborhoods even within a single metropolitan area, with blatant street-corner sales occurring in only some neighborhoods in any city. It should also be recalled that some of the initial research questions for the study had to do with racial/ethnic variations. The reality of most American cities is that multiple ethnic-group subsamples require multiple neighborhood samples as well. Further, the larger the white subsample desired in an urban crime study, the stronger the practical need to include more working-class or even middle-class areas; the neighborhoods with high crime rates are not generally white, and the white neighborhoods do not generally have high crime rates. The matter of sociodemographic subsamples is discussed in more detail later in this chapter, but the point here is that the "who" decision necessarily played a part in this "where" decision.

The second general sampling consideration is that of a sample selection technique. The new study's concern with interviewing only *serious delinquents, on the street* rather than in institutions, essentially defined the necessary technique in advance: a purposive sample, rather than a random sample. That is, serious delinquents still active on the street are one of the special populations for which it is impossible, in actual practice, to identify every population member—a process that is a prerequisite for drawing a random sample. The only way to interview a sample consisting solely of serious delinquents, therefore, is to define the characteristics of the group to be interviewed (what age, how much crime, etc.) and then go to the streets deliberately looking for persons meeting those definitions. As is discussed in more detail below, this approach requires detailed knowledge about local high-crime-rate areas, multiple contacts with participants in and observers of the local street scenes, preliminary interview questions to establish sample eligibility, and a great deal of effort to maintain confidentiality and to establish good rapport between respondent and interviewer.

The third and final sampling consideration—specific geographic locale(s)—was fairly much determined for the new study by decisions on the two previous questions: (1) multiple neighborhoods in a single metropolitan area with a high availability of cocaine, in which (2) the necessary information and contacts existed for a purposive sample of serious delinquents to be drawn. For this study, both of these needs were met by the *Miami/Dade County Florida metropolitan area*. The senior author had been conducting drug/crime research in this area for well over a decade and had built up numerous contacts on the street as well as with personnel in criminal justice and drug treatment agencies. He was thus aware that by

1984 Miami had a large crack problem, in addition to having been the major cocaine import site for the United States for many years.

## Locations for the New Study

Dade County has a population of about 1.9 million people, of whom some 45% are Hispanic, 39% non-Hispanic whites, and 16% non-Hispanic blacks (*Newsweek*, Jan. 25, 1988, p. 28). In 1980 the City of Miami had only about 347,000 people, but the Miami Standard Statistical Area population was ranked 21st in population size in the United States. By 1984 the Consolidated Metropolitan Statistical Area of which Miami is a part ranked 11th.

The Miami area encompasses numerous independently incorporated towns and small cities, ethnically defined communities within Miami proper, the usual assortment of locally known "areas" and neighborhoods both within and outside city limits, and a unique area known as "Liberty City." This large, high-crime-rate, high-poverty-rate neighborhood made national headlines early in the 1980s with a major riot. It includes part of Miami and some contiguous unincorporated areas and is well known to all local residents, but, since it is not a formally incorporated city, it is almost never included in area maps.

Specific goals for neighborhoods were not used, but, as shown in Table 4.2, the 611 interviews were spread over 20 neighborhoods varying

### TABLE 4.2
**Neighborhood Distributions (*N*s)**

|  |  |  | Ethnicity | | |
|---|---|---|---|---|---|
|  | Neighborhoods | Interviews | Black | Hispanic | White |
| **Totals** | 20 | 611 | 258 | 100 | 253 |
| **Metro area** |  |  |  |  |  |
| North | 4 | 56 | 2 | 6 | 48 |
| Northeast | 4 | 105 | 4 | 1 | 100 |
| Central | 4 | 287 | 202 | 52 | 33 |
| West | 3 | 80 | 7 | 26 | 47 |
| Southwest | 5 | 83 | 43 | 15 | 25 |
| **Predominant ethnicity** |  |  |  |  |  |
| White | 8 | 162 | 6 | 4 | 152 |
| White/Hispanic | 3 | 100 | 10 | 33 | 57 |
| Hispanic | 2 | 38 | 0 | 37 | 1 |
| Mixed (all three) | 3 | 80 | 24 | 21 | 35 |
| Black | 4 | 231 | 218 | 5 | 8 |

greatly in terms of location and ethnic composition. The major reason for this high degree of locational and ethnic variation is the sociodemographic subsample goals toward which the interviewers were working. Rationale and details for these goals are discussed in the next section, but the effect of these goals on neighborhood distributions was to force interviewing into many different areas in an effort to fill the subsamples.

These neighborhoods also vary greatly in socioeconomic terms—from the broken-down, burned-out slum areas of Liberty City to predominantly middle-class neighborhoods like Kendall and South Miami. The majority could be characterized as basically working-class areas, whether white (Carol City or North Miami), Hispanic (Westchester or Hialeah), or black (Opa-Locka or Perrine). However, interviews were conducted with youths from welfare families in 18 of the 20 neighborhoods, and serious delinquents from middle-class families were found in 13 of the 20. But although no neighborhood yielded more than a few interviews with youths from middle-class families, in eight different neighborhoods a third or more of respondents still living at home were from welfare families. Similarly, in seven areas over a third of youths residing with their families were living in households in which nobody—parent, sibling, or other—had graduated from high school; in four other areas this was the case for fewer than 10% of the families.

As expected, family socioeconomic indicators varied by the primary ethnic composition of the neighborhood. In Miami this is generally a black versus white/Hispanic contrast, because the great majority of Hispanics in Miami (and in this sample) are Cubans, for whom socioeconomic indicators are highly similar to those for non-Hispanic whites. The contrast is again evident in neighborhood distributions for the youths still living at home. For example, in all four black neighborhoods at least 40% of youths living at home were living in families with no high school graduate, whereas not even one white or Hispanic neighborhood had such a high figure. The same statement also applies to female-headed households.

# WHO:
# SOCIODEMOGRAPHIC
# SUBSAMPLES

As discussed in Chapter 2, recent studies of serious delinquency have devoted considerable attention to analyzing its sociodemographic distribution. Nearly all studies identify urban underclass males as the sociodemographic group most highly involved in serious delinquency, although considerably less consensus exists on why this should be so. One apparently relevant factor is that these studies rely on the juvenile justice system to identify serious delinquents, and justice system records show a clear overrepresentation of blacks compared to their percentage of the total population. The extent to which this situation reflects racial bias in criminal justice processing is unknown (see Pope and McNeely 1981). The National Youth Survey found no difference in the percentage of blacks and whites ever arrested but a higher probability of repeat arrests for blacks ever arrested than for their white counterparts; data on offenses committed showed no obvious explanation for this difference (Elliott and Huizinga 1984, pp. 59–60). Further, the National Youth Survey found weak and inconsistent relationships between race and *overall* drug/crime behaviors, even though lower- and working-class boys had clearly higher rates of *serious* offenses than their middle-class counterparts (Elliott, Huizinga, and Menard 1989, pp. 32–39).

It is also significant that recent studies of serious delinquency have found other sociodemographic groups involved in addition to urban underclass males (although as smaller percentages of their base populations): white as well as minority-group males, working-class and even middle-class youths as well as underclass youths, and females as well as males. Again, however, too little is known about the ways in which serious delinquency is related to these sociodemographic factors, in part due to the methodology of prior studies. Random-sample surveys locate too few serious delinquents for detailed analysis, and the large databases provided by juvenile justice records have limited types of information and an unknown degree of representativeness relative to all serious delinquents. Because of this situation, the new study's orienting questions, as described at the end of Chapter 3, include a concern with comparative analysis of serious delinquents from varied sociodemographic backgrounds.

Thus, the research goals of the new study dictated the use of *a multiple-sociodemographic-subsample design*: predetermined subsamples to permit comparative analysis. This kind of design cannot be used to discover the distribution of delinquency within any and all existing subpopulations, but, in practice, no study can serve both purposes. The random-sample surveys required to discover what distributions exist invariably have some subsamples that are too small for proper analysis. Generally, for example, they have included too few blacks, let alone Hispanics, to use ethnicity as a variable in data analysis (Schuster 1981); even the National Youth Survey sometimes had too few nonwhite females to include in their analyses (e.g., Huizinga and Elliott 1986).

Further, ethnic comparisons are most needed among those youths least likely to be included in random-sample studies: residents of inner-city areas, school dropouts, chronic truants, runaways, and youngsters "living at home" but so actively involved in street life as to be in their parents' homes only rarely (see Hindelang, Hirschi, and Weis 1981, pp. 33–36; R. Johnson 1980; Kandel 1975; Miller 1981; Thornberry and Farnworth 1982). Studies restricted to serious juvenile offenders also contribute very little information about ethnic comparisons, since studies of both street gangs and institutionalized youths have samples that are too specialized for this purpose. For the new study, therefore, the chance to study distributions of serious delinquency was given up, in favor of having large enough subsamples to permit comparative analysis.

## Target Subsamples for Miami

The subsample design problem, then, was a matter of selecting which categories to include. The choices were necessarily influenced by the new study's specific location as well as the findings of prior research. Both random-sample surveys and studies of juvenile justice samples indicate clearly that the main groups to be included should be black and white males. This was possible in Miami in spite of the small size of the non-Hispanic black population: at 16%, considerably smaller than in many other major cities. As elsewhere, however, blacks are overrepresented in Dade County criminal justice and drug treatment statistics, which suggested that securing interviews with large numbers of crime-involved black youths would not be problematic. Non-Hispanic whites constitute considerably more of the area population: 39%. Since they tend to appear in local crime and drug agencies in numbers proportionate to their total population, numerous interviews with white serious delinquents also appeared feasible.

Further, black and white male subsamples were anticipated to be so relatively simple to contact that a full "youth" age range of 12–17 seemed feasible for them. Securing enough interviews with the youngest boys to permit age comparisons meant that age had to be specified in the subsample plan, because serious delinquency is more common among older than younger adolescents (see, e.g., Elliott, Huizinga, and Menard 1989, pp. 41–44; FBI 1991; Inciardi 1979; Rutter and Giller 1984, pp. 47–53). Defining a target number for each individual age between 12 and 17 seemed overly restrictive, although a 12–14 versus 15–17 split might still provide too few of the very youngest offenders. Thus, targets were defined for three age groups, but with slightly smaller subsamples specified for 12–13-year-olds than for 14–15- and 16–17-year-olds: specifically, 60, 70, and 70, respectively, for a total of 200 boys of each race.

A female subsample also seemed desirable, since prior studies have made it clear that girls are in fact involved in serious delinquency. In studies of violent delinquents identified by the juvenile justice system, females appear as a small but significant minority—e.g., about one-sixth in both the New York court study (Strasburg 1978) and the Columbus arrest study (Hamparian et al. 1978). Gender comparisons for the National Youth Survey show that the greater involvement in delinquency by males is statistically significant and consistent across all types of delinquency, but of surprisingly small size (Canter 1982). This accords with our previous experience in interviewing young adult offenders in Miami, which suggested that locating young black and white females seriously involved in crime would not be a problem (Inciardi 1986, pp. 157–169; Inciardi and Pottieger 1986). In addition, race and age-group comparisons for females would help clarify any race and age comparisons made for males. Thus, a subsample of 100 girls was planned, to be split evenly between blacks and whites and between the two older age groups—14–15 and 16–17 (i.e., 25 respondents in each race/age group).

Finally, the large (45%) Hispanic population of the Miami area presented an opportunity to include this third ethnic group. Random-sample surveys only rarely include enough Hispanic youth for detailed analysis; official records typically track only race; and even when Hispanic ethnicity is recorded, there is an abundance of room for error (see Bondavalli and Bondavalli 1981). Hispanics in Miami, however, are se-verely *under*represented in local criminal justice and drug treatment statis-tics, especially females and very young offenders (see Page 1980). Thus, the decision was made to include only a small Hispanic subsample, con-fined to only males and only the older two age groups: 50 boys age 14–15 and 50 age 16–17.

The final sample was quite close to the subsample distribution tar-gets. As Table 4.3 indicates, the total of 611 was predominantly black (42%) or white (41%), with 100 Hispanics (16%). Mean age was 15.0, with nearly equal numbers of 16–17-year-olds (42%) and 14–15-year-olds (38%), plus 120 12–13-year-old boys (20%). About one in six respondents was female ($N = 100$), as planned.

**TABLE 4.3**
**Demographic Subsample Distributions**

| | Age (Ns) | | | Total | Percentage | |
|---|---|---|---|---|---|---|
| | 12–13 | 14–15 | 16–17 | N | Of Sex | Of Total |
| **Male** | | | | | | |
| Black | 60 | 67 | 82 | 209 | 40.9% | 34.2% |
| White | 60 | 68 | 74 | 202 | 39.5 | 33.1 |
| Hispanic | 0 | 50 | 50 | 100 | 19.6 | 16.4 |
| Male total | 120 | 185 | 206 | 511 | 100.0 | 83.6 |
| **Female** | | | | | | |
| Black | 0 | 25 | 24 | 49 | 49.0% | 8.0% |
| White | 0 | 25 | 26 | 51 | 51.0 | 8.3 |
| Female total | 0 | 50 | 50 | 100 | 100.0 | 16.4 |
| **Total by age** | 120 | 235 | 256 | 611 | | |

This subsample distribution was designed for purposes of statistical comparisons, with an additional concern for practical feasibility. However, it might also be noted that the final distribution is not unlike that for youths and young adults seen in the criminal justice and drug treatment systems of Dade County.

# How: Interviewing Serious Delinquents on the Street

The process of locating and interviewing young people on the street who are active criminals is not as difficult as it might seem, given the right preparation. The requirements for doing so are discussed in the first section below. Following this, the truthfulness and accuracy of self-report data collected from serious criminal offenders are discussed, including the variety of ways this issue has been studied empirically and the methods used to enhance the accuracy of the new study's data.

## On the Street

One of the most difficult parts of setting up an on-the-street crime study is finding interviewers with experience in talking to criminal offenders and with knowledge of the local street scene. For the new study, however, this was accomplished prior to even planning the research. The senior author and the three interviewers who were hired for the project all had extensive experience in talking to drug users and other criminal offenders, including over ten years of such experience specifically in Miami. During this time, each became familiar with a variety of the specific street scenes in the area and built up numerous contacts with offenders, ex-offenders, and drug treatment personnel. These contacts were starting points for interviews in particular neighborhoods. That is, the contact people went to the street with one or more interviewers and introduced them to youths who were actively involved in street crime.

The introduction included a frank statement that the research questions concerned the youth's illegal activities, but with assurances that names would not be collected and that none of the information would be turned over to law enforcement authorities. The contact person assured the youth that the interviewer was someone who could be trusted, someone whose questions should be answered truthfully, and someone whose safety was of personal interest to the contact person. The first questions asked constituted a brief screening interview to determine eligibility in terms of demographic background (for the age/sex/ethnicity subsamples) and criminality, including what kinds of crime the youth had committed most often in the last twelve months and how many such offenses were committed; in most instances, no further details were needed to confirm eligibility. A payment of $10 was promised for the 25–35 minutes anticipated to complete the interview.

The statement that no information would be turned over to law enforcement authorities was backed up with a Grant of Confidentiality issued by the National Institute on Drug Abuse. This is a document guaranteeing that no member of the research staff can be forced to divulge the identity of research subjects to any law enforcement agency, court, or grand jury, at the local, state, or federal level. Respondents were made aware of this document and given copies if they requested it.

The interview itself also made the confidentiality emphasis obvious. No names were asked. Location information recorded for place of interview was neighborhood, not specific address. The date-of-birth question specified only month and year, not day. Questions on illegal activities did not specify dates, places, or descriptions of particular crimes—only age at first time or number of activities in a given time period (for crime types, number in the prior twelve months; for drug use, number of days used in the prior ninety days). In short, none of the information collected was specific enough to identify a particular respondent.

Another feature of the interview that was helpful in assuring cooperation was its structure: it was set up so that interviewers could place most of their attention on the respondent rather than on reading questions and recording answers. Because questions were almost entirely about facts or events, rather than attitudes or opinions, the items were almost all very brief identifiers that the interviewer could glance at, phrase into a question while looking at the respondent, and jot the answer (most commonly a number or a single word) to very quickly, not interrupting the flow of conversation. This, along with the general knowledgeability of the interviewers about matters related to crime and drug use, helped establish rapport between interviewer and respondent.

Based on this rapport, respondents were asked to identify other offenders who might be included in the research. These individuals, in turn, were located and interviewed, with the process being repeated until the social network surrounding each user was exhausted or the applicable subsample targets had been filled. This process restricted the sample to only those offenders currently active enough to be known to other informants, eliminating former offenders as well as those not involved in or only peripheral to the local street scene. The focus on interviews with only serious delinquents was thereby maintained. Altogether, the refusal rate was less than 4%.

## The Truthfulness and Accuracy of Self-Reports

As discussed in Chapter 2, self-report studies have become a standard approach to examining illegal behavior among student and household populations since they were first tried in the 1940s. An extensive literature now exists to show that self-report methodology as used with normal youth populations gives results that are both sufficiently accurate and fairly compatible with the conclusions drawn from analyses of arrest data (for summaries, see Elliott, Huizinga, and Menard 1989, pp. 4–9; Hindelang, Hirschi, and Weis 1981, pp. 13–25; R. Johnson 1979, pp. 89–93). Further, studies indicate that the most accurate self-reported delinquency measures are those that (1) ask questions about serious as opposed to trivial behaviors and (2) use face-to-face interviews as opposed to paper-and-pencil written questionnaires (see Huizinga and Elliott 1986). The Miami study had both of these characteristics.

By the 1960s, self-reports also were being used to investigate the much more serious behaviors of adult participants in drug/crime street subcultures, particularly heroin addicts. This use raised more emphatic concerns about truthfulness: would addicts' greater criminal involvement make them likelier to hide the truth from interviewers? Several studies investigated this question by checking heroin addicts' self-reported activities against other indicators. Self-reported drug use was compared to medical records and urinalysis reports (Amsel et al. 1976; Ball 1967; Cox and Longwell 1974); self-reported crimes were compared to official criminal justice records (Amsel et al. 1976; Ball 1967; Bonito, Nurco, and Shaffer 1976); and self-reported income sources and drug use were compared to the reports of relatives and aftercare counselors (Stephens 1972). Some researchers have even compared addict self-reports of crime involvement to their own observations of such crimes (although not systematically; see Johnson et al. 1985, pp. 22–25). These studies consistently find that addict self-reports are surprisingly truthful and accurate. In fact, several of these investigators have commented on the incompleteness and inaccuracy they discovered in official records during the research process.

Self-report methodology for use with serious criminal offenders has also been bolstered by numerous discussions of ways to increase the quality of the data collected (see Amsel et al. 1976 for a listing especially pertinent to drug/crime studies). Ball (1967) provides a list of recommended procedures for obtaining good interviews with drug/crime-involved offenders in particular. His specifications relevant to street interviews were followed in our field procedures: use of a structured personal interview with probe questions and use of experienced interviewers with no police affiliation who were familiar with both the local drug scene and local high-drug/crime neighborhoods. In addition, interviewers were given intensive personal training (and a detailed field manual) concerning use of the interview schedule.

The most common source of unreliable self-report data comes not from deliberate lying but from recall difficulties. This can be a particular problem for those who commit crimes with great frequency. One solution is careful construction of questions, particularly so as not to ask the unanswerable—information the respondent would be unlikely to know (such as an assault victim's degree of injury) or unlikely to remember (e.g., number of crimes committed over a period longer than a year, at most).

Another solution to recall problems is interviewing techniques that help respondents reconstruct the time period being discussed. For example, current criminal activities are linked not to some vague "prior twelve months" but to significant life events during that time—birthdays, Christmas, the start of the school year, a serious injury experienced, a family death or wedding or birth, and so forth. The same general method is used to help respondents to remember how old they were when they began particular activities or to remember when and for what they were arrested. The interviewers for our new study had experience in these techniques with respondents who were 30–40-year-old offenders, people whose drug/ crime careers had begun 15 or even 30 years before. The comparatively brief life histories of the teenagers interviewed here therefore presented very few recall problems, since even the most chronic offenders were recalling only seven or eight years of history.

Survey data can also be troublesome if respondents balk at critical questions, resulting in large numbers of "missing data" responses. Balks were avoided for this study by being very frank in stating our interest in illegal activities and by asking a crime question almost immediately, as part of the screening questions. Cooperation was also enhanced by the previously discussed assurances of confidentiality and by our efforts to promote interviewer/respondent rapport.

## A Note about Statistics

The emphasis throughout the following chapters is on *description* of the drug and crime involvement of the serious delinquents interviewed, including the relationship of drug use and crime to each other and to respondents' backgrounds. In some cases the nature of these relationships is compared to predictions implied by the various theoretical perspectives developed to explain garden-variety delinquency, as discussed in Chapter 2. Two kinds of statistics are used throughout this analysis: measures of central tendency and correlations, both of which are defined and discussed below.

First, however, the reasons for using statistics in a study such as this must be examined. The motive for using them is that they can be very helpful in describing and interpreting findings. One utility of statistics is that they help summarize data, which is necessary because looking at a large number of specific observations can be confusing. For example, there may be a great variation from case to case in the number of crimes committed by a group of offenders, or in the age at which they first became involved in crime. Some statistics provide an idea of which observations—for example, crime frequencies or initiation ages—are *typical* for the sample. Other statistics provide a way of summarizing the nature of a relationship between observations—for example, age at initial crime in relation to level of current crime involvement.

Another special use of statistics is to help estimate the probability that a relationship, or a difference, is meaningful rather than accidental. What looks like a big difference between two groups—for example, 30% more heroin users among 10 females than among 10 males—might be only a happenstance result of which 20 youths were interviewed. If another 20 interviews were done, the difference might disappear or even be reversed. *Statistics provide ways of estimating the likelihood of potential data-interpretation problems*, which gives researchers a way of indicating how much confidence can be placed in their findings.

The problem is that statistical inference is legitimate only in a random sample—not in a purposive sample such as the Miami serious delinquents. This means that the only *proper* way to evaluate the meaning of the Miami findings is to use guesses, intuitions, personal judgment, and other estimating techniques subject to personal biases. Statistics were developed in order to help eliminate such biases so that different researchers would come out with the same sorts of guesses no matter what their personal prejudices. Thus, the authors of this book decided to be improper, providing statistics throughout the data-description chapters of this book. Readers offended by this impropriety are hereby invited to ignore it and implored to forgive the authors' desire for a tool beyond "eyeballing" to guess the likelihood that apparent differences or apparent relationships *would be* real if a random sample had been possible. A major justification for this violation of the rules, as the preceding chapters imply, is that *a random sample of serious delinquents is, in practice, an unattainable ideal.*

In terms of the specific kinds of statistics employed here, one type is measures of central tendency—means and medians. A **mean** is an arithmetic average: the sum of all the observations, divided by the number of observations. For example, the mean of 1, 4, and 16 is 7—1 + 4 + 16, divided by 3. Means use all the observations collected—but they don't necessarily represent a "typical" case when the observations include extreme values such as the 16 in the list above. If the 16 were a 7, a number markedly closer to the other numbers in the list, the mean would be 4—(1 + 4 + 7)/3—a number close to half the size of the original mean. In cases like this, a better measure of central tendency is a **median**, the middle number when all the observations are put into numerical order. The median of both example lists above—1, 4, 16 and 1, 4, 7—is 4.

In the following chapters, means are used for ages (e.g., age at first marijuana use, or age at first arrest). This is done because (1) means are the most commonly used indicators of central tendency in the literature on drug/crime ages, and (2) means work adequately for ages in this data set because there are no extreme age values.

For numbers of crimes committed, means will not work; for almost every crime type, a very small number of offenders committed an enormous number of offenses compared to the rest of the respondents. Thus, medians are much more useful to indicate the typical number of offenses. Where means are used to describe numbers of crimes, as in this chapter, it is for the purpose of comparing these findings to those of most other studies, which almost always use means (generally with little or no discussion of their adequacy as indicators of central tendency).

For the drug use measures, even a median would be of limited use—too many of the "number of days used in the last 90 days" variables have a median of 0 or 90. Therefore, drug usage descriptions are in terms of percentages within grouped and ranked usage-frequency categories (e.g., (1) daily, (2) 3+ days a week but less than daily, and (3) occasional). This means that drug use specifics are described with no measure of central tendency at all.

The other commonly used statistic in the following chapters is a **correlation**, a measure of the degree of relationship between two variables. Correlations range from –1.000 to +1.000, representing completely negative to completely positive correlations; a correlation near .00, whether positive or negative, means that the variables are not related at all. If, for example, age at first crime were always one year greater than age at first drug use for every serious delinquent in the Miami sample, the correlation between these two variables would be +1.000 (using most ways of calculating a correlation); the same would be true if crime age were always one year lower instead of higher. Either way, the observations would go in the *same* direction (thus the *positive* correlation): the offenders who were youngest at first crime would be consistently the youngest at first drug use. If, on the other hand, people with very high scores on one measure (e.g., alcohol use) almost always had very low scores on a second measure (e.g., number of illegal drug sales), and vice versa, the correlation would be near –1.000.

Correlations are also generally accompanied by probability estimates, denoted as "*p*." Ranging from 1.0 down to .0001 or less (which translates to 100% down to .01%—one-hundredth of one percent—or less), this number is the probability that a given correlation would occur purely by accident. Generally, a statistic with a probability of less than 5% (usually written as $p < .05$) is considered acceptable—a good bet to be real rather than happenstance. Even smaller probabilities indicate still better chances that the correlation is a real one.

The specific correlation used in the following chapters is the Spearman Correlation Coefficient, generally referred to as **rho**. This is a rank-order correlation coefficient, which means that it is based on the relative order of observations for each variable—a sequence of 1, 3, and 5 is treated in exactly the same way as 1, 4, and 16, since both sequences are in 1-2-3 rank order. Rho is used in preference to the more commonly seen Pearson Correlation Coefficient (*r*) for four reasons having to do with the Miami serious-delinquency data. First, calculation of the Pearson *r* is based on means (specifically, differences between each observation and the mean), and, as noted above, means are often inappropriate for this data set and are especially misleading for crimes—the primary variables to be described and explained. Second, and also as noted above, the drug usage indicators are most usefully described in terms of ranked ("ordinal") categories, which is what *rho* but not *r* was designed to handle. Third, many of the background variables are also ordinal measures estimating relative rank (e.g., higher versus lower family socioeconomic status), rather than measures in terms of absolute numbers ("ratio level measures," like dollars or years). Fourth and finally, even the numerical indicators that are used in this study—years of age, number of days, number of crimes—seem to be more usefully, and even validly, considered as relative/ordinal, rather than absolute/numerical, indicators. That is, although a respondent's best estimate of having done 95 burglaries is not necessarily a precise numerical report of crimes done, there is a very good chance it *does* mean that this respondent committed *more* burglaries than did another respondent who reported 40 burglaries.

This emphasis on ranked, or ordinal-level, interpretations of even data reported as numbers also has two important implications beyond the choice of specific statistics. Most importantly, this emphasis contributes to the confidence one can have in examining the Miami self-report data in terms of validity (how "real" is each observation?) and reliability (would a repeat of the study result in the same answers?). Both factors are enhanced by not expecting the number data to have actual numerical meaning and not looking at ordinal data with statistics designed for higher-level measures. Second, the limitations and peculiarities of this data set also contribute to the explanation, for those who wish it, of why this book focuses on basic descriptions rather than a full-blown, complex multivariate statistical model. Such analysis is simply beyond the scope of the Miami data. We are improper enough to provide statistical tests on a purposive sample, but only for simple statistics aimed at basic description of a large group of serious delinquents on the street—which is, after all, the primary goal of the study.

Finally, for readers who prefer not to be bothered with statistical particulars, the lengthier specifications for correlations and test results in the following chapters have been confined to footnotes and tables.

## POSTSCRIPT

In summary, 611 youths were interviewed between December 1985 and November 1987 (with continuing field contacts through the end of 1991); all of them were seriously delinquent in that they had committed either 10 or more Index crimes or 100 or more lesser profit-making crimes in the prior 12 months. Most respondents had exceeded this minimum by an extremely large margin. Interviews were done on the street, as opposed to in institutions, in 20 neighborhoods within the Miami/Dade County Florida metropolitan area. At the time of the interviews, both *powder* cocaine and *crack* cocaine were widely available in the Miami area, as they now are in most American cities.

Sociodemographic subsample requirements were used to ensure adequate statistical analysis of gender, age, and race/ethnicity. Black and white males ages 12 to 17 formed the bulk of the sample ($N = 411$); the 200 other youths were ages 14 to 17—100 black and white females and 100 Hispanic (primarily Cuban) males. Interviewer selection and training, questionnaire construction, and interviewing procedures were all designed to maximize interviewer/respondent rapport and hence accurate interview responses. Actual results closely matched the research plan for both the sociodemographic subsample target sizes and the "serious delinquency" eligibility requirements.

The purposive- rather than random-sampling procedure used for this study means that the youths interviewed cannot be considered a representative sample of serious delinquents in the Miami area. However, the resemblance of the sample to the sociodemographic distribution of youth in the Dade County treatment and justice system populations suggests that it is by no means unrepresentative of heavily drug/crime-involved youths in the area.

Further, it can be argued that the sample is *closer* to being representative of *serious* delinquents than (1) any sample studied in the last 20 years but also, ironically, (2) any sample that can be located through a random-sample survey of the general youth population. The latter will invariably locate only a small subsample of serious offenders, due to the relative rarity of extreme criminal involvement among all youths; for the same reason, this small subsample will even more invariably oversample the least serious of the serious offenders. As Cernkovich, Giordano, and Pugh (1985) point out, these random samples of serious delinquents will look "serious" by comparison to most youths in the total sample, but the minimal extent of their crime involvement will be quite obvious by comparison to the criminality of institutionalized delinquents. The purposive-sampling techniques used here, in contrast, permitted the research to focus on inner-city areas, to access youths who were not in school or not even living with parents, and to plan sociodemographic subsamples that would ensure interviews with a cross-section of serious delinquents by gender, age, and ethnicity regardless of their living arrangements or school status.

# CHAPTER 5

# TEENAGE COKE HEADS, BANDITS, AND HUSTLERS

The fundamental reason for this study was to determine just how much drug and criminal involvement serious delinquents on the street really engage in. What *kinds* of drug use and crime? At what frequency levels? How long had they been doing such things? No answers were available for these very elementary questions because, as explained in Chapter 2, street studies of serious, nongang delinquents simply had not been done for 20 years.

The drug and crime involvement of the serious delinquents interviewed is thus described in this chapter in some detail. Male and female patterns are discussed separately, although they are nearly identical for drug use and less markedly different for crime than might be expected.[1] Relationships of drug use and crime to age and race/ethnicity are also discussed.

## DRUG INVOLVEMENT

For garden-variety delinquents, drug involvement beyond alcohol and marijuana tends to be quite limited. As discussed in Chapter 3, it typically entails relatively inexpensive substances, low frequency of use, and rather

---

[1]Since the female subsample is more restricted in age and ethnicity, figures are reported for both (1) the male total and (2) only those males comparable in age and ethnicity to the female total (blacks and whites age 14–17—i.e., excluding the 220 males age 12–13 or Hispanic).

limited risks of addiction. The seriously crime-involved youths interviewed in Miami, in contrast, were almost all seriously drug involved too. This is indicated by the early age at which they began using drugs, the number and variety of drugs they had tried and were still using, and the frequency with which they were currently using some highly addictive substances.

## Drug Use Histories

As in other samples of delinquents and criminals, alcohol and marijuana were the earliest and most commonly used substances. Unlike those other samples, however, these youths had both universal and extremely early experiences with both drugs. Every youth interviewed had tried both substances; three out of four had used alcohol by age 10 and marijuana by age 11. This is startlingly younger than typical ages found among a street sample of adult heroin users interviewed in Miami in 1977–1978, slightly less than ten years before the delinquency study (Inciardi 1979). The heroin users first tried alcohol at a median age of 13 or 14—compared to a median of 7 for the serious delinquents. Similarly, the heroin users began marijuana use at a median age of about 15 or 16, compared to age 10 for the serious delinquents.

Further, unlike garden-variety delinquents, almost all 611 of the serious delinquents had also experimented with other drugs: 99.3% had used some additional drug, first doing so at a mean age of 11.6 years. The five "other drug" types, in order of prevalence, were:

- *Cocaine* (used at least once by 99.2% of the sample)—generally both *powder* cocaine (99.2%) and crack (95.7%) and, in a few cases, coca paste (12.9%).[2]

---

[2]Common in the drug-using communities of Colombia, Bolivia, Venezuela, Ecuador, Peru, and Brazil is the use of coca paste, known to most South Americans as *basuco, susuko, pasta basica de cocaina,* or just simply *pasta* (Jeri 1984). Perhaps best known as "basuco," coca paste is one of the intermediate products in the processing of the coca leaf into cocaine. It is typically smoked straight, in cigarettes mixed with either tobacco or marijuana, and its effects are similar to those of crack.

The smoking of coca paste became popular in South America beginning in the early 1970s. It was readily available and inexpensive, had a high cocaine content, and was absorbed quickly. As the phenomenon was studied, however, it was quickly realized that paste smoking was far more serious than any other form of cocaine use. In addition to cocaine, paste contains traces of all the chemicals used to initially process the coca leaves—kerosene, sulfuric acid, methanol, benzoic acid, and the oxidized products of these solvents, plus any number of other alkaloids that are present in the coca leaf (Almeida 1978). One analysis undertaken in Colombia in 1986 found, in addition to all of these chemicals, traces of brick dust, leaded gasoline, ether, and various talcs (Bogota *El Tiempo,* 19 June 1986, p. 2-D). Coca paste is periodically available in Miami and in Caribbean locales, but typically in limited quantities (Inciardi 1987).

- *Hallucinogens or inhalants* (79.2%)—most commonly PCP (74.3%) but sometimes inhalants such as glue (38.3%) or LSD and other hallucinogens (27.3%).
- *Prescription depressants* (75.8%)—especially minor tranquilizers such as Valium (71.8%) but also narcotic analgesics such as codeine or Percodan (64.6%).
- *"Speed"* (59.9%)—the street name for prescription stimulants such as amphetamines (whether legally or illegally manufactured), usually in pill form (57.3%) but sometimes injected (24.5%).
- *Heroin* (56.5%), either intravenously (33.6%) or by other methods (49.4%) such as snorting or "skin popping" (i.e., injecting under the skin, as opposed to into a vein).

Over 95% of the youths interviewed had tried at least two of these five drug types, and the majority (58.8%) had tried four or all five of them.

First use of these other drugs occurred only after use of alcohol and marijuana, but this was still at very young ages: a mean of about 12 years for hallucinogens or inhalants and 13 for depressant pills, speed, cocaine, and heroin. Table 5.1 shows exact means, by gender. These ages are again markedly younger than for the 1977–1978 heroin users: the delinquents who had tried heroin did so at a median age of 13, compared to 18 for the adult heroin users. Cocaine was first tried by (92% of) the heroin users at a median age of 19 or 20, compared to a median age of 12 for (99% of) the serious delinquents. Further, these ages indicate that most of the youths in this delinquency sample meet the previously noted definition of "precocious" drug involvement offered by Carpenter and her associates (1988, p. 11)—use of drugs other than alcohol or marijuana by age 13. This description fits 91.2% of the 611 youths we interviewed.

A chronological curiosity reflected in Table 5.1 is that, in this sample, the use of cocaine *always* preceded crack use. This pattern occurred because crack did not become readily available in Miami until after these youths had already begun to use cocaine. This historical circumstance also explains why mean ages for first crack use are higher than those for any other drug. As one 16-year-old user commented on the matter in 1987:

> Most of us were already usin' coke [cocaine] when crack really got here. Yeah, it's been around here [Miami] since maybe 1981–1982, in some neighborhoods anyway, but we didn't go runnin' around and knockin' ourselves out tryin' to find it. We had coke, lots of coke, and cheap coke, so we were already doin' coke, ya know?

## TABLE 5.1
### Drug Involvement History by Gender

*(handwritten: Serious Offenders)*

| | Male Total (N = 511) | Only Black or White and Age 14–17 | |
|---|---|---|---|
| | | Female (N = 100) | Male (N = 291) |
| **Percentage ever using** | | | |
| Alcohol | 100.0% | 100.0% | 100.0% |
| Marijuana | 100.0 | 100.0 | 100.0 |
| Hallucinogen/inhalant | 78.9 | 81.0 | 82.8 |
| Rx-type depressant | 74.2 | 84.0* | 70.8 |
| Speed | 57.1 | 74.0* | 60.5 |
| Cocaine powder | 99.4 | 98.0 | 99.3 |
| Crack cocaine | 96.1 | 94.0 | 94.5 |
| Heroin | 56.4 | 57.0 | 54.0 |
| **Mean age at first use of** | | | |
| Alcohol | 7.4 | 8.3 | 8.2 |
| Marijuana | 10.3 | 10.8 | 10.7 |
| Hallucinogen/inhalant | 11.6 | 12.1 | 11.8 |
| Rx-type depressant | 12.4 | 13.2* | 12.8 |
| Speed | 12.6 | 13.1 | 13.0 |
| Cocaine powder | 12.2 | 12.8 | 12.8 |
| Crack cocaine | 13.4 | 14.2 | 14.1 |
| Heroin | 12.7 | 12.8 | 13.2 |
| **Mean number of types tried** (of 7; cocaine counted as one type) | 5.7 | 5.9* | 5.7 |
| **Ever in drug treatment** (including alcohol) | 13.5% | 13.0%* | 21.0% |

*Spearman (rank-order) Correlation Coefficient ("rho") significant at $p < .05$ for gender = male (0 = no, 1 = yes) with "ever" (0 = no, 1 = yes), age, or number of types. All rhos are in the .08 to .15 range.

Interestingly, however, the cocaine-to-crack progression seemed to persist even after crack had become a fact of life in Miami's street drug cultures. In 1990, for example, a 17-year-old daily crack user explained:

> I started using crack in, well, let's see, I was 14, so I guess it was 1987. Before that I was into

grass [marijuana] and some PCP. I wanted to do
some crack, try it, see what it was like, see what
all the fuss was about. Everybody I knew, that I
heard of, that did crack had done cocaine first.
That's just the way it is. Hey, you don't learn to
drive on a 16-gear truck, do ya? . . . That's just
the way it is.

Table 5.1 also indicates that gender differences are almost nonexistent in the drug histories of these serious delinquents. Girls were slightly more likely to have used prescription depressants and stimulants; boys tended to be younger when first using various drugs and were more likely to have been in drug treatment. However, these gender/drug-history correlations are extremely weak, as is also implied by the small gender differences displayed in mean ages and percentages ever involved.

Age was considerably more important than gender. This is reflected indirectly in the lower mean ages shown in Table 5.1 for the total male sample, which includes 12–13-year-olds, as compared to the 14–17-year-old black and white males. The tendency for younger youths to start drug use earlier is especially pronounced for more serious drugs.[3]

Earlier drug use among younger respondents does not necessarily indicate a cohort or historical change. Such change may be *part* of the explanations for these correlations, given the well-documented trend toward decreasing ages for initial drug use, as discussed in Chapter 3. However, the total age range for this sample is quite small, which severely restricts the degree to which the sample is capable of reflecting true cohort or historical change. A second and thus probably more important factor is that sample-selection criteria restricted respondents to only serious delinquents. Youths age 12 and 13 who are already seriously crime involved may also be more drug involved than their age peers who become serious delinquents only at age 14 or 15. Some of the 16- and 17-year-olds interviewed were not committing enough crime at age 12 and 13 to have qualified for sample inclusion; their drug use at that point may have been correspondingly minor.

The data indirectly confirm this idea. Age at initial serious delinquency can be approximated for the sample by age at starting "regular crime"—meaning crime of one type (e.g., drug sales or shoplifting) done at least three times a week. Age at first drug use was significantly correlated with age at initial serious delinquency for all five of the major drug types used by the respondents—alcohol (rho = .56), marijuana (rho = .65), cocaine (rho = .77), prescription-type depressants (rho = .63), and heroin (rho = .75).

---

[3]For the total 611 delinquents, the rho between age at interview and age at first use is .14 for alcohol, .33 for marijuana, and .51–.57 for speed, prescription depressants, cocaine powder, and heroin. The correlation is extreme for crack use—.82—because it was only among the youngest respondents that crack was available to be used at an especially early age.

More importantly for the present context, these correlations are consistently larger than those between the same drug initiation ages and *current* age, and they are obviously much larger for the two drug types used earliest—marijuana (.65 vs. .33) and alcohol (.56 vs. .13). The greater association of early drug use with early serious delinquency than with younger current age suggests that the younger respondents started drug use earlier than the older respondents not because of a cohort effect but because (1) early drug use and early crime tend to occur together, and (2) only those 12–13-year-olds already involved in serious crime were eligible for the sample.

Finally, ethnic variations in drug history were smaller than might be expected. Since whites in this sample were almost always from a higher-socioeconomic-status background than blacks and Hispanics, their access to drugs at an early age might be predicted to be correspondingly lower. That is, higher-status neighborhoods tend to have lower rates of illicit drug use and less of a problem with street-corner drug sales. But although the supposition of later drug initiation ages for whites is supported, the differences are small. Among 14–17-year-olds, mean age at first use was only about a year later for whites (male or female) than for blacks (male or female) or Hispanics (males only): alcohol at 10 instead of 9 (or 8 for Hispanics), marijuana at 11 instead of 10, cocaine at 13 instead of 12.

Similarly, white males age 14–17 had tried fewer of the seven drug types (mean 5.1) than had boys this age who were black (6.3) or Hispanic (6.0), but 5/7 versus 6/7 is a small difference. And for girls the mean number of drug types tried was the same for whites (5.9) and blacks (6.0). Finally, significantly fewer 14–17-year-old whites, especially the males, had ever tried heroin. Among males, heroin had been used by 30% of whites compared to 68% of Hispanics and 77% of blacks; for females the comparison is 45% of whites, 69% of blacks. Racial differences in drug history were thus larger for 14–17-year-old males than for their female counterparts. However, a racial difference is not as apparent among the 12–13-year-old boys, since 55% of blacks and 50% of whites had tried heroin, at similar mean ages (11.0 black, 11.2 white), and the difference in mean number of drug types ever tried is not as large—5.1 for whites and 5.6 for blacks, as opposed to 5.1 and 6.3 for 14–17-year-old boys.

## Current Drug Use

Drug use in the 90 days prior to interview reflected a continuation of the involvement with multiple substances shown in the drug history of this sample. Thus, normal drug use for these serious delinquents was **polydrug use**—use of multiple psychoactive substances, including use at such levels that the effects of one drug were necessarily modifying the effects of another. Of the seven drug types investigated, the 611 youths interviewed had tried a mean of 5.7 types, were using a mean of 4.6 types *currently* (i.e., in the 90 days prior to interview), and were currently using a mean of 2.6 types *regularly* (at least three days a week). Almost every respondent (94.8%) was using at least two different drug types regularly, and almost half (49.9%) were using three different drug types that often.

The base for this polydrug pattern was marijuana and cocaine. When respondents were asked their *two* most preferred drug types (hence totaling 200%), the two most common answers by far were cocaine in some form (92.6%) and marijuana (83.5%). Markedly fewer cited alcohol (17.5%) or heroin (4.1%), and almost no one named prescription depressants (1.0%), speed (0.5%), or PCP (0.2%). Thus, as combination answers (totaling 100%), cocaine/marijuana was much more popular than any other—76.4%, compared to 11.9% for the second most frequent combination (cocaine/alcohol) and 5.8% for the third (marijuana/alcohol).

Further, marijuana and cocaine were typically used at high frequencies during the 90 days prior to interview and had been used regularly for several years. Table 5.2 shows that current *typical* marijuana use for this sample was *daily use*—i.e., use on every one of the prior 90 days. Four out of five respondents were using marijuana daily, almost all the rest were using at some lower level of "regular," and 100% reported marijuana use at least "once or twice a week." Further analysis for the 583 youths (95.4% of the sample) using marijuana regularly indicated that they had been using at this level for a median of four years; 90% began regular use two or more years before we interviewed them.

Cocaine, a far more dangerous and addicting drug, was used almost as many days as marijuana was. Since most respondents were both snorting powder and smoking crack (and a few—3.4%—were using coca paste), a "total cocaine use" variable was constructed by adding the days of use reported for all three cocaine forms. The total-cocaine computation showed that 98.5% were currently using cocaine in some form, 91.2% had a cocaine usage total indicating regular use (3+ days per week, over 13 weeks, to total 39+ of 90 days), and 64.2% had totals amounting to daily use of cocaine, in one form or another. Further, as with marijuana, regular use was not a new pattern. Of the 266 regular users of powder cocaine, 91% had been using regularly for over a year and the majority (63%) had done so for over two years. Crack was a much more recently introduced drug, but 73% of the 424 regular crack users had been using it regularly for over a year and 29% had used at this level for over two years.

The marijuana/cocaine pattern was almost always supplemented with use of at least one depressant—alcohol or pills or heroin. Alcohol was the most commonly used (at 95.9%), and the majority of 14–17-year-olds were drinking regularly, as shown in Table 5.2. Regular use of depressant pills was less common, but two out of three youths had used such drugs at least once in the prior 90 days. Heroin use was even more likely to be sporadic; of the 265 users, 66% used it no more than two days a month (1–7

**TABLE 5.2**
**Current Drug Use: Main Drug Types by Gender**
**(Cumulative Percentages)**

| | Male Total (N = 511) | Only Black or White and Age 14–17 | |
| --- | --- | --- | --- |
| | | Female (N = 100) | Male (N = 291) |
| **Marijuana** | | | |
| Daily | 84.3% | 70.0%* | 85.2% |
| Regular | 96.9 | 88.0 | 97.3 |
| 1–2+/wk | 100.0 | 100.0 | 100.0 |
| **Cocaine** | | | |
| Daily | 12.3% | 24.0% | 15.5% |
| Regular | 42.9 | 47.0 | 44.3 |
| 1–2+/wk | 74.2 | 78.0 | 74.6 |
| Any | 98.8 | 96.0 | 98.6 |
| **Crack** | | | |
| Daily | 38.4% | 46.0%* | 32.3% |
| Regular | 68.9 | 72.0 | 61.9 |
| 1–2+/wk | 83.6 | 85.0 | 77.7 |
| Any | 93.9 | 90.0 | 91.8 |
| **Alcohol** | | | |
| Daily | 13.1% | 33.0% | 22.0% |
| Regular | 45.4 | 55.0 | 58.8 |
| 1–2+/wk | 69.7 | 71.0 | 74.2 |
| Any | 96.1 | 95.0 | 97.6 |
| **Depressant pills** | | | |
| Daily | 2.3% | 5.0%* | 2.4% |
| Regular | 21.3 | 28.0 | 21.3 |
| 1–2+/wk | 38.6 | 54.0 | 36.8 |
| Any | 66.5 | 70.0 | 60.1 |
| **Heroin** | | | |
| Daily | 2.3% | 13.0%* | 4.1% |
| Regular | 3.1 | 13.0 | 4.8 |
| 1–2+/wk | 5.9 | 21.0 | 7.9 |
| Any | 42.9 | 46.0 | 41.2 |

*Spearman (rank-order) Correlation Coefficient ("rho") significant at $p < .05$ for gender = male (0 = no, 1 = yes) with drug use during the last 90 days coded 4 = Daily (90 days); 3 = Regular but less than daily (39–89 days); 2 = Semiregular (18–38 days); 1 = Occasional (1–17 days); 0 = No use (0 days). All rhos are in the .08 to .18 range.

days) and only 7% used it at least twice a week (26+ days). However, 24 youths (3.9% of the total sample) were using intravenous heroin daily (all 90 days). When days of use for all three depressant types are added together, the total is at least 90—amounting to daily use—for 35.0% of the sample; 64.8% had a total of at least 39 use-days, corresponding to regular use; and 99.0% were currently using at least one depressant.

Hallucinogens, inhalants, and speed, in contrast, were not used often and thus are not included in Table 5.2. Almost all of the 22.1% of respondents reporting current hallucinogen/inhalant use were using PCP (21.1%) rather than other hallucinogens (3.9%) or inhalants (1.1%), and almost all PCP use (87% of the 129 users) was confined to 1–6 days out of the last 90 days. Altogether, fewer than 2% of the 611 respondents used hallucinogens and/or inhalants even once a week (13+ days), and only two youths (0.3%) used any such drug regularly. Speed was used by somewhat more respondents (32.1%), but, again, even weekly use was rare—only 5.2% of the 611 youths used speed 13 or more of the prior 90 days. Speed by pills was considerably more common than speed by needle—a 28.8% vs. 8.0% contrast. Of the 196 speed users, 75% used it exclusively in pill form and 10% were exclusively intravenous (IV) users. IV speed use was especially likely to be only occasional—55% of the 49 IV speed users injected speed only once or twice in the prior 90 days, and none injected on more than 15 days. Speed pills were used at only slightly higher frequencies. Of the 176 pill users, 73% used on only 1–6 days, only 3% used regularly, and no one used speed pills daily.

The gender differences for current drug usage frequencies shown in Table 5.2 are slight, as they were for the drug history indicators. Males used somewhat more marijuana (and hallucinogens/inhalants), but females used more depressant (and speed) pills, crack, and heroin. None of the gender/drug-usage correlations, however, are even .20—indicating, as for the drug history measures, very weak relationships between gender and drug use patterns.

Age relationships to current use of the same drug types are only slightly stronger than those for gender. The largest correlation is for alcohol: older youths were clearly drinking more (for the total sample, rho = .38). They were also using slightly more heroin and hallucinogens/inhalants (rho = .11 to .12) and somewhat more speed and cocaine powder (rho = .23 to .24), but younger respondents were using slightly more crack (rho = -.09, $p < .02$). There was no relationship between age and drug usage level for marijuana or prescription depressants.

Analysis of ethnic differences also showed some variations, but many were small and/or entangled with gender differences. The most marked concerned heroin use. Among 14–17-year-olds, the percentages of each subsample currently using (1) any heroin, (2) heroin 8+ days, and (3) daily IV heroin were:

|               | (1)  | (2)  | (3)  |
|---------------|------|------|------|
| White males   | 21%  | 7%   | 1%   |
| Hispanic males| 51%  | 8%   | 0%   |
| Black males   | 60%  | 19%  | 7%   |
| White females | 35%  | 20%  | 18%  |
| Black females | 57%  | 31%  | 6%   |

Most dramatically, this listing indicates that over half of nonwhite respondents could be labeled current heroin users. Whereas low-level use may be relatively harmless in itself, it requires distinctly criminal contacts and is the way a heroin addiction starts. Most interestingly, however, the "8+ days" and "daily IV" percentages indicate that this is more than a black/white difference: black male and white female percentages are the same at the 8+ days level, and, even though white males were by far the least likely to use heroin at all, it was white females who were the most likely to be daily IV heroin users in our sample.

Among males age 14–17, whites (compared to blacks and Hispanics) were using less heroin and cocaine, fewer prescription depressants (rho = −.30 to −.35), slightly less crack (rho = −.21), and slightly more alcohol (rho = .22). Blacks were using more heroin (rho = .30) and a little more cocaine powder (rho = .18), and Hispanics were using slightly more crack, cocaine powder, and prescription depressants (rho = .13–.18) and less alcohol (rho = −.23). Among girls, on the other hand, correlations with race were not significant for crack, cocaine powder, heroin, pills, or alcohol; the only difference, oddly, was less marijuana use among whites (rho = −.28). A smaller majority of white females were using marijuana daily—59%, compared to 82% for both black females and white males the same age (and 88–90% for black and Hispanic males age 14–17).

The most striking aspect of the gender, age, and ethnicity analyses of current drug use is the small number and size of the apparent differences among the sociodemographic subsamples. Only three differences stand out: slightly less overall drug use among white males than among the other subsamples, slightly more drug use among older than younger youths, and more disturbingly high rates of heroin experimentation among minority youths than among whites.

Finally, it should be noted that this sample displays much greater drug involvement than has been described for previously studied samples of serious delinquents. In the 1976 National Youth Survey (when respondents were 11–17 years old), only 15.8% of the 146 "serious delinquents" could be classified as multiple illicit drug users (Elliott and Huizinga 1984, p. 37), compared to 99.3% of this sample. Higher figures were reported for the 1982 Midwest city survey discussed in Chapter 4 (Cernkovich, Giordano, and Pugh 1985), probably because of more exclusive definitions in identifying the most serious offenders, and because of an older sample (ages 12–19). Still, only 38% of the serious delinquents in the Midwest city study used drugs other than alcohol or marijuana even once in the prior 12 months, and only one in six used such a drug at least twice a week. The institutionalized delinquents interviewed in the same study, on the other hand, reported drug involvement much more comparable to (although still less than) that of our sample: prior-year use of some drug beyond alcohol and marijuana for 83% of males and 91% of females, with 70–73% using such drugs at least twice a week.

There are three major reasons why the serious delinquents interviewed for this study were more drug involved than previous samples, especially prior samples of active (as opposed to institutionalized) serious delinquents. First, for reasons discussed in Chapter 2, the Miami respondent-location techniques resulted in a sample of much *more* seriously delinquent youth than can ever be located by use of random-sample surveys, the methodology used in prior studies. Second, the Miami research took place after the mid-1980s explosion in the availability of cheap cocaine, including crack, which resulted in much more cocaine use among teenagers than ever seen before. Third and finally, this cocaine availability factor was enhanced by the selection of Miami as a research site, since it had long been the preeminent cocaine import site for the entire country. In the time since these interviews, however, many other cities around the nation have been flooded with cheap cocaine too, so that high rates of inner-city cocaine use are now common nationwide.

## Current Drug Use
## Summary Variables

In subsequent chapters, current drug use is discussed in relation to both crime and background factors such as school and family variations. Two overall summary variables for current drug use were constructed to assist in these analyses. The rationale for these summaries is that it seems desirable to get an overall indicator for a given respondent's drug involvement, disregarding the details of which specific substances were used. This rationale seemed particularly appropriate for our sample since the same *general* pattern—marijuana/cocaine/depressant polydrug use—was displayed so consistently. The summary variables, it should be noted, were designed to supplement, rather than replace, drug-usage-level variables for drugs of special concern such as crack and heroin.

Construction of the drug summaries is based on three concerns: (1) relative drug usage levels—daily, less regular, or less than regular—for all drug types; (2) a focus on more-than-casual use, so that only use on 10+ days is included; and (3) some consideration as to the overall dangerousness of each drug type—e.g., daily use of cocaine or alcohol was given more weight than daily use of marijuana. Specifics are shown in Table 5.3, including details for the two summary variables: a score ranging from 2–20

TABLE 5.3
**Construction of Drug Score and Drug Level Summary Variable**

| Definition = Points | % Yes | Definition = Points | % Yes |
|---|---|---|---|
| **Marijuana** | | **Speed** | |
| Daily (90 days) = 3 | 82.0% | Regular, < 90 = 2 | 1.1% |
| Regular, < 90 = 2 | 13.4 | 10–38 days = 1 | 8.3 |
| 10–38 days = 1 | 4.6 | | |
| **Hallucinogens/inhalants** | | **Heroin** | |
| Daily (90 days) = 3 | 0.2% | Daily (90 days) = 4 | 4.1% |
| Regular, < 90 = 2 | 0.2 | Regular, < 90 = 2 | 0.7 |
| 10–38 days = 1 | 3.1 | 10–38 days = 1 | 9.3 |
| **Cocaine total** | | **Other** (1 point each) | |
| Daily (90 days) = 4 | 64.2% | Heavy alcohol = yes* | 35.0% |
| Regular, < 90 = 2 | 27.0 | IV user = yes | 23.4 |
| 10–38 days = 1 | 6.2 | Crack = daily | 39.6 |
| **Alcohol** | | **Drug level** | |
| Daily (90 days) = 4 | 16.4% | "High" = 13–20 | 20.6% |
| Regular, < 90 = 2 | 30.6 | "Typical" = 8–12 | 53.8 |
| 10–38 days = 1 | 39.4 | "Low" = 2–7 | 25.5 |
| **Rx-type depressants** | | **Mean scores:** High | 14.3 |
| Daily (90 days) = 4 | 2.8% | Typical | 10.0 |
| Regular, < 90 = 2 | 19.6 | Low | 5.5 |
| 10–38 days = 1 | 27.7 | Drug score total | 9.8 |

*Heavy alcohol: 5+ drinks on 9+ days, 3+ drinks on 30+ days, 1+ drinks on 75+ days.

(median = 10) and a three-category ordinal variable ("Low/Typical/High") based on this score.

To check that some major drug was not given too small or too large a weight in constructing the drug score, we examined correlations between this summary (range 2–20) and days of use (range 0–90) for the major drugs of concern. Results did not vary much by subsample.[4] Alto-

[4]For girls, correlations were highest for the depressants—alcohol, pills, and heroin (rho = .58 to .64)—and a bit lower for total cocaine (rho = .49). For boys of the same age as the girls, total cocaine was the drug most highly correlated with the summary score (rho = .66), but correlations with the three depressant types were only slightly lower than for the girls (rho = .49 to .55). For the youngest boys (those age 12–13), heroin correlated with the drug score at about the same strength as in the 14–17-year-old groups (rho = .55), and correlations for alcohol, pills, and total cocaine were even higher (rho = .74 to .82).

gether, these correlations reflect satisfactorily on the drug score as an over-all drug involvement indicator—they are large enough to indicate substantial correlation between the summary and the major specific drugs of interest; they are far enough below 1.00 to indicate that the drug score does not simply duplicate any specific drug usage variable; they vary among subsamples, but not by much; and they vary among specific drug types, but not by much.

When this overall summary variable is examined in relation to age, gender, and ethnicity, the results are about the same as the conclusions from the more detailed examination above looking at specific drug types. Specifically, we see (1) somewhat more drug use with increasing age, among both males (rho = .28) and females (rho = .34); (2) a little more overall drug use for the females in this sample than the males (rho = .18); and (3) only slightly more drug involvement for black males than for their white and Hispanic counterparts (rho = .14), but no black/white differences for females.

# CRIME INVOLVEMENT

For garden-variety delinquents, legal infractions are almost entirely minor—even trivial—offenses. As discussed in Chapter 2, these behaviors are much more likely to be status offenses than actual crimes, and crimes are almost entirely minor offenses such as petty theft, vandalism, or limited numbers of to-friends-only drug sales. The serious delinquents interviewed in Miami, by contrast, were all committing either substantial numbers of serious crimes such as robbery and burglary or enormous numbers of lesser crimes such as petty theft, selling or trading of stolen goods, drug sales, and prostitution. Further, as detailed below, they began these criminal activities at an early age and thus had been deeply crime involved for at least several years by the time they were interviewed.

## Crime Involvement History and the Role of Drug Use

The 611 youths interviewed first committed a crime at a mean (and median) age of 11.0 years—compared to a mean of 10.3 for first use of an illicit drug (which was marijuana for 95.1% of the sample). Studies of garden-variety delinquency, in apparent contrast, report that delinquency almost always precedes drug use. These studies, however, are not directly comparable, since the garden-variety delinquency preceding drug use is only rarely actual criminal behavior. One of the serious delinquents in this study, a 16-year-old from Miami's Liberty City area, explained how *his* early introduction to crime started:

> It be really hard figurin' when was *first*, when
> was *second*, like that. I was young, shit, *I-WAS-
> YOUNG*, maybe 8, I guess. I was with my brother.
> Fuck! He dead now, cut by some motha-fucka, who's
> also dead. He asked me if I had the balls to climb
> in somebody's window. I said yes, so we walked to
> this place with nice houses around a small lake. I
> was scared, but we found a house with a lot of
> trees an' stuff in the back an' a window I could
> get in. . . . We looked in the place for a long
> time, tryin' to find some money. We had some sodas
> we found, and then I saw $20 under a magnet on the
> side of the refrig. . . . That's all we got, that
> an' a couple of watches. . . .

The drug/crime sequencing for the serious delinquents is much more comparable to that of a sample of adult heroin users interviewed in Miami during 1977–1978 (Inciardi 1979). The heroin users' first illicit drug use occurred at a median age of 15.2; median ages at first crime were 15.2 for males and 15.9 for females. For the serious delinquents, mean drug/crime initiation ages were 10.3/11.0 for males and 10.8/10.8 for females, as shown in Table 5.4. For both the heroin users and the serious delinquents, crime was initiated at about the same time as, or slightly later than, illicit drug use. It might also be noted that, for crime, as for drug use, typical ages at initial involvement are markedly younger for the serious delinquents than for the heroin users—10 or 11 instead of 15 or 16.

Examination of which crime type was the first one committed provides some degree of explanation for the drug/crime sequencing comparisons. Perhaps not surprisingly for such a drug-involved sample, the first crime committed by 67.1% of the 611 youths interviewed was a drug sale or some other drug-business crime. A 14-year-old male remarked in this regard:

> I was sort of a scout, a lookout, for Mr. George.
> That was the name of the man who delivered the
> *stuff* [cocaine] to the places that sold it. That's
> all everyone knew him as. I was 11, an' Mr. George
> had a kid like me probably on every block where he
> brought the stuff in.
>
> I'd be in my front yard, see, watchin' for cops.
> Mr. George would drive by my house in his car,
> sometimes in somebody else's car. He'd drive by a
> few times. I'd watch and see if he was being fol-
> lowed. If everything looked OK, I'd go over to his
> car an' he'd give me the stuff, and tell me where
> to take it, or who to give it to. Sometimes he'd
> just give me a key an' say somethin' like "blue
> Pontiac 75/25." That would mean that near the cor-
> ner of 75th Street and 25th Avenue there'd be a

**TABLE 5.4**
**Crime Involvement History by Gender**

*Serious Offenders* (handwritten annotation)

| | Male Total (N = 511) | Only Black or White and Age 14–17 | |
| --- | --- | --- | --- |
| | | Female (N = 100) | Male (N = 291) |
| **First crime type done** | | | |
| Drug sale | 71.4% | 45.0%* | 64.6% |
| Theft | 27.6 | 41.0 | 34.7 |
| Prostitution | 0.2 | 14.0† | 0.3 |
| Robbery | 0.8 | 0.0 | 0.3 |
| **Percentage who ever** | | | |
| Did drug sale | 97.8% | 83.0%* | 97.6% |
| Did theft | 99.6 | 98.0 | 99.3 |
| Did prostitution | 5.9 | 89.0‡ | 4.8 |
| Did robbery | 67.1 | 51.0* | 71.5 |
| Were arrested | 91.8 | 81.0* | 90.4 |
| Were adjudicated | 74.6 | 72.0 | 78.0 |
| **Age at first** | | | |
| Drug sale | 11.5 | 11.9 | 12.1 |
| Theft | 11.7 | 11.4* | 11.9 |
| Prostitution | 12.6 | 12.6 | 13.1 |
| Robbery | 12.9 | 13.3 | 13.5 |
| Crime (earliest) | 11.0 | 10.8* | 11.3 |
| Arrest | 12.1 | 12.3 | 12.6 |
| Adjudication | 12.8 | 12.6* | 13.4 |

*Spearman Correlation Coefficient significant at $p < .05$ for gender = male (0 = no, 1 = yes) with crime type (for each, 0 = no, 1 = yes), ever (0 = no, 1 = yes), or age; rhos are in the .10 to .19 range.

†As above but rho = −.31 ($p < .001$).

‡As above but rho = −.83 ($p < .0001$).

blue Pontiac. The stuff, and instructions, or maybe something else, would be in the trunk. Mr. George was real careful. When I'd drop it off I'd collect the money too. Sometimes he'd tell me "get in." He'd drive me somewhere an' give me a package to deliver somewhere. Sometimes he'd drive me back home. Mostly I had to walk back. For each job I'd get $10.

Drug-business offenses are the one crime type that prior delinquency studies have identified as almost always following rather than preceding drug use (see White 1990). Thus, the gender contrast in the sequence of mean ages for first drug use and first crime—same age for females; crime slightly later for males—is probably related to the gender difference in the importance of drug sales as a first crime. For boys, drug sales were twice as likely as theft to be the first crime (71%, 28%), whereas for girls they were almost equally likely (45%, 41%).

The large percentages of youths interviewed who reported drug sales as the first crime suggest that drug use was instrumental in the initiation of their serious delinquency. Comparison to the adult heroin users is again instructive. Selling drugs was reported as the first crime committed by only 13% of female and 10% of male heroin users—percentages only one-fourth to one-seventh the size of those for the serious delinquents. This difference suggests a major cohort/historical change in *how* drug/crime offenders first get involved in both drug use and criminal activities.

Further analysis of the drug/crime sequence issue was done with additional data. It is at least possible that either first crime or first illicit drug use might be a relatively meaningless event in the career of a serious delinquent—just a happenstance "first" that is chronologically isolated from subsequent drug use or crime. With this in mind, interviewers asked respondents about the start of *regular* drug use and crime—that is, starting to use a particular drug or commit a particular crime type at least three times a week. For the total 611 youths, mean age at starting regular illicit drug use was 11.4, compared to 12.5 for starting regular crime. The start-regular ages not only confirm the difference seen with the first-time ages but also suggest a slightly larger gap.

The percentage of respondents exhibiting this drugs-before-crime history was computed by comparing the ages, for each respondent, at starting regular illicit drug use versus starting regular crime. The results showed that three out of four youths (74.5%) began regular drug use first, rather than starting both at the same age (20.1%); only a few (5.2%) began regular crime before regular drug use. By and large, then, age at starting regular crime (mean 12.5) was virtually the same as age at first doing both regular crime *and* regular illicit drug use (mean 12.6).

The implication of the preceding figures for chronicity should also be noted. That is, as might be expected from the current age of the respondents (mean 15.0), the youths interviewed had been doing *regular* crime for an average of 2.5 years by the time of interview. Regular crime for less than a year was rare (8.0% of the 611 total), and most respondents (70.7%) had been seriously crime involved for at least two years.

The gender comparison in Table 5.4 indicates that, among blacks and whites age 14–17, boys were slightly more likely to have done a drug sale as a first crime, to have done a drug sale or robbery at all, and to have been arrested and adjudicated (rhos with being male = .13 to .19), whereas girls were more likely to have done prostitution as a first offense (rho with being female = .31) and enormously more likely to have done prostitution at all (rho = .83). Except for the importance of prostitution in female offense patterns, these are rather small gender differences.

Age variations showed the same general tendency seen in the drug use histories of these youths: younger respondents tended to have started earlier. Correlations between current age and age at first crime for the total 611 youths showed that this association was particularly strong for age at first robbery (rho = .60 for the 394 youths who had ever committed a robbery), only somewhat lower for drug sales (rho = .46, N = 583) and prostitution (rho = .46, N = 119), and lowest for age at first theft (rho = .32, N = 602). Younger respondents were also arrested earlier (rho = .47 for the 550 ever arrested) and adjudicated earlier (rho = .54, N = 453), although they were somewhat less likely to have been adjudicated in the first place (rho = .21 between current age and yes-adjudicated). As explained above for drug use histories, this younger-now/earlier-start correlation is most likely a result of our restriction of the sample to serious delinquents.

Race/ethnicity correlations with crime history indicators were again rather small. Among the 411 black and white males age 12–17, blacks were slightly more likely to have drug sales as a first offense whereas whites were correspondingly likelier to have first done a theft (rho = .20 in both cases). This is consistent with findings of slightly later ages at first drug use for whites than blacks. Black boys age 12–17 were slightly more likely to have done drug sales, prostitution, and robbery than their white counterparts (rho = .12 to .20, $p < .01$); they were also more likely to have been arrested and adjudicated (rho = .23, .24). But, overall, there was no relationship at all among these boys between race and age at first crime, or first arrest, or first adjudication (rhos of .01 to .03). Hispanic ethnicity (among the 391 black, white, and Hispanic boys age 14–17) was significantly correlated ($p < .01$) with a first crime of drug sales (and not theft), with younger age at first drug sale, with no robberies ever committed, and with no arrest record—but all rhos were in only the .14 to .21 range, indicating rather weak associations.

Among female respondents as among males, whites were slightly more likely than blacks to have theft as a first offense (rho = .21, $p < .02$), and blacks were more likely to have ever committed a robbery (rho = .32, $p < .001$). In addition, black girls tended to be somewhat younger than their white counterparts when first committing particular crime types other than theft—by about a year for drug sales and prostitution (rho = .21 and .26, $p < .03$) and by almost two years for robbery (rho = .46, $p < .001$, N = 51). Black girls were also typically about a year younger at first arrest and first adjudication (rho = .31 and .23, respectively, $p < .03$). However, there was no correlation with race for females in (1) likelihood of the first crime being drug sales or prostitution; (2) probability of ever having done drug sales, thefts, or prostitution; (3) age at first theft; or (4) probability of having been arrested or adjudicated.

## Current Criminality

Crime during the prior 12 months was analyzed primarily in terms of four crime types: major felonies, petty property crimes, vice offenses, and drug-business activities. Table 5.5 presents information for (1) these four categories, (2) the specific offenses included in each, and (3) the grand totals. The latter figures indicate large numbers of offenses for the male respondents—

**TABLE 5.5**
**Current Crime by Gender (Percentage Doing Any Offense in the Prior 12 Months and Median Number of Offenses Done If Any\*)**

|  | Male Total (N = 511) | | Only Black or White and Age 14–17 | | | |
|---|---|---|---|---|---|---|
|  |  |  | Female (N = 100) | | Male (N = 291) | |
|  | Any | Mdn | Any | Mdn | Any | Mdn |
| Grand total | 100% | 516 | 100% | 640 | 100% | 520 |
| **Major felony** | 81% | 20 | 63% | 10 | 86% | 20 |
| Robbery | 62 | 10 | 45 | 10 | 66 | 10 |
| Assault | 13 | 2 | 23 | 3 | 19 | 3 |
| Burglary | 64 | 10 | 41 | 3 | 67 | 10 |
| Motor vehicle theft | 46 | 2 | 24 | 1 | 48 | 2 |
| **Petty property** | 98% | 163 | 98% | 196 | 97% | 151 |
| Shoplifting | 93 | 75 | 96 | 100 | 88 | 50 |
| Theft from vehicle | 59 | 3 | 52 | 2 | 65 | 3 |
| Pickpocketing | 5 | 1 | 33 | 5 | 4 | 2 |
| Prostitute's theft | 2 | 3 | 73 | 30 | 1 | 7 |
| Other larceny | 3 | 25 | 6 | 15 | 5 | 25 |
| Confidence games | 22% | 5 | 38% | 5 | 21% | 5 |
| Bad paper | 26 | 10 | 50 | 15 | 24 | 10 |
| Stolen goods offense | 85 | 75 | 59 | 100 | 78 | 94 |
| Property destruction | 30 | 2 | 21 | 1 | 28 | 1 |
| Other crime | <1 | 106 | 2 | 2 | <1 | 12 |
| **Vice** | 15% | 5 | 88% | 250 | 13% | 10 |
| Prostitution | 4 | 7 | 87 | 200 | 3 | 10 |
| Procuring | 13 | 5 | 57 | 55 | 12 | 10 |
| **Drug business (any)** | 97% | 300 | 89% | 200 | 97% | 300 |

\*I.e., medians are for offenders only, excluding youths with no offenses of that type.

a median of 516 offenses per person—and even larger numbers (median = 640) for the female respondents.

Gender differences in current crime patterns are apparent in Table 5.5 in terms of both crime types and level of involvement in particular crimes. Much of this difference is attributable to the importance of vice offenses in the crime patterns of the girls: 88% of them did some prostitution, and those 88 girls did a median of 200 prostitution offenses each.[5] Further, contrary to the common image of prostitutes working with (male) pimps, these girls often worked with a female partner and solicited for each other; two out of three female prostitutes reported such an arrangement. As one of them explained:

> Me and my friend Mary have this arrangement. If the *john* [customer] don't want me, then maybe he'd like Mary. See, I'm light skinned, and real slim. Some guys like that, some don't. Mary ain't fat, but she's real dark, an' bigger, especially on top. So if I can I take him to Mary, if that's what he want. I don't get nothin' for it, except Mary do it back for me. Sometimes the john remembers, too. One time this date come by an' say "Hey sweets, where's that big black nigga bitch friend o' yours?" So I take him by where Mary stands.

Because of these arrangements, the girls were almost five times more likely than their male counterparts to report procuring offenses, and the median number of procuring offenses per offender is five times higher for females than for males. This is not to say, however, that female crime patterns consisted entirely of vice offenses. Most of these girls (89%) were selling drugs, almost all (98%) were doing petty property crimes, and offenders doing each type did a median of about 200 such offenses each in the prior 12 months.

Among males, on the other hand, vice offenses were relatively uncommon, drug-business offenses were nearly universal (97%) and more numerous per offender than among the girls, and the most serious offenses—major felonies—were done by more respondents and at a median per offender that was twice that for the girls. Correlations between gender and number of crimes, however, were surprisingly small, except for prostitution (rho = .86 with being female). Among 14–17-year-olds, being male was positively correlated with number of major felonies and number of drug offenses, and being female was positively correlated with number of petty larcenies—but all these correlations were in only the .17 to .22 range, indicating rather weak gender/crime relationships.

---

[5]The extent of female prostitution, the topic of sex-for-crack exchanges, and implications for HIV/AIDS acquisition and transmission are discussed at length in Chapter 9.

Age variations in amounts of crime done were also quite small. Among the 511 males, there was some tendency for older offenders to do more drug-business offenses but fewer shopliftings and other petty larcenies. However, the rhos were only .16 and −.17—quite low, although statistically significant ($p < .001$). Similarly, among the 100 females, older offenders tended to do fewer drug-business offenses and more prostitution, but these correlations were also low (−.18 and .18, p < .001). Number of major felonies committed was not related to age for either males or females.

Differences by race/ethnicity were considerably fewer and smaller than one might expect based on prior studies. As discussed in Chapter 2, many researchers have suggested that black males commit a disproportionate amount of serious juvenile crime; among serious delinquents they might therefore be expected to appear as the *most* serious offenders. This expectation is not supported by the findings. For the 511 males interviewed, correlation between being black and number of major felonies is nonexistent (rho = .02), and correlations with being black are also quite small for number of petty larcenies (rho = .11, $p < .01$) and number of drug-business offenses (rho = .17, $p < .001$). Among females, no statistically significant correlations between race and numbers of crimes were found.

Finally, it might be noted that this sample is considerably more crime involved than previously studied samples of serious delinquents at large in the community. For example, the Miami youths averaged 10 robberies, 112 thefts (felony plus petty), and 493 drug-business plus prostitution "illegal services" offenses—compared to 2, 23, and 27, respectively, for the "serious career offenders" in the 1976–1977 National Youth Surveys (Dunford and Elliott 1984, Table 5). As another example, 26% of the Miami respondents did at least 12 burglaries in the prior 12 months, compared to 1% of the 128 "chronic offenders" interviewed in the community during the Midwest metropolitan area survey by Cernkovich, Giordano, and Pugh (1985, Tables 4–5). Similarly, of the 80 male chronic offenders in the Midwest study, only 33% sold marijuana and a mere 11% did so at least 130 times in the prior year; among the Miami males, 97% were involved in drug-business activities (which were as likely to involve cocaine as marijuana) and 80% did so at least 130 times in the prior year. Among females, 10% of the 48 Midwest chronic offenders did 130+ marijuana sales and 4% did 130+ prostitution offenses in the past year—compared to 89% and 69% of the 100 girls in the Miami sample.

## Current Crime
## Summary Variables

Summary variables for current crime involvement were constructed for the same reasons motivating construction of the current drug use summaries.

One possibility for a crime summary is a simple sum of all offenses. The problem with such a total as an indicator of overall crime involvement is that it gives no more weight to 100 burglaries, for example, than to 100 drug sales, even though the burglaries would appear to reflect a considerably more serious offense pattern. Thus, determining approximate equivalences among specific crime types, to indicate "overall crime," requires some sort of balance between smaller numbers of more serious crimes and larger numbers of less serious offenses.

Construction of the crime summary variables therefore began with necessarily arbitrary categorization of the four major crime types (as defined in Table 5.5) into levels that are arguably comparable across types. To do this, we reduced the full range of data for each crime type to five ordinal categories scored 0, 1, 2, 4, and 8. This scoring system permits a sum of the four types that is weighted rather than equivalent to a simple sum of the raw data; i.e., 100 burglaries contributes much more than 100 drug sales to the total score. The zero category is defined as "garden-variety delinquency"—up to a dozen petty property crimes, up to two dozen drug sales, but no major felonies and no vice offenses. The other end of the scale, scored as 8, is defined as indicating "extreme" involvement—namely, on a weekly basis, 1+ major felonies, 6+ petty property crimes, 7+ vice offenses, or 10+ drug sales; annually, this was taken as 50+, 300+, 350+, and 500+, respectively. The minimum cutoff level for the 4-point category is defined as half the 8-point category minimum—25, 150, 175, and 250, respectively; similarly, the cutoff level for the 2-point category is taken as half the 4-point category minimum—13, 75, 63, and 125. The 1-point category is then simply the range between the zero category and the 2-point category. Correlation of the resulting five-category crime-type summaries with the full-range variables indicates that they capture the essence of the full variables quite well, since the rhos are all in the .965 to .998 range.

The overall crime score was then computed by simply adding the points for the four ordinal-level crime-type variables. The resulting overall range is 1 to 32 points, with a median of 10 points. In subsequent chapters this score is used in correlations reported for "overall current crime." Finally, a three-category "crime level" variable was also constructed for use in cross-tabulation displays; score definitions and percentage distributions for this variable are shown in Table 5.6, along with specifics for the four component crime-type variables and the overall crime score. It should be kept in mind that the crime summary variables indicate *relative* crime, considered as a whole, in a sample composed entirely of youths who were *seriously* crime involved. Hence, even the lowest scores include youths who are considerably more crime involved than delinquents interviewed in the community in other studies.

**TABLE 5.6**
**Construction of Crime Score and Crime Level Summary Variable**

| Component Types (= Points toward Crime Score)/ Summary Variables | Male Total (N = 511) | Only Black or White and Age 14–17 | |
|---|---|---|---|
| | | Female (N = 100) | Male (N = 291) |
| **Major felony** | | | |
| None (= 0) | 19.0% | 37.0% | 13.7% |
| 1–12 (= 1) | 31.5 | 36.0 | 34.4 |
| 13–24 (= 2) | 11.4 | 7.0 | 12.4 |
| 25–47 (= 4) | 15.5 | 6.0 | 17.9 |
| 50+ (= 8) | 22.7 | 14.0 | 21.6 |
| **Petty property crime** | | | |
| 0–12 (= 0) | 6.3% | 3.0% | 9.6% |
| 13–74 (= 1) | 23.1 | 21.0 | 27.1 |
| 75–145 (= 2) | 16.2 | 19.0 | 14.4 |
| 150–298 (= 4) | 36.8 | 31.0 | 28.5 |
| 300+ (= 8) | 17.6 | 26.0 | 20.3 |
| **Vice** | | | |
| None (= 0) | 85.1% | 12.0% | 86.6% |
| 1–72 (= 1) | 14.3 | 13.0 | 12.4 |
| 100–160 (= 2) | 0.2 | 11.0 | 0.3 |
| 175–320 (= 4) | 0.4 | 37.0 | 0.7 |
| 350+ (= 8) | 0.0 | 27.0 | 0.0 |
| **Drug business** | | | |
| 0–20 (= 0) | 6.1% | 22.0% | 7.9% |
| 25–120 (= 1) | 12.9 | 19.0 | 13.1 |
| 125–225 (= 2) | 16.4 | 17.0 | 13.7 |
| 250–475 (= 4) | 39.1 | 26.0 | 36.4 |
| 500+ (= 8) | 25.4 | 16.0 | 28.9 |
| **Crime score (sum of points)** | | | |
| 24+ | 2.9% | 11.0% | 3.8% |
| 20+ | 10.4 | 23.0 | 11.7 |
| 16+ | 22.7 | 30.0 | 22.7 |
| 12+ | 40.9 | 51.0 | 39.9 |
| 8+ | 66.5 | 70.0 | 66.7 |
| 4+ | 92.6 | 92.0 | 93.8 |
| (Median score) | (10.0) | (12.0) | (9.0) |
| **Crime level (3-point category)** | | | |
| Highest (16+) | 22.7% | 30.0% | 22.7% |
| Typical (6–15) | 56.8 | 53.0 | 56.7 |
| Lowest (1–5) | 20.5 | 17.0 | 20.6 |

Correlations were examined between the overall crime score (range = 1 to 32) and the four specific crime-type summaries included in it. Except for vice, the results did not vary much by gender.[6] Altogether, correlations between the crime score and the specific types suggest that the summary is adequate. The small gender differences for crimes other than vice are in accord with the relatively small differences between male and female crime patterns (again except for vice). That one offense type does not predominate is suggested by the similarity in the size of the correlations both within and between demographic subgroups (except for vice among the male subgroups, the overall range is .58 to .82). Further, none of the correlations are so high as to suggest total overlap between a given offense type and the crime score, indicating that the summary does contribute new information.

Finally, the crime score was examined in relation to gender, age, and ethnicity. These correlations indicate (1) no relationship between overall crime level and being male (rho = –.09, not significant at the .01 level for the 611 total respondents); (2) no relationship between overall crime level and current age (rho = .04, again not statistically significant); and (3) a fairly weak relationship between overall crime level and being black among 14–17-year-old males (rho = .25, $p < .001$) and females (rho = .23, $p < .01$) and no relationship to race among the 12–13-year-old boys (rho = –.02, not significant).

## POSTSCRIPT

The preceding discussions and tables indicate that both drug use and crime vary in this sample. That is, the serious delinquents interviewed can be categorized as less or more seriously delinquent, less or more seriously involved in drug use or crime. However, this variation is *not* primarily a variation by gender, age, or race/ethnicity, since only minimal differences were found among sociodemographic subsamples in drug use or crime, in terms of either history or current activities. In fact, very striking similarities were found across these groups.

Specifically, the great majority of serious delinquents interviewed demonstrated the following characteristics:

---

[6]For females, all four crime types are similarly correlated with the total crime score: major felonies (rho = .60), petty property crime (rho = .77), vice (rho = .65), and drug-business offenses (rho = .66). For males of the same age as the females, the correlation for vice is markedly lower (rho = .23), but the others are virtually identical: major felonies (rho = .58), petty property crime (rho = .73), and drug-business offenses (rho = .62). For boys age 12–13, the correlations with the crime score are slightly stronger for major felonies (rho = .82) and drug-business offenses (rho = .71), but about the same as for 14–17-year-olds for petty property crime (rho = .69); the correlation for vice (rho = .46), as in the case of the older boys, is markedly lower than for the other offenses within the same subsample.

1. Very early initiation into drug use, starting with alcohol and marijuana.
2. Experience with a wide variety of different drug types.
3. A current polydrug use pattern consisting of regular (and typically daily) marijuana and cocaine use plus at least semiregular use of at least one depressant.
4. Very young age at first crime, which typically followed first illicit drug use and which was almost always either a drug sale or a theft.
5. Current crime involvement well in excess of sample eligibility requirements: either a considerable number of serious crimes or a massive number of lesser crimes (and, not uncommonly, both).

By comparison, the list of sociodemographic *differences* in drug use and crime patterns is considerably less impressive than the preceding list of near-uniformities. Gender differences are virtually nonexistent for drug use and surprisingly small for crime, with the exception of the importance of prostitution in female crime patterns. Younger age is correlated with earlier drug and crime initiation ages, but this appears to be a function of our restriction of the sample to only serious delinquents; relationships between current age and current drug use or current crime are slight. Race/ethnicity correlations are also relatively small: whites tend to start drug and crime involvement later than blacks, but only a little later; white males are less drug involved than youths of any other gender/ethnicity category, but not by much; and the generally weaker relationships of current drug use and crime to race for females compared to males suggest that male race/ethnicity differences are not due directly to race/ethnicity as such.

The small sociodemographic differences reported in this chapter appear especially miniscule given the heavy emphasis in prior studies on two factors: (1) serious involvement in youth crime as male and not female behavior, and (2) black males as the most serious of serious delinquents. It should be recalled in this context that this study can say nothing about the relative distribution of serious delinquency among all youth. It may be, as prior studies suggest, that adolescent black males are the youths most likely to become serious delinquents and that the probability of a youth becoming involved in violent crime is at least six times larger for boys than for girls. However, among the serious delinquents interviewed here, black males can be characterized as no more than "slightly" more drug or crime involved than other serious delinquents, and the females—although less prone than males to major felonies—were clearly as enmeshed as the males in a drug/crime lifestyle.

# STREET KIDS AND CRACK COCAINE

Crack cocaine is the newest substance included in discussions of the relationship between drug use and crime. Since it made its first appearance on the streets of urban America during the mid-1980s, media attention has focused on how the high addiction liability of the drug instigates users to commit crimes to support their habits, and on how rivalries in crack distribution networks have turned some inner-city communities into urban "dead zones," where homicide rates are so high that police have written them off as anarchic badlands.[1]

Of special emphasis in press reports on crack has been the involvement of inner-city youths in the crack business. As *Time* magazine explained in its May 9, 1988, cover story:

> With the unemployment rate for black teenagers at 37%, little work is available to unskilled, poorly educated youths. The handful of jobs that are open—flipping burgers, packing groceries—pay only minimum wages or "chump change," in

---

[1]See *New York Times*, November 29, 1985, pp. 1A, B6; *Newsweek*, June 16, 1986, pp. 15–22; *USA Today*, June 16, 1986, p. 1A; *Newsweek*, June 30, 1986, pp. 52–53; *New York Times*, August 25, 1986, pp. B1–B2; *New York Times*, November 24, 1986, pp. 1A, B2; *Newsweek*, April 27, 1987, pp. 35–36; *New York Times*, March 20, 1988, p. E9; *Miami Herald* ("Neighbors" supplement), April 24, 1988, pp. 21–25; *New York Times*, June 23, 1988, pp. A1, B4; *Time*, December 5, 1988, p. 32; *New York Doctor*, April 10, 1989, pp. 1, 22; *U.S. News & World Report*, April 10, 1989, pp. 20–32.

the street vernacular. So these youngsters
turn to the most lucrative option they can
find. In rapidly growing numbers, they
are becoming the new criminal recruits of
the inner city, the children who deal
crack. (p. 20)

Other stories have targeted the "peewees" and
"wannabees" (want-to-be's), the street-gang acolytes
in grade school and junior high who patrol the
streets with walkie-talkies in the vicinity of crack
houses, serving in networks of lookouts, spotters,
and steerers, and aspiring to be "rollers" (short for
high rollers) in the drug distribution business (see
*Newsweek*, March 28, 1988, pp. 20–27). Yet with all the
media attention on youths in the crack scene, only
minimal empirical information has been collected on
their use of the drug, their complicity in the drug
business, and their specific criminal behaviors, including violent activities.

In early 1985, few people nationally had heard of
crack, but it was already a problem in Miami
(Inciardi 1987). This awareness permitted crack to be
included in the drug history section of the interview
schedule being planned for this street study of serious delinquents. Preliminary analysis of the first
interviews showed a surprisingly high prevalence
and incidence of crack use. Of the first 308 youths
interviewed, 95.5% reported having used crack at
least once, and 87.3% reported current regular use—
i.e., in the 90 days prior to being interviewed, use
three or more times a week. These unexpected figures motivated the design of a supplementary crack-
data instrument, which was ultimately used during
the last 254 interviews, from October 1986 through
November 1987. This chapter is a report of the findings from this crack-data subsample.

# Drug Use and
# Crack–Business Involvement

As indicated in Table 6.1, the crack-data subsample was very similar to the
total sample in terms of distribution by gender, ethnicity, age, and school
experience. General drug histories were likewise similar. For crack use spe-

**TABLE 6.1**
**Demographic Characteristics of the Crack-Data Subsample**
**(versus the Total Sample)**

|  |  | Crack-Data Subsample (N = 254) | Total Sample (N = 611) |
|---|---|---|---|
| **Sex** | Male | 85.0% | 83.6% |
|  | Female | 15.0 | 16.4 |
| **Ethnicity** | Black | 39.4% | 42.2% |
|  | White | 43.3 | 41.4 |
|  | Hispanic | 17.3 | 16.4 |
| **Age** | 12–13 years | 24.4% | 19.6% |
|  | 14–15 years | 42.1 | 38.5 |
|  | 16–17 years | 33.5 | 41.9 |
|  | (Mean age) | (14.7) | (15.0) |
| **Schooling** | Attending   grades 5–8 | 38.6% | 26.5% |
|  | grades 9–10 | 31.1 | 33.4 |
|  | grades 11–12 | 8.3 | 11.1 |
|  | High school graduate | 0.0 | 0.3 |
|  | Dropped out of school | 22.0 | 28.6 |
|  | (Mean grades completed) | (8.0) | (8.5) |
|  | Ever suspended/expelled | 89.4% | 87.9% |

cifically, this means that involvement with this new drug occurred only *after regular* use of alcohol, marijuana, and powder cocaine.

Current drug use rates were also high but varied considerably by degree of participation in the crack trade. Of the 254 youths under analysis here, all but 50 (19.7%) had some type of involvement in the crack business. Twenty subjects (7.9%) had only "minor" involvement, since they sold the drug only to their friends, worked for dealers as lookouts and spotters, or steered customers to one of Miami's approximately 700 crack houses. Most of the youths (138, or 54.3%) were crack "dealers," involved directly in the retail sale of crack. Finally, 46 subjects (18.1%) were designated as "dealer+," since they not only sold the drug but also manufactured, smuggled, or wholesaled it. The differences among cases designated as "minor," "dealer," and "dealer+" are readily illustrated by three adolescents—Erica, Wilson, and Pete—interviewed by the senior author during field studies in early 1991.

Erica, a 16-year-old crack user, had been a part-time model since age 11. Erica lived with her mother and sister in the Kendall section of South Dade County and attended the local high school, where she was a cheerleader and played field hockey. She modeled clothing at local department stores and fashion shows and did occasional television commercials. The modeling jobs paid for Erica's crack use, which was sporadic—"sometimes every weekend, sometimes just once a month, with an occasional binge here and there, but *very* occasional," as she explained it. As for her involvement in the crack business, she indicated:

> I'm not really *in* the crack business. I just know someone who is and help him out once in a while. Sometimes I just carry the product for him, and once I picked up a payment. He usually pays me with crack, some of which I sell to friends when we get together to smoke.

Wilson, age 17 and a high school dropout, was a bonafide crack dealer who grew up on the streets of Liberty City. Wilson began his career in drugs at age 12 with marijuana, followed by amphetamines, cocaine, heroin, and then crack at 16. He reported having been in and out of jails and drug treatment programs "for years," and at the time of interview he was a daily user of alcohol, crack, marijuana, and heroin. As for his crack sales, he explained:

> I sell the cracks for money and for cracks. The man, he give me *this much*. I sell most of it, and I get the rest for me, like *this much*. Every day I do this. Every fucking day.

Pete was the entrepreneur of the three. Also a daily crack user and high school dropout, he had been using drugs for half his short life of 16 years. He prided himself on his ability to purchase cocaine by the quarter-ounce, converting it to crack in his mother's microwave oven while she was out at work:

> The formula is simple--cocaine, water, baking soda, and a little *comeback* [a cocaine analog, such as lidocaine, that will bind with cocaine during the cooking and serve to increase the volume of the end product]. Put it in a fucking measuring cup, cook it for two minutes, and there it is--*ready rock*.

When we examine drug use within the context of a youth's level of involvement with the crack business (none, minor, dealer, and dealer+), a number of relationships quickly become evident. As indicated in Table 6.2, the greater a youth's involvement in the crack business, the more likely was the daily or at least regular use of such drugs as marijuana, depressants, and crack. Whereas 66% of the youths with no business involvement were daily users of marijuana, daily use increased to 80% for those with

**TABLE 6.2**
**Current Drug Use by Crack-Business Involvement**

| | Crack-Business Involvement | | | | Total Crack Sample (N = 254) |
|---|---|---|---|---|---|
| | None (N = 50) | Minor (N = 20) | Dealer (N = 138) | Dealer+ (N = 46) | |
| **Alcohol** | | | | | |
| Daily | 4.0% | 5.0% | 7.2% | 8.7% | 6.7% |
| Regular | 14.0 | 15.0 | 39.9 | 56.5 | 35.8 |
| Occasional | 78.0 | 80.0 | 48.6 | 34.8 | 54.3 |
| No use | 4.0 | 0.0 | 4.3 | 0.0 | 3.1 |
| **Marijuana** | | | | | |
| Daily | 66.0% | 80.0% | 91.3% | 100.0% | 87.0% |
| Regular | 30.0 | 20.0 | 6.5 | 0.0 | 11.0 |
| Occasional | 4.0 | 0.0 | 2.2 | 0.0 | 2.0 |
| **Prescription depressants** | | | | | |
| Regular | 2.0% | 5.0% | 32.6% | 50.0% | 27.6% |
| Occasional | 56.0 | 55.0 | 52.9 | 37.0 | 50.8 |
| No use | 42.0 | 40.0 | 14.5 | 13.0 | 21.7 |
| **Powder cocaine** | | | | | |
| Daily | 10.0% | 15.0% | 2.9% | 0.0% | 4.7% |
| Regular | 44.0 | 60.0 | 21.0 | 8.7 | 26.4 |
| Occasional | 36.0 | 25.0 | 76.1 | 91.3 | 66.9 |
| No use | 10.0 | 0.0 | 0.0 | 0.0 | 2.0 |
| **Crack** | | | | | |
| Daily | 2.0% | 5.0% | 70.3% | 87.0% | 54.7% |
| Regular | 26.0 | 50.0 | 15.2 | 6.5 | 18.5 |
| Occasional | 48.0 | 45.0 | 14.5 | 6.5 | 22.1 |
| No use | 24.0 | 0.0 | 0.0 | 0.0 | 4.7 |
| **Cocaine total (all forms)** | | | | | |
| Daily | 16.0% | 30.0% | 82.6% | 95.7% | 67.7% |
| Regular | 58.0 | 70.0 | 17.4 | 2.2 | 26.8 |
| Occasional | 16.0 | 0.0 | 0.0 | 2.2 | 3.5 |
| No use | 10.0 | 0.0 | 0.0 | 0.0 | 2.0 |

minor involvement, 91% for dealers, and 100% for those in the dealer+ group. The most pronounced differences are apparent with crack use, with the proportions using crack daily ranging from 2% of those with no crack-business involvement to 87% of those in the dealer+ group.

Considering all forms of cocaine together, the percentage of daily users increases from 16% of those with no involvement to 95.7% in the dealer+ group. These figures reflect total cocaine use, regardless of form, and hence include powder cocaine, crack, and coca paste (basuco).

The only data in Table 6.2 not following the same general trend of more frequent use as involvement in the crack market increases appear in the proportions of daily users of powder cocaine. None of the dealer+ group and only 2.9% of the dealers were daily users of this form of cocaine, and only 8.7% and 21%, respectively, were "regular" users. Consequently, there were considerably more daily and regular users of this drug among those having little or no involvement in the crack trade. One reason for this difference becomes clear in Table 6.3.

When the 246 youths who had some experience with both powder *and* crack cocaine were asked to indicate their two most preferred drugs,

**TABLE 6.3**
**Drug Preferences and Bad Crack Highs**

|  | Crack-Business Involvement | | | | Total Who Ever Tried |
|---|---|---|---|---|---|
|  | None (N = 42) | Minor (N = 20) | Dealer (N = 138) | Dealer+ (N = 46) | Crack (N = 246) |
| **Two most preferred drugs** | | | | | |
| Cocaine (any form) | 100.0% | 100.0% | 100.0% | 100.0% | 100.0% |
| Marijuana | 95.2 | 90.0 | 94.2 | 95.7 | 94.3 |
| Alcohol | 2.4 | 5.0 | 2.9 | 4.3 | 3.3 |
| Heroin | 2.4 | 5.0 | 2.9 | 0.0 | 2.4 |
| Other | 0.0 | 0.0 | 0.0 | 0.0 | 0.0 |
| **Cocaine preference** | | | | | |
| Crack cocaine | 28.6% | 55.0% | 86.2% | 93.5% | 75.2% |
| Powder cocaine | 69.0 | 30.0 | 9.4 | 4.3 | 20.3 |
| No preference | 2.4 | 15.0 | 4.3 | 2.2 | 4.5 |
| **Ever bad highs on crack?** | | | | | |
| Never | 33.3% | 40.0% | 66.7% | 71.7% | 59.8% |
| Once or twice | 45.2 | 40.0 | 29.7 | 26.1 | 32.5 |
| 3+ times | 21.4 | 20.0 | 3.6 | 2.2 | 7.7 |

every one of them named cocaine, in one form or another; marijuana was almost as popular a choice. These preferences remained constant regardless of level of involvement in the crack market. Differences clearly emerged, however, with preferences for crack cocaine versus powder cocaine—the greater one's involvement with the crack business, the greater the preference for crack over powder.

These differences can be explained in a number of ways. First, as shown in Table 6.3, some two-thirds of those with no crack-business involvement and three-fifths of those with minor involvement had bad experiences with crack. Almost the reverse was the case with those in the dealer and dealer+ groups. More importantly, however, market access determines a customer's ability to obtain a desired commodity, regardless of whether that commodity is diamonds, truffles, chocolate-covered grasshoppers, or crack cocaine.

This access, furthermore, went beyond the obvious one of dealers having convenient opportunities to purchase crack for personal consumption. As Table 6.4 indicates, almost nine out of ten crack users actually received crack directly, on at least an occasional basis, as part of their pay for drug sales. This was reported as a *frequent* occurrence by almost all (85%+) of the subjects in the two crack-dealer groups. Further, the majority of crack users who had only minor or no crack-business involvement were

**TABLE 6.4**
**Getting Paid in Crack and Paying for Crack**

| | Crack-Business Involvement | | | | Crack Users in Subsample |
|---|---|---|---|---|---|
| | None (N = 38) | Minor (N = 20) | Dealer (N = 138) | Dealer+ (N = 46) | (N = 242) |
| **Paid in crack for dealing, last 12 months** | | | | | |
| Never | 44.7% | 10.0% | 7.2% | 2.2% | 12.4% |
| Occasionally | 39.5 | 55.0 | 8.0 | 6.5 | 16.5 |
| Often (6+ times) | 15.8 | 35.0 | 84.8 | 91.3 | 71.1 |
| **Money spent on crack for personal use, last 90 days** | | | | | |
| $2,400 or more | 0.0% | 0.0% | 36.2% | 52.2% | 13.2% |
| $1,000 or more | 2.6 | 0.0 | 70.3 | 93.5 | 58.3 |
| Median amount | $75 | $225 | $2,000 | $2,500 | $1,650 |

paid in crack at least sometimes, even though their dealing entailed some drug other than crack for all of the no-involvement group and unknown numbers of the minor-involvement group.

The last part of Table 6.4 shows, however, that being paid in crack for dealing was not sufficient to support the crack use patterns of most crack dealers. In fact, the greater the crack-business involvement, the more money that was spent buying crack for personal use. The money rarely came from legal sources, since only 6.7% (N = 17) of the 254 youths were employed at the time of interview. Rather, as the following section indicates, the primary source of this money was profit-making crime of all sorts.

# THE DRUGS/VIOLENCE CONNECTION

The general relationship between drugs and violence within this population can be examined within the context of Goldstein's (1985) "tripartite" conceptual framework. The serious delinquents interviewed for this study, like most drug/crime samples, demonstrate the impact of three simultaneous connections between drug use and violent behavior. Goldstein labels these the *psychopharmacological, economically compulsive,* and *systemic* models of violence.

The *psychopharmacological model of violence* suggests that some individuals, as the result of short-term or long-term use of certain drugs, may become excitable, irrational, and violent. Some 5.4% of the sample reported committing this form of violence at least once during the 12-month period prior to interview, and 4.6% reported being the *victims* of it during this same period. In both cases, the impatience and irritability associated with drug withdrawal or the paranoia and edginess associated with stimulant abuse were the typical causes of this behavior. During mid-1989 a 17-year-old daily crack user summed up both situations:

> It doesn't seem to matter whether you're on or off crack . . . you're crazy both times. If you're high, you think someone's goin' ta do something to you, or try an' take your stuff. If you're comin' down or are waiting to make a buy or just get off, you seem to get pissed off easy. . . . A lot of people been cut just because somebody looked at them funny or said somethin' stupid.

Similarly, a 16-year-old female crack user reported in 1990:

> . . . I was in this *graveyard* [a room in an abandoned building used for selling and smoking crack or for exchanging sex for crack] off 103rd

> [Street], givin' this man a blow job [oral sex]
> for a *taste* [a share of drugs; in this case, a
> *hit* from a crack pipe] of his crack. But he was
> so strung out, so wasted, so fucked up from doin'
> crack that he couldn't *get it up* [get an erec-
> tion]. Like it was my fault, the mother fucker.
> . . . The touchy asshole. He keeps slappin' me,
> sayin' that I couldn't give good *head* [oral sex].
> . . . Another time I saw this same man, with some
> other lady, and the same thing was happenin' and
> he got fuck-all kick-ass mad and beat her up bad.

A second view, the *economically compulsive model of violence,* holds that some drug users engage in economically oriented violent crimes to support their costly drug use. As already indicated in the previous chapter (see Table 5.5), the majority of respondents in this study participated in robberies during the 12-month period prior to interview. That most robber-ies were committed to purchase drugs is suggested by answers to the ques-tion "Of the money you make illegally, how much goes to buying drugs?" Some 61.9% of all 611 respondents said 90% or more, and 91.0% said over half their crimes went toward purchasing drugs. In this regard, a 17-year-old male reported in 1988:

> To get enough money for whatever we wanted to do
> [whatever drugs], sometimes me an' a friend would
> go downtown, maybe down the street from some nice
> restaurants, and wait for them [potential victims]
> to go to their cars. We'd know what cars they'd be
> goin' to. It was the rental cars--Hertz, Alamo,
> you know, those cars--for the tourists. When the
> guy would bend down to unlock the door, we'd run
> from across the street real fast, knock him with a
> club an' kick him a few times, take his wallet,
> jewelry. And the guy would always have a lady with
> him, and she would stand there in shock, so I'd
> run around the car an' take her bag, a chain from
> the neck if she had it.

In addition, 24.1% of the 611 respondents had taken drugs away from another drug user in the prior 12 months by means of force or threat of force, and 21.1% had themselves been the *victim* of a drug robbery dur-ing that time. An additional 39.9% were not robbed of drugs in the past year but had been victimized this way at some previous time. For example, a 15-year-old female explained in 1989 that, because of her size and her sex, she had been continually victimized by the drug users and sellers that she dealt with:

> Maybe it was because I'm a girl, maybe because I'm
> little, but everybody was rippin' me off. I'd get
> my stuff and somebody would knock me down and take

> it. I would lie to my mother about the bruises.
> Once I was beat so I had two black eyes, and I
> told my mother somebody tried to rape me, and she
> went crazy, wanted to call the police. . . .

Third, the *systemic model of violence* maintains that violent crime is intrinsic to involvement with any illicit substance, due to the traditionally aggressive patterns of interaction within illegal drug-trafficking and -distribution systems. Many of the youths interviewed in this study reported involvement in systemic violence as both perpetrators (8.3%) and victims (9.0% in the last 12 months; another 7.2% earlier). The violence typically emerged in this population as fights resulting from territorial disputes, the sale of poor-quality drugs, and instances of "messing up the money." One incident involved the execution in 1987 of two crack user/dealers in Miami's Liberty City community who were suspected of being police informants. As the reported perpetrator of these homicides indicated:

> I'm not sayin' *when* I did it, *how* I did it, or
> *where* I did it. But I will say why. Because they
> were cheatin', lyin' mother fuckers, takin' money
> from cops and sellin' out. . . . So I was told to
> teach 'em a good lesson, and make a good example
> of 'em. (Inciardi 1990a, p. 100)[2]

Table 6.5 suggests a clear relationship between a youth's proximity to the crack market and his or her overall involvement in crime, *including violent crime*. Specifically, the more involved a youth is in crack distribution, the earlier he or she first committed a crime and was first arrested, convicted, and incarcerated. Moreover, the greater the crack-business involvement, the higher the likelihood of an arrest resulting in incarceration. This suggests that the youths most likely to become deeply involved in the crack trade were those with the earliest and most serious general crime history.

Current crime—i.e., crime in the year prior to interview—shows the same pattern: the greater the crack-business participation, the greater the level of other crime commission. As indicated in Table 6.6, this held for both major felonies and property offenses. This pattern was not seen for the vice offenses, due primarily to the small number of females in the sample.[3]

---

[2]The perpetrator of these executions, sampled for the study in 1987, was interviewed by the senior author two years later, in early 1989. A black male and high school dropout, he was 17 years of age at the time of the homicides. In his neighborhood he had the reputation of being an aggressive youth who had been arrested on several occasions for serious assaults. Local crack-using informants never doubted his assertions about the 1987 killings. In fact, they claimed that from 1986 through early 1989 he was responsible for at least four killings in the Miami-Dade drug community.

[3]Only 15% of the sample were females ($N = 38$), who were distributed in the crack-business categories as follows: "None" ($N = 13$), "Minor" ($N = 1$), "Dealer" ($N = 22$), and "Dealer+" ($N = 2$).

**TABLE 6.5**
**Crime and Arrest-Related Histories (Mean Age and Percent Involved)**

| | Crack-Business Involvement | | | | Total Crack Sample (N = 254) |
|---|---|---|---|---|---|
| | **None** (N = 50) | **Minor** (N = 20) | **Dealer** (N = 138) | **Dealer+** (N = 46) | |
| **Drug sale** | | | | | |
| First marijuana | 12.6 | 12.3 | 10.1 | 9.9 | 10.6 |
| % ever | 86.0% | 100.0% | 100.0% | 100.0% | 97.2% |
| First other | 13.1 | 13.1 | 11.2 | 11.3 | 11.7 |
| % ever | 70.0% | 100.0% | 100.0% | 100.0% | 94.1% |
| Start regular | 13.7 | 13.4 | 11.4 | 11.5 | 12.0 |
| % ever | 84.0% | 100.0% | 100.0% | 100.0% | 96.9% |
| **Theft** | | | | | |
| First time | 12.0 | 12.6 | 10.8 | 10.7 | 11.2 |
| % ever | 94.0% | 100.0% | 100.0% | 100.0% | 98.8% |
| Start regular | 13.4 | 13.5 | 11.7 | 11.7 | 12.0 |
| % ever | 74.0% | 55.0% | 89.9% | 100.0% | 85.8% |
| **Crime (earliest)\*** | | | | | |
| First time | 11.7 | 12.1 | 9.8 | 9.7 | 10.3 |
| Start regular | 13.2 | 13.2 | 11.2 | 11.2 | 11.7 |
| % ever regular | 100.0% | 100.0% | 100.0% | 100.0% | 100.0% |
| **Arrest** | | | | | |
| First | 12.8 | 13.1 | 10.6 | 10.4 | 11.1 |
| % ever | 68.0% | 100.0% | 98.6% | 93.5% | 91.7% |
| **Adjudication** | | | | | |
| First arrest resulting in adjudication | 14.1 | 14.6 | 10.9 | 10.9 | 11.3 |
| % ever | 20.0% | 45.0% | 84.8% | 93.5% | 70.5% |
| **Incarceration** | | | | | |
| First | 14.2 | 15.0 | 12.6 | 12.8 | 12.8 |
| % ever | 12.0% | 25.0% | 61.6% | 71.7% | 50.8% |
| **Treatment for drug/alcohol** | | | | | |
| First entry | N/A | N/A | 13.2 | 13.0 | 13.1 |
| % ever | 0.0% | 0.0% | 4.3% | 8.7% | 3.9% |

\*In each case (first, regular) age at time of first such occurrence, whether for drug sales, theft, prostitution, or robbery (the latter taken as "regular" at the tenth occurrence rather than at starting 3+ times/week).

**TABLE 6.6**
**Specific Crimes in the 12 Months Prior to Interview**

|  | Crack-Business Involvement | | | | Total Crack Sample (N = 254) |
|---|---|---|---|---|---|
|  | None (N = 50) | Minor (N = 20) | Dealer (N = 138) | Dealer+ (N = 46) |  |
| **Major felonies** | 44.0% | 65.0% | 87.7% | 95.7% | 78.7% |
| Robbery | 12.0% | 40.0% | 66.7% | 73.9% | 55.1% |
| Assaults | 4.0 | 0.0 | 8.0 | 17.4 | 8.3 |
| Burglary | 24.0 | 25.0 | 70.3 | 91.3 | 61.4 |
| Motor vehicle theft | 30.0 | 35.0 | 57.2 | 73.9 | 53.1 |
| **Property offenses** | 94.0% | 95.0% | 100.0% | 100.0% | 98.4% |
| Shoplifting | 90.0% | 95.0% | 100.0% | 100.0% | 97.6% |
| Theft from vehicle | 34.0 | 30.0 | 75.4 | 84.8 | 65.4 |
| Pickpocketing | 2.0 | 5.0 | 13.0 | 10.9 | 9.8 |
| Prostitute's theft | 8.0 | 5.0 | 20.3 | 4.3 | 13.8 |
| Other larcenies | 4.0 | 0.0 | 0.7 | 0.0 | 1.2 |
| Con games | 6.0% | 5.0% | 53.6% | 63.0% | 42.1% |
| Bad paper | 10.0 | 5.0 | 60.1 | 73.9 | 48.4 |
| Stolen goods | 76.0 | 85.0 | 94.9 | 97.8 | 90.9 |
| Property destruction | 16.0 | 0.0 | 35.5 | 34.8 | 28.7 |
| Other crimes | 0.0 | 0.0 | 0.7 | 0.0 | 0.4 |
| **Vice offenses** | 18.0% | 5.0% | 33.3% | 17.4% | 25.2% |
| Prostitution | 18.0% | 5.0% | 22.5% | 6.5% | 17.3% |
| Procuring | 4.0 | 5.0 | 30.4 | 15.2 | 20.5 |
| **Drug business (any)** | 86.0% | 100.0% | 100.0% | 100.0% | 97.2% |

Of particular interest in Table 6.6 are the figures regarding violence—robberies and assaults. Specifically, the greater the crack-business participation, the greater the involvement in violent crime. Moreover, those in the "dealer" and "dealer+" groups committed more violent crimes on a per capita basis than those in the "none" and "minor" groups. Of youths who committed *any* robberies, those with no or only minor crack-market ties averaged 6.1 robberies each, compared to 13.9 for dealers and 18.2 for the dealer+ group.

In terms of absolute numbers, these 254 youths were responsible for a total of 223,439 criminal offenses during the 12 months prior to interview. Some 61.1% of these offenses were drug sales, 11.4% were vice offenses, 23.3% were property offenses, and 4.2% were major felonies, including robberies, assaults, burglaries, and motor vehicle thefts. As indicated in

**TABLE 6.7**
**Crimes and Arrests in the 12 Months Prior to Interview**

|  | Crack-Business Involvement | | | | Total Crack Sample (N = 254) |
|---|---|---|---|---|---|
|  | None (N = 50) | Minor (N = 20) | Dealer (N = 138) | Dealer+ (N = 46) | |
| **Number done** | | | | | |
| Major felonies | 444 | 164 | 5,857 | 2,938 | 9,403 |
| Property offenses | 5,479 | 3,937 | 32,360 | 10,203 | 51,979 |
| Drug business | 9,785 | 6,630 | 70,365 | 49,766 | 136,546 |
| Vice offenses | 3,115 | 2,020 | 18,006 | 2,370 | 25,511 |
| Total offenses | 18,823 | 12,751 | 126,588 | 65,277 | 223,439 |
| **Mean number per respondent** | | | | | |
| Major felonies | 8.9 | 8.2 | 42.4 | 63.9 | 37.0 |
| Property offenses | 109.6 | 196.9 | 234.5 | 221.8 | 204.6 |
| Drug business | 195.7 | 331.5 | 509.9 | 1081.9 | 537.6 |
| Vice offenses | 62.3 | 101.0 | 130.5 | 51.5 | 100.4 |
| Total offenses | 375.9 | 637.6 | 917.3 | 1419.1 | 879.6 |
| **Percent arrested for** | | | | | |
| Major felonies | 6.0% | 10.0% | 17.4% | 26.1% | 16.1% |
| Property offenses | 30.0 | 25.0 | 46.4 | 32.6 | 39.0 |
| Drug business | 46.0 | 90.0 | 76.1 | 58.7 | 68.1 |
| Vice offenses | 4.0 | 5.0 | 6.5 | 2.2 | 5.1 |
| Any offense | 64.0 | 100.0 | 94.9 | 84.8 | 87.4 |

Table 6.7, the relationship between crack-trade participation and level of other criminal involvement is quite clear. The mean number of crimes per subject during the 12-month period ranges from 375.9 for those with no involvement in the crack business to 1419.1 offenses for those in the dealer+ category. Furthermore, this pattern was apparent not only for total crimes but also for three of the four primary crime categories: major felonies, property crimes, and total drug-business offenses (it did not hold for vice offenses).

Table 6.7 also indicates that, although less than 1% of the 223,439 offenses resulted in arrest, some 87.4% of the respondents were arrested during the 12 months prior to interview. The fact that the subjects were youths, that 358 (88.4%) of the 405 crimes resulting in arrest were either drug, vice, or petty property offenses (i.e., not major felonies), and that Miami-Dade has a seriously overburdened criminal justice system, explains why these youths were still in the free community at the time of interview.

# STREET KIDS, STREET CRIME

Recent media reports appear to be correct in assessing youthful involvement in the crack business as a significant crime trend in some locales. If anything, media reports may underestimate its importance, for three reasons: (1) the crack trade is related to not only heavier crack use but also more use of other drugs, (2) young crack dealers commonly violate not just drug laws but also those protecting persons and property, and (3) the crack business appears criminogenic in ways that go beyond any potential it may have as a *lure* into crime.

This last point is particularly well illustrated by the data in this study. For these youths, money to be made in the crack business was *not* the motive for initial criminal activities. Future research may show such cases, but, as it happened, crack was not widely available until most of these subjects had been engaged in some sort of regular crime for at least a year or two. Due to this timing, most had actually *sold* marijuana before ever *using* crack. But this means that, crime initiation aside, the crack business is criminogenic in that it leads serious delinquents to become even more seriously involved in crime.

In particular, these data suggest that it is not drug sales in general but specifically the crack business that is so highly problematic. Tables 6.6 and 6.7 show that 86% of the no-crack-business group were selling *some* drug, averaging around 200 sales per year. But the involvement of this group in major felonies and petty property crime was distinctly lower than that of youths with even minor involvement in the crack business, let alone compared to that of crack dealers. At the other end of the scale, one might expect that more crack-trade participation would lead to less time for, or less interest in, other crime. But there is only a slight dropoff in petty property crime for the dealer+ group compared to other dealers, and for the most serious offenses—major felonies—the dealer+ group averaged nearly 50% more crimes per offender than other crack dealers, who in turn committed nearly five times as many crimes as subjects with minor or no crack-trade participation.

So what explains the criminogenic effects of the crack trade? The general drugs/crime literature, as discussed in Chapter 3, suggests that one factor is the interactive pattern typical of crime/drug relationships for addictive, expensive drugs: crime finances use; use encourages more use; more use encourages more crime. Crack certainly appears eligible for this general pattern, since it is highly addictive and, although cheaper than other forms of cocaine, is expensive for unemployed users with anything more than a sporadic use pattern. At retail prices, a big crack habit—dozens or even scores of hits per day—can be at least as expensive as a big heroin habit, since the latter entails considerably fewer daily doses.

Thus, one major problem with the crack trade is that it facilitates crack addiction. Every single youth in the subsample who was involved in the crack business to even a minor degree was a crack user; of the crack dealers, over 70% used crack every day whereas under 15% used it less than regularly. Furthermore, even though greater crack-trade participation meant more crack earned directly, as payment for drug sales, it also meant heavier use patterns, so that crack dealers were paying an average of over $8,000 a year to purchase crack for personal use. The fit to the classic crime/drug interactive cycle seems clear: crack dealing finances crack use, crack use encourages more crack use, and more crack use requires more profit-making crimes of all sorts to support an ever-growing addictive use pattern.

This cycle was readily apparent in the lives of many of the youths interviewed. As one stated:

> It's like the vicious circle--the more cracks you use, the more cracks you want, and the more you have to do to get the cracks.

Another remarked:

> Ya get to a step in the business that everyone is out t' get ya. They know'd ya have stuff an' they want it, but they'd just as soon take it first. So ya have t' start protectin' yerself, 'cause they're carryin' [weapons] too. And when yer carryin' yer gonna use it. An' so ya use it to protect yerself, an' also t' *take off* [rob], because yer so far into it [using so much drugs] that yer money's burnin' up fast.

And a third:

> Dan Rather says that we street kids are into this for the gold chains, the leather coats, the sunglasses, the designer jeans. . . . I believed that shit too, once. Ol' Dan never been out on the street. He don't know what the fuck he's talking about. I work hard, but there's not that much money in dealin' crack. The more you use, the more you have to sell, and hustle. You get caught up in it, like a big snowball going down a hill. You end up doing all kinds of things. . . .

To the degree that one driving force for this cycle is indeed crack use, one possibility for breaking the cycle is forced intervention into the addiction pattern. This step requires that these youths be located, but the criminal justice system is in fact finding them: 92% of the crack-data subsample had been arrested at some time (true for almost 98%—199/ 204—of those with any crack-business involvement at all). Further, over 87% had been arrested just within the 12 months prior to interview. This is a much higher percentage than that typical of young adult heroin users in street studies 10 or 20 years ago. But although these youths have been located, intervention has not occurred. Fewer than 4% of this extremely drug-involved sample had *ever* been in drug treatment. This reflects not only an overburdened juvenile court system but also inadequate treatment resources for adolescents. Both problems are commonplace across the nation.

But an additional criminogenic aspect of the crack business—and another reason why compulsory intervention is required—is the crack trade's strong attractiveness as a lifestyle to the youths involved in it. This fascination is reminiscent of descriptions applied some years ago to the heroin-user subculture: the joys of hustling and "taking care of business," the thrills of a "cops and robbers" street life (see Preble and Casey 1969; Sutter 1969). Interviews with some young crack dealers give the impression that the crack trade is, for them, not only all this but much more. Demand for crack makes dealing it remarkably easy and sometimes profitable—more so than selling heroin used to be. Further, crack-business networks give the appearance of upward mobility and therefore a feeling of achievement; movement up the ranks is rare for heroin dealers. A likely additional factor is that the rewards for crack dealing include a drug that makes its users feel not merely unworried but omnipotent. Finally, the sheer youth of these young crack dealers means that dangers—street violence, arrest, overdose, and potential death—are perceived with particularly giddy enthusiasm as challenges to be outwitted and overcome. Participation in the crack trade, in short, provides its own kind of intoxication for many youths entangled in it.

In conclusion, the crack/crime dynamic, at least for adolescent crack dealers, represents an intensified version of the classic drug/crime relationship originally described for (adult) heroin users. Both patterns rest on addiction; however, for crack, addiction onset appears to be more rapid, and maximum physiological intake—and thus financial requirements—seems more limitless. For both, sales of the drug of choice are the most common criminal offense, but the rewards of the crack trade go well beyond those of "getting by" through heroin dealing. Finally, whereas both patterns ensnare youth in their formative years, young crack dealers are astonishingly more involved in a drugs/crime lifestyle at an alarmingly younger age.

# POSTSCRIPT

The data in this chapter address a number of points about the relationships among crack, crime, and violence in Miami and perhaps elsewhere.

First, whereas media reports suggest that homicide is a concomitant of crack distribution among inner-city youths, this may not be the case in Miami-Dade. Moreover, much of the current focus on crack-related violence may be more the result of a media event than an emergent trend. Consider, for example, the trends indicated in Figure 6.1. The data represent homicide rates per 100,000 population in six selected cities for the years 1985 through 1990. Rates were computed for the cities themselves rather than for Metropolitan Statistical Areas (MSAs), because the former offer better reflections of inner-city crime. That is, *city* crime rates tend to reflect the more acute crime picture, as opposed to MSA data that are diluted by lower crime rates in many suburban areas. The year 1985 was used as the starting point because it represents the year prior to popularization of crack in inner cities.

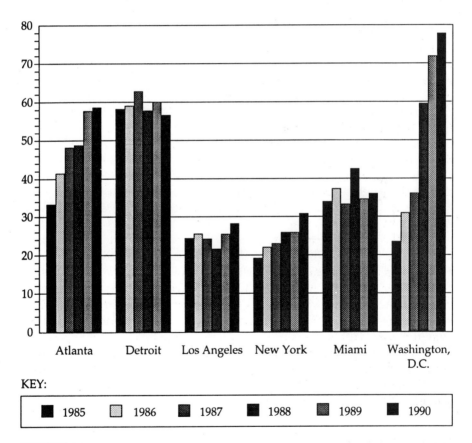

KEY:

| 1985 | 1986 | 1987 | 1988 | 1989 | 1990 |

**FIGURE 6.1**
**Homicide Rates per 100,000 Population**
SOURCE: *Uniform Crime Reports, 1985–1990.*

According to the DEA (Drug Enforcement Administration 1989), all six of these cities have high rates of crack availability and distribution. In addition, they are urban areas that are known for their high rates of crime and violence. Interestingly, they reflect a number of very divergent trends in homicide. For example:

- *In New York*, the homicide rate reflected steady upward movement—a 46.7% increase from 1985 through 1988—followed by a two-year stabilization and then a 19% increase in 1990.
- *In Detroit*, the rate peaked in 1987, followed by a decline in 1990 to a pre-1985 level.
- *In Los Angeles*, with some fluctuations in interim years, the homicide rate was only slightly higher in 1990 than in 1985.
- *In Atlanta*, the homicide rate increased dramatically over the six-year period.
- *In Miami*, where the homicide rate increased some 25% from 1985 through 1988, more recently it has fluctuated in a downward trend.
- *In Washington, D.C.*, where the homicide rate increased by some 154% from 1985 through 1988, the rate increased during 1989 by yet another (and rather significant) 21%, with an additional increase in 1990.

Since there are many demographic and ecological differences among the cities targeted here, generalizations and explanations about the alternative homicide rates are difficult. What is clear from the data is that higher rates of homicide do not necessarily go hand in hand with higher rates of crack use and distribution. *In fact, what happened in Washington, D.C., appears to be unique.*

*Second*, adolescent involvement in crack distribution does not necessarily mean *youth gang* involvement in crack distribution. The exploits of the "Crips," "Bloods," and other violent street gangs have become legend in Los Angeles and other parts of the United States, but gangs do not appear to be major participants in *every* active inner-city crack market. Miami illustrates this point.

Miami's juvenile street gangs apparently have yet to establish themselves in the underworlds of drug use and crime. In 1985, the Dade County Grand Jury (1985) noted that there were some 2,800 youths involved in 36 known gangs in Miami-Dade but that:

> Dade County gangs appear to have advanced to a point, but no further. We have learned that there is an additional evolutionary step which brings the gang from fighting and relatively disorganized criminality to the level of organized criminal activity with adult participation. . . .

Three years later, the Dade County Grand Jury (1988) reexamined the gang problem. Although they found that the number of gang members had expanded 25% (to some 3,500), they could present no evidence that juvenile gangs had become enmeshed in drug distribution. And, indeed, of the 611 hard-core adolescent offenders interviewed in our new study, only 1.8% (N = 11) were gang members at the time of interview, and only 2.5% (N = 15) were former members. As to why *not*, a 17-year-old black male commented in 1989:

> The gangs in this town are just not where it's at. They're kid stuff. Most of 'em are just "tag crews," markin' up the buildings with graffiti, bein' macho about when and where the next fight'll be, and struttin' for the ladies. Crimewise some are doin' shotgun robberies, but most of it is snatchin' purses and gold chains from the old Jews in South Beach or from neighborhood geeks. . . . If you want to make some money, ya don't have time for that shit.

*Third*, although Miami received international attention during the early 1980s because of the number of drug-related homicides, much has changed in the years since. Miami's worst year for murders was 1981, with a total of 621. As indicated in Table 6.8, the homicide rate has dropped by almost half since then. The violence earlier in the decade was related primarily to Miami's "cocaine wars" (see Eddy, Sabogal, and Walden 1988; Gugliotta and Leen 1989). For years the balance of power in the cocaine-trafficking hierarchy had been on a relatively even keel. Colombians bought coca paste in Bolivia and Peru, processed it into powder cocaine in their

**TABLE 6.8**
**Miami Homicide Rates per 100,000 Population**

| Year | City of Miami | Miami-Dade SMA |
|------|---------------|----------------|
| 1981 | 58.8 | 34.5 |
| 1982 | 51.9 | 29.7 |
| 1983 | 38.4 | 22.2 |
| 1984 | 42.4 | 23.7 |
| 1985 | 33.9 | 21.8 |
| 1986 | 37.3 | 21.6 |
| 1987 | 33.2 | 20.1 |
| 1988 | 42.5 | 24.6 |
| 1989 | 34.6 | 19.9 |
| 1990 | 36.0 | 19.9 |

SOURCE: *Uniform Crime Reports*, 1981–1990.

own country, and shipped it north to Miami, where Cuban middlemen distributed it locally and/or transhipped it elsewhere. Beginning in the late 1970s, however, the Colombians decided to cut out the middlemen and take over cocaine distribution in South Florida. The struggle reached its peak in Miami during 1981, with the Colombians winning the takeover.

Currently, Miami-Dade police officials estimate that perhaps one-third of the county's homicides are drug related, with the balance classified as of either "other felony" or domestic origin. As such, it would appear that Miami's crack-distribution networks may be "kinder and gentler" than elsewhere.

*Fourth*, although crack distribution by hard-core adolescent offenders in Miami may not reflect the gang-related violence seen in Los Angeles and elsewhere, it is nevertheless highly criminogenic. As the data in this chapter have demonstrated, young crack dealers commonly violate not just drug laws but also those protecting persons and property. Moreover, greater involvement in the crack business is associated with larger numbers of other crimes. As indicated in Table 6.7, for example, those in the "dealer+" group averaged almost 50% more major felonies per offender than other crack dealers, who in turn committed nearly five times as many as the youths with no crack-trade participation. The most obvious reason for this association between crack distribution and other crime is that participation in the crack trade facilitates crack addiction, which necessitates raising money for even more crack purchases.

# CHAPTER 7

# STREET KIDS IN STRAIGHT WORLDS

Families, schools, and employment experiences are the three primary influences on young people toward conventional behavior—"the straight life." Americans have long debated the relative importance of these factors and even what each ought to be doing for teenagers. In fact, the only thing that is agreed upon—and has been for decades—is that all three are failing to help youths become contributing members of society. But even in this historical context, the attractions of a conventional adult life appear particularly difficult to promote successfully today. Life in the streets is not only fun but can sometimes be economically rewarding. A 12-year-old drug dealer, a child not old enough for a legal job, can easily earn $100 a week plus a daily bonus of two or three crack rocks. A 17-year-old in the drug business may earn $500 a week, as well as a larger daily crack bonus; a few of these older youths get free trips to New York City or even Colombia. No such rewards are given for good school grades, and a student's part-time job bagging supermarket groceries would just barely pay for the small-time dealer's free crack.

Yet most serious delinquents still live with their families, and many are young enough to be required to attend school. The question explored here is the relationship between these ties to conventional life and drug/crime involvement patterns. The analysis begins with the most basic indicators of attachment to family, school, and legitimate work: absence or presence of these links at the time we were interviewing. In subsequent sections, more specific influences of family and school are discussed.

# LACK OF TIES TO CONVENTIONAL LIFE

According to social control theory, lack of ties to conventional life—family membership, school attendance, work experience—increases the chance that a youth will be involved in drug use and crime (see Hirschi 1969). This perspective is supported by research reporting that rates of delinquency for school dropouts rise after the youths leave school (Bachman, O'Malley, and Johnston 1978; Thornberry, Moore, and Christenson 1985) and that both drug use and crime are more frequent among dropouts than among students (Fagan and Pabon 1990; Kandel 1975). In contrast, strain theory (for example, Cohen 1955) posits school as a source of threat and disappointment for lower- and working-class boys, which can lead to delinquency. The implication is that, by decreasing the strains and stresses felt by troubled youths, dropping out also should decrease their delinquency (Elliott and Voss 1974).

Evidence on the drug/crime effects of leaving home is more scarce, but, as discussed in Chapter 1, drug use and crime appear to be much more common behaviors among runaways than in the general youth population. There is still less evidence concerning employment, but the logic is similar: working at a legitimate job should mean less need for, less interest in, and less time for criminal behavior. Recent research on young adults has shown that drug users have higher-than-average rates of changing jobs, getting fired, and being unemployed (Kandel and Yamaguchi 1987; Newcomb and Bentler 1988).

Our study of Miami youths provides the opportunity to examine relative degrees of serious delinquency for those who are still at home or still in school or legally employed, compared to serious delinquents without such ties to conventional life. However, the study's evidence on the fewer-ties/more-deviance hypothesis is limited, since no before-versus-after data for drug/crime behavior are available relative to leaving home, dropping out, or working. More drug use and crime, as well as dropping out, for example, could be primarily the result of influences from delinquent peers. Drug/crime involvement may have preceded, and helped cause, weaker attachments to family, school, and conventional work roles, rather than the other way around. However, the data can be used to examine the logical first question of whether absent ties to conventional life are in fact associated with earlier and greater current drug/crime involvement.

## Leaving Home

All of the 12–15-year-old boys interviewed, and 96% of the 14–15-year-old girls, were still living with a family. Among 16–17-year-olds, however, 18% of the 206 males and a surprising 76% of the 50 females had moved away from home. There were no differences by race/ethnicity for either gender. Relatively few lived alone—4 males and 4 females (10.5% of both the 38 males and the 38 females age 16–17 not living at home). Girls were especially likely to live with same-sex friend(s) or a group of mixed-sex friends (58%, compared to 34% of boys), whereas boys were more likely to live with a single friend of the opposite sex (55%, compared to 29% of girls). Mean age at leaving home for these 16–17-year-olds was 16 years for males and 15.7 years for females. Thus, the great majority had been out on their own for only a year or less; 24% of the girls, however, had left home about two years before.

The 16–17-year-olds living on their own were also disconnected from conventional life in other ways. All of them were school dropouts, compared to 55% of males and 42% of females the same age who were living with their families. Further, fewer of them had legal jobs when interviewed—11% of males and 8% of females, compared to 18% and 33% of their counterparts living at home. And more of them had never in their lives held a legal job—58% of males and 63% of females, compared to 35% and 42% of males and females the same age still with their families.[1]

Looking specifically at drug/crime comparisons, initiation ages were slightly earlier for 16–17-year-olds living on their own, compared to those living with families. As shown in Table 7.1, mean ages at starting regular substance use (whether alcohol or an illegal drug) tend to be about a year earlier for those now on their own. Age differences for first crime and starting regular crime are even smaller, except for the first crimes of females: girls now on their own began at a mean age of 11 years, compared to 12.3 for girls still living with families. As specified in Table 7.1, correlations between drug/crime initiation ages and living with a family generally show a positive, and statistically significant, relationship.

Current drug and crime involvement is also somewhat more intense for 16–17-year-olds living on their own, compared to those living with families. For the drug usage summary variable, both males and females living on their own are about three times likelier than their peers still at home to be in the highest category. At the other extreme, the lowest usage category includes 20–25% of the 16–17-year-olds still living at home but none of those out on their own. Current drug usage is thus more highly correlated with living-at-home status than are the drug initiation ages discussed above.

---

[1]Both the school and work-experience comparisons are statistically significant for both males and females: chi square $p < .00001$ for the dropout/not comparisons and $p < .05$ for the never-past/now-work comparisons.

**TABLE 7.1**
**Drug/Crime Involvement of 16–17-Year-Olds Living with Families versus on Their Own, by Gender**

| | Male | | Female | |
|---|---|---|---|---|
| | **On Own** (N = 38) | **Family** (N = 168) | **On Own** (N = 38) | **Family** (N = 12) |
| **Age start regular use** | | | | |
| Mean:   Any substance | 10.4 | 11.4 | 11.3 | 12.6 |
| Illicit drug | 11.2 | 11.8 | 11.9 | 13.1 |
| Alcohol | 11.1 | 12.4 | 12.3 | 13.0 |
| Cocaine | 13.4 | 14.0 | 14.0 | 14.6 |
| Rho:*   Any substance | +.24 | | +.29 | |
| Illicit drug | +.23 | | +.29 | |
| Alcohol | +.20 | | — | |
| Cocaine | +.22 | | +.22 | |
| **Current drug usage** | | | | |
| Summary category: | | | | |
| High usage | 52.6% | 16.7% | 55.3% | 16.7% |
| Typical | 47.4 | 62.5 | 44.7 | 58.3 |
| Low usage | 0.0 | 20.8 | 0.0 | 25.0 |
| Rho:*   Score (2–20) | −.36 | −.46 | | |
| **Age start crime** | | | | |
| Mean:   First ever | 11.3 | 11.6 | 11.0 | 12.3 |
| Start regular | 12.9 | 13.4 | 13.2 | 13.7 |
| Rho:   First ever | — | +.30 | | |
| Start regular | +.16 | — | | |
| **Current crime level** | | | | |
| Summary category: | | | | |
| Highest | 36.8% | 18.5% | 26.3% | 16.7% |
| Typical | 55.3 | 62.5 | 71.1 | 50.0 |
| Lowest | 7.9 | 19.0 | 2.6 | 33.3 |
| Rho:*   Total score (1–32) | −.25 | | — | |
| Major felony | −.17 | | −.34 | |
| Petty property | −.14 | | — | |
| Vice | −.27 | | −.43 | |
| Drug business | −.18 | | — | |

*Spearman Correlation Coefficient significant at $p < .05$ for the relationship between the listed drug/crime variable and living arrangement coded 0 = On own, 1 = Family.

Current crime is also negatively related to living with a family, although not as strongly as current drug use. As the correlations reported in Table 7.1 indicate, for males offenses of all types are somewhat more numerous among youths out on their own; the relationship is consistent, although not strong. For females there is no overall correlation between crime involvement and living at home versus on one's own because there is no relationship for two of the four offense types—petty property crimes and drug-business offenses. Girls still at home were committing as many of these crimes as girls out on their own. However, girls out on their own were committing significantly more major felonies and vice offenses—i.e., more of the most serious crimes and more of the offense types easiest for girls to make a living from on the street. Also, in both cases, the correlations are somewhat stronger than those seen for boys.

For those youths who *were* on their own and *were* more heavily involved in crime, the reasons were clear. For example, a 17-year-old boy reported:

> Having my own place now means that there's no one
> to fall back on. I got to pay the rent an' all,
> and when I get back from work there isn't any nice
> home-cooked meal on the kitchen table. Now I'm
> responsible for everything. I pay the rent, I eat
> out mostly, and that takes cash. Hustling for
> drugs, *and* food and rent is a lot of work--more
> ripoffs than before. . . .

Similarly, a 16-year-old female prostitute living with a friend stated:

> I left home in the first place because I was being
> hassled all the time about comin' home stoned,
> about my dates, the way I looked, missing school,
> and all the rest. I can't blame them for bein'
> upset, and in some ways it was easier bein' home.
> . . .
>
> Now it don't matter what time I come in, or who I
> bring in with me, but I gotta be having a lot more
> *johns* [customers]. Everything is so darn expen-
> sive. Forget about the drugs, just the cost of my
> clothing keeps me on the *stroll* [locations for
> soliciting customers] and doing *car tricks* [pro-
> viding sex to motorists] much later every night.

## Dropping Out of School

Most of the 16–17-year-olds interviewed were school dropouts (63% of the males and 86% of the females); the rest were still in school, except for two boys who had graduated. These figures are much higher than the 29%

dropout rate for Dade County public school students as a whole in 1985 (Dade County n.d., p. 13). When they left school, dropouts had completed a mean of only 9.6 grades (males 9.6, females 9.7). There were no significant differences by race/ethnicity in dropout rates for either males or females.

As a group, dropouts got into trouble in school at an earlier age than the others in their cohort. Male dropouts age 16–17 were first suspended or expelled in a mean grade of 6.8, compared to 7.4 for their age peers who were not dropouts; for the females, corresponding grades were 7.5 and 7.2, respectively (not a significant difference). But both male and female dropouts were first high on drugs while at school in an earlier grade (means of 6.4 vs. 7.0 for boys, 6.0 vs. 6.5 for girls) and began skipping school earlier (mean grades of 6.4 vs. 7.1 for boys; 6.1 vs. 6.5 for girls). And dropouts had especially high frequency rates for cutting school during at least their last year: 83% of males and 84% of females cut classes three or more days a week, compared to 49% of males age 16–17 who were still in school and none of the seven female students this age. Also consistent with the general association between earlier start and worse problems, those who dropped out also had more total suspensions and expulsions. Whereas 16–17-year-old males who remained in school averaged 2.4 suspensions, the dropouts averaged 4.2; for females the contrast was 2.8 for students and 3.4 for dropouts.

Clearly, none of this bodes well for the future school achievement of the 12–15-year-olds interviewed. These younger students first got high at school or cut classes in an even earlier grade than did the 16–17-year-old *dropouts*—fifth or sixth grade instead of seventh. Further, 86% of the 12–15-year-old boys already had at least one suspension or expulsion on their records, as did 74% of the 14–15-year-old girls. (School problems for younger students are discussed in detail later in this chapter.)

Differences in drug/crime history between 16–17-year-old male dropouts and their counterparts still in school are very similar to those for males living on their own versus with families.[2] Further, being a dropout was associated with greater current involvement in both drug use (rho = .42) and crime (rho = .25), particularly major felonies (rho = .25) and drug-business offenses (rho = .20).

For 16–17-year-old girls, on the other hand, dropout status was less important than it was for males, and much less important than living with a family versus having left home. Drug/crime initiation age was not related to being a dropout; nor were current overall crime level, current major felonies, current petty property crime, or current vice offenses. However, female dropouts had higher current drug use scores than female stu-

---

[2]Specifically, dropout status is correlated with younger age at starting regular substance use, whether alcohol (rho = –.25) or illicit drugs (rho = –.21); male dropouts were also slightly younger at first regular cocaine use, first crime, and first regular crime (rho = –.13 to –.15, $p < .04$).

dents (rho = .38), perhaps because school attendance interferes with drug use opportunities. These higher drug use scores were not due to more *overall* drug involvement for female dropouts, since dropping out was correlated with *fewer* drug sales (rho = –.29).

## Working in a Legal Job

Many of the 16–17-year-olds interviewed had worked at some legal job for at least a short period—61% of the boys and 42% of the girls. The percentage of 16–17-year-olds with any job experience varied greatly by gender and ethnicity—29% for black females, 50–54% for black and Hispanic males and white females, 77% for white males. Among younger respondents, on the other hand, markedly fewer had ever worked—25% of 14–15-year-old boys, 12% of 14–15-year-old girls, and 7% of 12–13-year-old boys. Ethnic differences for the three younger age/gender groups were minimal.

For 16–17-year-old males, the most frequent job types (for present or last job) were unskilled labor (24% had such experience) and semiskilled trades (13%); relatively few had ever had a full-time job—19% of the total, about a third of those with any job experience. White males with job experience (N = 78) were especially likely to have worked full time—40% did so, compared to 24% of their black counterparts (N = 55) and only 5% of Hispanics (N = 39). The best blue-collar jobs—semiskilled or trade positions—were also markedly likelier for whites (24%) than Hispanics (13%) or blacks (7%). Unskilled labor, on the other hand, was a likelier job experience for blacks (51%) and Hispanics (44%) than for whites (27%).

For females age 16–17, the most common positions typically pay less than jobs held by males of this age—unskilled services (26% had such experience) and office or store clerical positions (10%). However, girls with work experience were more likely to have worked full time; 24% of all 16–17-year-old females had done so, which is 57% of those with any job experience. Job types did not vary by race nearly so much as among males; present or last job was an unskilled service position for 55–56% of both white and black females ever employed.

Current legal employment was uncommon even among 16–17-year-olds (16%); as previously discussed, it was especially uncommon for youths living on their own rather than with families. Thus, data on working at a legal job was examined in terms of (1) any versus no lifetime job experience and (2) a three-category variable coded 0 = Never worked, 1 = Job in the past but not now, and 2 = Employed now.

The relatively limited experience of 16–17-year-old serious delinquents with legal employment might lead to the assumption that such work is a fairly unimportant consideration in their drug and crime involvement. Not surprisingly, then, the analysis indicates that job type and full-time/part-time status are unrelated to drug/crime history or current levels. However, among 16–17-year-olds, greater job experience (0 = never, 1 =

past, 2 = current) is more strongly connected to later age at drug/crime initiation than are being in school and living with a family.[3] Job experience also shows a clearly negative relationship to current drug use and crime involvement.[4]

   This consistent association of legal work experience with less drug/crime involvement suggests that the connection is commitment to a drug/crime lifestyle. Legal work experience appears to demonstrate less commitment to the streets and more potential for eventually taking up a conventional adult lifestyle. The term *demonstrates* is used here rather than *influences* or *helps lead to* because of the clear age differences between first legal work experience and first drug/crime behaviors. Initial drug and crime experience occurred very early in the lives of the serious delinquents interviewed, typically at age 10–12, whereas work experience was common only by age 16. Thus, among youths who are now age 16–17, legal work experience is least common among those with the longest histories of drug/crime involvement and the strongest participation rates in heavy drug use, the most serious crime (major felonies), or career street crime (especially drug sales and prostitution).

## Social Control Variables and Serious Delinquents

Altogether, the preceding findings indicate support for a social control perspective on the importance of ties to conventional life even among older youths (age 16–17) who are very seriously involved in drug use and crime. Family, school, and job experience variables are more strongly related to early and current drug/crime involvement than are the sociodemographic variables of age, gender, and race/ethnicity discussed in Chapter 5.

   It should be recalled that this is a very specialized analysis: one of early versus extremely early drug/crime initiation, and heavy versus extremely heavy current drug/crime involvement, in a group consisting en-

---

[3]Correlations for the four drug variables shown in Table 7.1 in relation to living with a family are in the .20 to .24 range for males and .22 to .29 (except alcohol, for which the rho was not significant) for females. Correlations for the same variables with the work experience variable are .40, .31, .58, and .42 for males (any, illicit, alcohol, cocaine) and .49, .48, .49, and .51 for females (all significant at $p < .001$). Similarly, living-with-family correlations with ages at first crime and starting regular crime are .11 and .16 for males and .30 and .10 for females—but the equivalent statistics in relation to job experience are .28 and .42 (males) and .33 and .56 (females).

[4]Correlations with current drug use score are −.32 for males and −.27 for females. For the crime involvement score, the correlations are −.34 for males and −.51 for females. The specific crime types most negatively related to job experience are major felonies (rho = −.25 for males, −.27 for females) and career street crime—i.e., drug-business offenses (rho = −.27 for males, −.42 for females) and female vice offenses (rho = −.55).

tirely of serious offenders. However, this is also a type of comparison that has not been done before. Prior tests of social control variables in relation to delinquency have compared presence or absence of much less seriously delinquent behaviors in the general household youth population. It would not have been surprising if we had found no such relationship, perhaps indicating that older serious delinquents have uniformly weakened ties to conventional institutions. But some do have such ties, and those ties still have a dampening impact on their drug use and criminal behavior.

The finding that ties to conventional life are related to both early and current drug/crime indicators suggests an interactive as opposed to one-way relationship. That is, youths with missing ties—those who are not living with a family, who are school dropouts, and who have no work experience—are also those who were youngest at the initiation of deviant activities. This typically preadolescent deviance most likely contributed to weaker ties to conventional institutions during early and middle adolescence—more family conflict, more school problems, less interest in or chance of getting a legal job. Finally, by age 16–17, these weakened ties probably helped account for greater commitment to drug use, crime, and their accompanying street values.

# FAMILY DISADVANTAGE

Social class is by far the most commonly investigated family variable in delinquency research. Yet, as discussed in Chapter 2, the relationship of social class and delinquency—especially serious delinquency—remains a source of much debate among researchers. On one hand, lower-class youths are clearly overrepresented in the juvenile justice system. On the other, the degree of such overrepresentation varies markedly by geographical location; moreover, among serious offenders in the juvenile justice system, variations in seriousness or number of offenses are only weakly correlated with social-class differences. These assorted conflicting findings, however, are from studies of violent youth in the juvenile justice system, a clearly limited and possibly biased sample of serious delinquents. Among youths still actively committing serious offenses in the community, the 533 youths still living with families when we interviewed them displayed considerably more variation in social-class indicators than one would expect if serious delinquency were an exclusively lower-class phenomenon.

## Indicators of Social Class

Today, the influence of social class on delinquency is most often viewed as one of differences in access to conventional opportunities and resources, including role models for socially valued activities such as graduating from school and getting a job (Brownfield 1986; Rosen 1985; Sorrells 1980). Family economic resources also have a strong effect on where families can live, so neighborhood influences beyond the family also play a role in providing social-class-related models for conventional behavior. However, neighborhoods are never completely homogeneous in regard to income, job status, education, and other socioeconomic characteristics. Family social class is therefore most often estimated by looking at parental economic circumstances—education, employment type, and job-versus-welfare income.

During the street interviews, questions about family social class were simple enough so that even very young adolescents had enough information to answer: (1) job types for each person providing legal employment income in the youth's household; (2) the gender of each of these job holders; (3) presence or absence of household income from three types of nonjob income: unemployment compensation, AFDC/welfare, and retirement or disability income; and (4) of the total number of persons in the household, the number with a high school diploma or GED. Responses to these questions were used to construct four simple indicators of social class, which were then combined into a summary variable.

The most direct indicator of social class is type of family income, in four categories ordered by relative prestige. The lowest category—welfare income—accounts for the largest number of respondents—39% of the 533 youths living with a family. The second lowest category is other low-income sources (such as unskilled labor or service jobs, unemployment compensation, or retirement income); this type includes 22% of the sample, so that, altogether, 61% of youths living with a family were from very-low-income households. Most of the rest (34% of youths at home) lived in families with one or more persons holding jobs that could be classified as "stable working-class" positions—semiskilled or skilled blue-collar jobs or low-level white-collar jobs such as clerical and sales work. Only a few (5%) lived with a parent who had a clearly middle-class occupation.

A second social-class measure was a simple "number of employees" (in the household) variable, which indicates both relative number of income sources and relative number of conventional role models for the respondent. Thus, job versus nonjob income in the "other low income" category could be distinguished, as could two-job versus one-job working-class families. Even in welfare families, there was often someone present who had a job—sometimes the respondent's older brother or sister, sometimes the mother's boyfriend. Any legal job was counted, regardless of who in the household held it. Totals indicated that 37.5% of the 533 youths living at home were from families with no employees, 44% lived in a family with one job holder, and 18.5% lived with two or more.

A third indicator was a similar count of "number of high school graduates" in the household, again including not only parents but anyone else living with the respondent. As with the employees count, this indicates the number of conventional models in the household, and it also has implications for the household income level. Some 38% of the 533 youths living with families were from households with no high school graduate; in 39% there was one graduate, and in 24% there were two or more.

The fourth indicator of social class was presence of a female head of household. Single mothers have traditionally been blamed for delinquency because they cannot provide male role models for sons and supposedly are unable to adequately supervise either sons or daughters. This attribution is not confirmed by more recent research, which finds that the single-parent family, or "broken home," is only slightly related to even trivial offenses such as running away and being truant (Rankin 1983; Rosen and Neilson 1982; Wells and Rankin 1986). Moreover, these small correlations become even smaller when the effects of home quality (amount of supervision, abuse, conflict, affection, enjoyment) are controlled (Van Voorhis et al. 1988). Other studies have reported that single-parent families are more of a delinquency risk for girls than for boys (Johnson 1986) or for blacks than for whites (Matsueda and Heimer 1987). However, when the single parent is female, there is almost always a markedly lower family income than when the single-parent head of household is male (see, e.g., Hewlett 1986; Sidel 1986). This makes "female head of household" at least as much an indicator of family economic circumstance as parental education level. Almost half of the sample (49.5%) lived in female-headed households.

Finally, these four very simple variables—each with only limited information about family income or status—were combined into a single variable to summarize "family disadvantage." This summary is a simple addition for the four indicators described above, with assigned points for each level:

- Income type (middle-class job type = 0 through welfare = 3)
- Number of employees (2+ such persons = 0, only one = 1, no such persons = 2)
- Number of high school graduates (2+ = 0, only one = 1, and none = 2)
- Female-headed household (no = 0, yes = 1)

The resulting total score of 0–8 indicates the relative socioeconomic disadvantage of the respondent's family.[5] For the total 533 youths living at home, the correlation between family disadvantage score and being black is .55—which is substantial but which also indicates that the two variables are by no means identical.

---

[5]The four indicators contributing to the score are all highly correlated with it (rhos of .76 to .92).

For use in the crime/class analysis, the disadvantage score reduced fairly readily to a three-category variable.[6] The three levels included similar percentages of the 533 youths living with a family, but each had clearly different socioeconomic characteristics:

1. Families with little disadvantage (score 0–2, 34% of the with-family cases) tended to have:
   a. Incomes from stable working-class jobs (86%).
   b. Two or more people working (84%).
   c. At least one high school graduate (100%).
   d. A male head of household (99%).
   Some 89% of these families were white or Hispanic.
2. Families with only some disadvantage (scores 3–6, 36%) had an assortment of disadvantage combinations:
   a. Some were welfare families (26%), whereas many had an income type that was not welfare but was nonetheless low income (58%).
   b. Many were female-headed households (53%).
   c. Some had no high school graduate (35%), and very few had two+ graduates (11%).
   The racial/ethnic distribution of this middle category—41% black, 42% white, 17% Hispanic—was almost identical to that for the total 533 youths living at home.
3. Families with severe disadvantage (scores 7–8, 30%) showed the following characteristics:
   a. All were female-headed households (100%).
   b. Most were receiving welfare (98%).
   c. Most had no high school graduate (84%).
   d. Often there were no employees (56%), but never were there two+ employees.
   Some 79% of these families were black.

Altogether, this description suggests that the Miami sample had an adequate range of "family disadvantage" to permit analysis of its relationship to relative seriousness in drug and crime involvement.

## Family Disadvantage and Serious Delinquency

To analyze drug/crime initiation ages, correlations with family disadvantage category were examined for 11 age variables: (1) first crime; (2–6) first drug use in five categories: any substance, any illegal drug, alcohol, co-

---

[6]The three-category version yields statistical results almost identical with the total 0–8 point score (rho = .95).

caine, and any drug beyond alcohol and marijuana; (7) first regular crime; and (8–11) first regular drug use in four categories: any substance, any illegal drug, alcohol, and cocaine. It was expected that, if "family disadvantage" were related at all to drug/crime involvement in this sample, the relationship would probably be most strongly indicated in earlier initiation for more disadvantaged youths, since they typically grow up in areas with high drug/crime rates. Once a serious level of such behaviors is initiated, less disadvantaged youth may well pick their friends and behavioral locales in accordance with it, giving family disadvantage relatively little influence on levels of current drug/crime behaviors. However, the results suggest that family disadvantage has about the same degree of relationship to drug/crime initiation age as that discussed in the last chapter for race/ethnicity. Youths from the poorest families tended to begin drug use and crime earlier—but only a little earlier, so that the others soon caught up.[7]

Not surprisingly, then, overall current drug use is not associated with family disadvantage at all, for any age group or either gender, using either the 0–8 score or the 3-category variable. There is very little association even with specific type of current drug use. The single drug type for which family disadvantage score is significantly correlated ($p < .05$) with more days of current use is heroin (rho = .17, .26, and .30 for 12–13-year-old males, 14–17-year-old males, and 14–17-year-old females, respectively). This suggests that, of the street drugs available to youth, only heroin remains identified with underclass neighborhoods, but even that identification is not a strong one.

Finally, current criminal behavior is only slightly more strongly related to family disadvantage than is current drug use or drug/crime involvement history. Of the 15 correlations shown for this relationship in Table 7.2, only 5 are statistically significant correlations in the predicted direction and none are even as high as .30.

The total crime score is correlated with family disadvantage score for only one of the three primary subgroups—males age 14–17. But even for them, family disadvantage is not related to major felonies (rho = .03); only the less serious offenses of petty property and drug-business crimes are related to family disadvantage in the expected direction. For females, overall crime and petty property offenses are not related to disadvantage, but major felonies and vice are. These fluctuations by crime type and

---

[7]Among 12–13-year-old boys the results indicated that family disadvantage was basically irrelevant to age at drug/crime initiation: only one of the 11 correlations was statistically significant, and it was low (for age at first alcohol use, rho = .17).

Among 14–17-year-olds (unlike younger youths), a totally consistent pattern of negative correlations appeared—more disadvantage, earlier starts. But for females none of the correlations were statistically significant, and for males 8 of the 11 were –.13 or less. The three largest indicated earlier starts for disadvantaged boys in cocaine use (rho = .25 first use, –.19 regular use) and regular drinking (rho = .31).

**TABLE 7.2**
**Current Crime by Family Disadvantage for Youths Still at Home**

| Gender, Age, and Family Disadvantage | (N) | Median Crime Score | Median Number Done Last 12 Months | | | |
|---|---|---|---|---|---|---|
| | | | Major Felony | Petty Property | Vice | Drug Business |
| **Male 12–13** | | | | | | |
| Little | (27) | 14.0 | 52 | 167 | 0 | 300 |
| Some | (52) | 8.5 | 7 | 150 | 0 | 177 |
| Severe | (41) | 10.0 | 10 | 177 | 0 | 300 |
| Rho* | | — | –.17 | — | — | — |
| **Male 14–17** | | | | | | |
| Little | (134) | 9.0 | 11 | 103 | 0 | 250 |
| Some | (120) | 9.0 | 8 | 128 | 0 | 300 |
| Severe | (99) | 12.0 | 11 | 216 | 0 | 350 |
| Rho* | | +.26 | — | +.28 | — | +.23 |
| **Female 14–17** | | | | | | |
| Little | (20) | 10.0 | 0 | 234 | 13 | 275 |
| Some | (19) | 12.0 | 3 | 110 | 201 | 300 |
| Severe | (21) | 12.0 | 4 | 175 | 175 | 250 |
| Rho* | | — | +.24 | — | +.27 | — |

*Spearman Correlation Coefficient significant at $p < .05$ for Family Disadvantage Score (range 0–8, least to most disadvantage) as related to Crime Score (range 1–32, least to most crime) or level of crime type (five categories, as used to construct the Crime Score). Crime medians are listed for the full-range variables.

gender are what one would expect if an underlying relationship between crime and family disadvantage exists, but it is only a weak one.

In this context, the figures shown in Table 7.2 for the youngest boys appear to require further discussion. This subgroup shows a weak reverse relationship for major felonies. That is, 12–13-year-old boys from *less* disadvantaged families are slightly *more* involved in these serious crimes (rho = –.17). Half of the least disadvantaged boys of this age committed over 50 major felonies in the prior 12 months—a median five times that for their more disadvantaged counterparts. In addition, they committed as many petty property and drug-business offenses as the most disadvantaged 12–13-year-olds. Seriously delinquent youths in poor neighborhoods are likely to be living in high-crime-rate areas in which their illegal behavior is at least partially a function of local youth subcultures. But 50 major felonies by a fairly well-off 12–13-year-old boy suggests that a boy this young and this economically advantaged who is seriously delinquent *at all* may be more likely than a young underclass boy to be *extremely* delinquent.

Although family disadvantage appears to be related to current crime in somewhat different ways for different age/gender groups, it must be repeated that these relationships are all relatively weak. None of the correlations are even as large as .30, which means that family disadvantage bears less relationship to current crime among serious delinquents than does living with a family versus alone, dropping out of school, or having work experience in a legal job. Further, family disadvantage is even less strongly related to current drug use or drug/crime involvement history than to current crime. In short, in this sample of serious delinquents, youths from more economically disadvantaged families were only a little more seriously drug/crime involved than less disadvantaged youths.

# FAMILY IMPACT ON DRUG/CRIME BEHAVIORS

Of the 611 serious delinquents interviewed, 87.2% were still living at home. This raises several questions about the relationship between family interaction and the serious delinquency of these youths. What impact, if any, did families have on the drug use and criminal behavior of these teenagers? Were there arguments about drugs, crime, and related topics? Were girls subject to a greater amount of such criticism than boys? What about younger versus older boys? Were adult attitudes toward drug use related to the drug involvement of their children? The interviews included two sets of questions that provide some information on this topic. The first was a series of questions about arguments with families; the second set pertained to starting alcohol use with peers versus with an adult present.

## Family Arguments

Arguing can be both a method of communicating and an indication of the quality of family relations (Hirschi 1969). One young man in this study who had moved out of his family's home commented to the interviewer that many neighbors knew when his family argued and sometimes called the police. Another stated:

> The whole world knew when my parents and me were going at it. My father would be screaming "fucking kid" this and "fucking kid" that, and everything. My mother would be screaming at me to show some

> respect and at the both of us to quit fighting
> because "what will the neighbors say?" That
> bullshit. One time my father started hitting me
> and she threw a vase at him that hit the window
> instead and made a hell of a racket. . . . Our
> family bouts were notorious in the neighborhood.

Few become that intense. However, this was one sort of possibility kept in mind when the family-argument questions were constructed. It seemed that frequent arguments in general might indicate a problem in family functioning, which in turn might be related to more adolescent drug/crime behaviors. But it turned out that almost the only youths who *never* argued with their families were those no longer living at home. A common response for them was "We used to argue all the time, but now we don't because I never see them since I moved out." Because the questions about arguments were phrased in terms of current behavior ("How often *do* you argue with them about. . ."), for consistency the 78 youths no longer living with their families were excluded from this analysis. Also excluded were the two youths living at home for whom there were missing answers.

Of the 531 remaining youths living with families, 96% reported at least some family arguments about money, school, drug use, crime, or friends' crime. More tellingly, arguing about a particular topic "often" (as opposed to only "sometimes") was very common, especially regarding money, drugs, and crime (59–65%). Prostitution was a major topic for argument in some of the girls' families: For example, a 17-year-old from South Miami recalled in 1990:

> My mom gets so mad sometimes. She sees me goin'
> out, the way I'm dressed an' all, and she knows
> what I'm up to. I just have to tell her off. What
> I do is my own business. Once she called me a "no
> good, fucking whore," an' I told her back, "no,
> Mom, I'm the daughter of a fucking whore."

Many also argued "often" about school or the crimes of the respondent's friends (45–48%). For example, a 15-year-old boy from Miami Beach remarked:

> When my father found out that instead of being in
> school I was out smokin' dope, that did it. He
> yell a lot at me, tellin' me that if I miss any
> more school he's gonna throw me out of the house.

Specific percentages are reported in Table 7.3 for all respondents combined because frequency of family arguments had absolutely no relationship to gender, age, or age with gender controlled; this held for all five argument topics.

**TABLE 7.3**
**Arguments with Family If Still Living at Home***

| | | | Subject of Argument | | |
|---|---|---|---|---|---|
| | | Money | School | Drug Use | Own Crime | Friends' Crime |
| **Percentage** | | | | | | |
| Often | | 63.1% | 47.8% | 65.3% | 59.1% | 44.6% |
| Ever | | 90.6 | 82.1 | 90.8 | 80.6 | 68.9 |
| **Correlation with drug use score** | | | | | | |
| Male | 12–13 | .65 | .25 | .56 | .57 | .34 |
| | 14–17 | .35 | .18 | .29 | .34 | .26 |
| Female | 14–17 | .61 | .41 | .50 | .52 | .51 |
| **Correlation with crime score** | | | | | | |
| Male | 12–13 | .54 | .27 | .44 | .60 | .31 |
| | 14–17 | .24 | .12 | .16 | .23 | .12 |
| Female | 14–17 | .52 | .44 | .36 | .45 | .29 |

*Total $N$ of 531 excludes 78 youths not living with family and 2 missing-data cases: 120 males age 12–13, 351 males age 14–17, 60 females age 14–17. Correlations are Spearman Correlation Coefficients significant at $p < .05$ between frequency of arguments (0 = never, 1 = sometimes, 2 = often) and summary scores for current drug use (range 2–20) and current crime (range 1–32).

The commonality of arguing, and of arguing often, indicates that the arguments data are not useful for identifying unusual family problems. However, family arguments are of interest in examining parents' attempts to deal with their teenagers' serious delinquency. If arguing is an effort to control behavior regarded as undesirable and important by the parent, then arguing about a particular behavior should be correlated with the youth's level of involvement in that activity. As shown in Table 7.3, this is exactly what was found. The amount of arguing with family about drug use is significantly correlated with the level of current drug use, and family arguments about crime are correlated with level of current criminal behavior. This can be taken as evidence that the parents of these serious delinquents were communicating their displeasure with drug use and crime.

The correlations in Table 7.3 indicate a weaker relationship between family arguments and a youth's level of drug/crime involvement for 14–17-year-old boys than for girls the same age or for 12–13-year-old boys.

However, as previously noted, neither age nor gender was related to the frequency of family arguments about drug use and crime. This suggests that, even though parental criticism of the drug and crime involvement of older boys is less related to *specific* drug/crime behaviors than it is among girls and younger boys, such criticism is still occurring at a general level. In short, among the serious delinquents interviewed who were still living at home, families were apparently trying to control the drug and crime involvement of both their sons and daughters, including both their younger and older teenagers.[8]

## Early Alcohol with an Adult

Even a family that strongly disapproves of the use of illegal drugs may have a relatively casual attitude toward alcohol use by teenagers. Alcohol is, after all, a legal drug (at least for adults), and many grownups use it without apparent problems. Prior research suggests that both parental attitudes toward drugs and parents' own drug use influence their children's drug use behaviors (see, e.g., Jensen and Brownfield 1983; Kandel 1980).

One obviously pertinent factor in this discussion is whether adults actually help initiate a youth's alcohol use. Even if alcohol is the only drug a parent uses, permitting its use by a child may have a more extensive influence than delivering a "drinking is OK" message. Most of the 611 youths interviewed did not drink regularly but did consume large quantities of illegal drugs. It may be, for example, that very early alcohol use provides early experience with being high, which then encourages a youth to try other kinds of drugs offered later by peers.

An example of adult involvement in initiating alcohol use was provided by a 15-year-old male who stated:

> When I was around 9, it was my sister's wedding and everyone was giving me a sip of champagne. I remember getting real high, an' me stumbling all over and acting silly. They thought it was real cute. . . . I remember getting sick and vomiting, but the high was good before I got sick. . . .

---

[8]Also examined were ethnic/racial differences in family arguments. Among the 471 boys still at home, there was little if any difference by race/ethnicity in the frequency of arguments about money, drug use, or crime, but being white was correlated with more family arguments about school (rho = .16, $p < .001$) and about friends' criminal behavior (rho = .24). Among the 60 girls at home, being white was significantly related only to more family arguments about drug use (rho = .25, $p < .03$). Thus, of ten correlations (five topics, two genders) with race = white, only three were .10 or larger and none were greater than .25. This suggests minimal relationships to race/ethnicity in family arguments.

> Then I remember being in the fifth grade and going
> into the Publix [supermarket] and stealing small
> bottles of wine to get a little high, and then
> staying out late so they [parents] wouldn't smell
> it on me.

The interview questions for both alcohol and illicit drugs asked how old the youth was at the time of (1) first trying the substance and (2) first starting to use "regularly" (defined as three or more times a week for at least a month). But for alcohol there were two additional age questions: (3) age at first getting high or drunk and (4) age at first drinking without an adult present. A clear pattern of adult involvement in early drinking is shown by the sequence of mean ages for these four variables and by the size of the gaps between them:

- 7.6  First try alcohol ($N = 611$)
- 8.8  First time drunk ($N = 608$)
- 9.5  First alcohol without an adult present ($N = 608$)
- 11.0  Start regular drinking ($N = 328$)

Adult involvement was further investigated by comparing the sequence for each respondent, to determine whether an adult was present at first alcohol use or first intoxication. The results indicated that *most* youths—80%—first tried alcohol with an adult present. Further, this experience was not just a sip on a holiday, since 81% of the 608 who had ever been drunk were first drunk with an adult present. As the mean age sequence shown above suggests, youths whose first alcohol use was in the presence of an adult ($N = 491$) had their first drink much earlier (mean age 6.8) than those who started with their peers (mean age 10.8). Thus, the correlation between first drinking with an adult present (1 = yes, 0 = no) and younger age at first alcohol use is substantial (rho = $-.54$, $p < .001$). Even more importantly, those who first drank with an adult got high for the first time much earlier (66.4% by age 9; mean age 8.3) than those who first drank with peers (12.5% by age 9; mean age 11.3).[9]

The importance of adults giving youths their first drink is that it means alcohol use begins at a younger age. And (as noted in a different

---

[9]Results differed somewhat by gender, age, and ethnicity. First drinking with an adult present was more likely for black, Hispanic, and 12–13-year-old males (89–98%) than for females or 14–17-year-old white males (57–64%). Those girls who did have their first drink *with an adult* present, however, did so at a younger mean age than boys the same age (6.5 rather than 7.0). Consequently, the correlation between first drinking with an adult and younger age at first high is even greater for females (rho = -.69) than for males (rho = -.48). But among 14–17-year-olds who first drank *with peers*, mean age at first alcohol use was younger for males (10.6) than for females (11.4). Thus, the gap between mean ages at first alcohol with an adult versus with peers is markedly larger for females (4.9 years) than for males of the same age (3.6 years).

context in Chapter 5) the younger these youths were when they had their first drink, (1) the younger they were when they started regular illicit drug use (age/age rho = .63) and regular crime involvement (rho = .56) and (2) the more seriously involved they are now in overall drug use (age/summary-score rho = −.47), and overall crime (rho = −.53). In short, adults who gave children alcohol were also giving them a head start in a delinquent career, compared to delinquents who first started drinking with their peers, and this earlier start meant more serious drug/crime involvement. The approximate size of these correlations was quite consistent across demographic subgroups by age group, gender, ethnicity, and combinations of these three factors.

Finally, first having alcohol with an adult was also examined in relation to "family disadvantage," the general measure of social class discussed earlier in this chapter. For the 533 youths still living at home, the correlation between these variables was significant, although not large: the more disadvantaged a youth's family, the more likely the youth was to have first tried alcohol with an adult present (rho = .26). But the correlation between age at first drink and family disadvantage is weak (rho = −.19), so that, although those from disadvantaged families are more likely to first drink with an adult present, they are not necessarily that much younger than other youths.[10]

## Summary: Family Impact on Serious Delinquency

The findings discussed in this section suggest that serious delinquency both influences and is influenced by family interactions. The latter is indicated by the finding that, in this sample of seriously drug-involved adolescents, a surprisingly large percentage were in the presence of an adult when they first used a psychoactive substance, namely alcohol. Since first alcohol use, when with an adult, occurred at a mean age of 6.8 years, the logical presumption is that the adult was a parent or other family member. Further, this was significant alcohol use, in that most youths in the sample were not only first drinking but first drinking to the point of intoxication with an

---

[10]However, there is a substantial gender difference in the association between drinking first with an adult and growing up in a disadvantaged family. The correlation between these variables is markedly higher for both black and white girls (rho = .41 and .46, respectively; $p < .01$ for both) than for males of the same age (rho for whites = .22, $p < .01$; for blacks and Hispanics, rho is nonsignificant at .13 and .07, respectively). This gender difference is consistent with the often-noted greater emphasis on traditional gender roles in working-class families. That is, in such families girls would be expected not to drink and would not be given alcohol by adults, although those same families would not be particularly concerned if their sons drank (Gans 1962; Horowitz 1983; Komarovsky 1962; Suttles 1968). It may be that, in the most disadvantaged families, the gender-role expectations for girls are less protective and restrictive, making it as acceptable for girls as for boys to drink.

adult present. Mean age at first alcohol use for youths first drinking with peers, in contrast, was 10.8, a full four years later. Early introduction to alcohol is particularly important because alcohol use was the first stage in the drug/crime careers of these serious delinquents. Younger age at first drinking was strongly related to both younger age at first regular use of illegal drugs and younger age at starting regular crime. Further, since earlier drug/crime initiations are correlated with more serious current drug/crime involvement, younger age at first alcohol use is also significantly associated with higher levels of current drug use and criminal behavior.

The influence of serious delinquency on family interaction is shown by the finding that the current drug and crime involvement of these youths is related to—and most likely causes—family friction. In most instances, greater drug involvement is correlated with more arguments with families about drug use, and more crime is correlated with more arguments with families about crime. These associations suggest that families are aware of and struggling against the serious delinquency of their teenagers. Although there is no direct evidence on the matter, unsolicited comments from many youths interviewed suggest that these arguments may lead to leaving home, particularly for girls. As discussed in the prior section of this chapter, seriously delinquent youths living on their own tend to be even more strongly drug and crime involved than their peers who are still living at home.

# SERIOUS DELINQUENTS STILL IN SCHOOL

Researchers generally agree that schooling and delinquency are strongly related, but the nature of the relationship is still debated. Many studies have emphasized student characteristics such as intelligence (see Hirschi and Hindelang 1977) and academic performance (e.g., Bachman, O'Malley, and Johnston 1978; Hindelang, Hirschi, and Weis 1981), whereas others have focused on school characteristics such as tracking (e.g., Colvin and Pauly 1983) and the treatment of poor and minority youth by school personnel (e.g., Kelly 1982). The primary argument, however, is the disagreement between research supporting control theory (e.g., Hirschi 1969; Johnson 1979; Kruttschnitt, Heath, and Ward 1986; Simcha-Fagan and Schwartz 1986; Thornberry, Moore, and Christenson 1985; Wiatrowski, Griswold, and Roberts 1981) and research supporting strain theory (e.g., Cloward and Ohlin 1960; Cohen 1955; Elliott and Voss 1974; Kvaraceus 1966; Schafer and Polk 1967).

Strain theory argues that school problems leading to frustration and failure are major factors in the initiation of delinquency. Schools are especially likely to place this kind of strain on poor and working-class students, who become frustrated at being unable to achieve in the system that will determine their later chances of economic success. Particularly in combination with the peer influences prevalent in school, these strains may lead youths to reject both school expectations and other conventional rules and values. Control theory, on the other hand, suggests that delinquency results from the characteristics of individual youths, particularly their degree of attachment to conventional institutions such as school and family.

That both strain and control theory are supported by research evidence suggests that characteristics of both schools and individual youths contribute, each interacting with the other in the creation of delinquency. Liska and Reed (1985) argue that the impact of student/school relationships on delinquency is further complicated by causal feedback from delinquency itself. That is, delinquency reduces attachment to school, and this in turn encourages further delinquency. Moreover, this complex process may work quite differently for middle-class and lower-class youth. Liska and Reed tested their arguments with longitudinal data from a national probability sample of 15–17-year-old male high school students. They found different relationships among delinquency, school attachment, and parental attachment for black and white students. For whites, parental attachment had an effect on delinquency, but school attachment did not; rather, delinquency often affected school attachment. But for blacks, school attachment was an important causal factor in delinquency, perhaps because school is the only relationship underclass youths have with the wider society. In short, a major reason for the continuing debate about the school/delinquency relationship is that it is probably a more complex phenomenon than either strain theory or control theory suggests.

The recent studies on this issue have all been done with samples of ordinary students involved in nothing more than garden-variety delinquency. The Miami interviews with serious delinquents permit analysis of these issues with a sample that could be expected to show much higher degrees of detachment from school than found in the normal youth population. Included were questions about three aspects of student/school relationships: student attitudes toward school, student in-school behaviors, and school disciplinary actions. As discussed below, each set of variables indicates that, on the whole, these seriously delinquent youths were in fact quite detached from their schools. There is considerable variation, however, in the degree to which this detachment is related to early or current drug/crime involvement.

## Attitudes:
## The Unimportance of School

The 436 respondents still in school (70.4% of the total sample) were asked to rate the importance to them of (1) graduating from high school, (2) getting good grades, and (3) being liked by teachers. These items used a three-category scale of Very, Somewhat, and Not important. Graduating received the highest importance ratings, since only 24% said a diploma was not important, compared to "not important" reports of 45% for getting good grades and 43% for being liked by teachers. On the other hand, only 10% said that graduating is *very* important, about the same as for getting good grades (4%) and being liked by teachers (10%). Translating none-to-very as 0-to-2 for each of the three items, and then adding them for a 0-to-6 total score, 58% had totals of 2 or less and only 14% had totals of 4 or more.

Probably because of the virtual universality of poor school attitudes in this sample, only two variations by sociodemographic category were apparent. First, 16–17-year-old females still in school appeared more uniformly decided than their male counterparts that school is important. At a minimum, they had all apparently resolved to graduate, since *all* of them said graduating was at least somewhat important.[11] However, it may be recalled from the discussion of school dropouts that, among all 16–17-year-olds in the sample, a higher percentage of females than males had dropped out of school—86% versus 63%.

Second, among 16–17-year-old males, ethnic differences are apparent in attitudes toward graduation. Over 40% of black and Hispanic males of this age said graduation was *not* important, whereas 45% of their white counterparts said it was *very* important (and none of the whites said it was not important). This difference in attitudes is not surprising in the context of at least a decade of markedly higher unemployment probabilities for young minority males than for their white counterparts.

Overall, however, findings on the school-attitudes questions indicated most clearly that the serious delinquents we interviewed who were still in school assigned relatively little importance to good grades or teachers' attitudes toward them, and only a bit more to school graduation. Since this sample is composed entirely of serious delinquents, the finding that these youths attribute very little importance to school is consistent with control theory. Not surprisingly, then, school attitudes among these serious delinquents are relatively unrelated to how early they began their drug/crime involvement or to the relative degree of their serious delinquency now.[12]

---

[11]Females appeared to have slightly more positive attitudes toward all aspects of school. Being female correlated significantly ($p < .05$) although weakly with importance of graduating (rho = .11), getting good grades (rho = .12), and being liked by teachers (rho = .22) among 14–17-year-old blacks and whites. The correlation coefficients were similar when race was controlled. Being liked by teachers, the most gender-related attitude, was reflected in male versus female percentage contrasts of 50% versus 27% who said it was *not* important and 4% versus 14% who said it was *very* important that teachers like them.

[12]Six correlations with the school-attitudes total (the sum of the three importance ratings, a possible 0 to 6 points) were examined for males age 12–13, males age 14–17, and females: (1–4) ages at first and first regular drug use and first and first regular crime and (5–6) the summary scores for current drug use and crime. None of the 12 correlations for male students were statistically significant ($p < .05$). For female students, four were significant but not strong: rhos of .25 with age at first drug use, .22 with age at starting regular crime, −.31 for current drug use, and −.23 for current crime. As with the attitude/demographic relationships, a likely explanation is that there is not enough variation in the school attitudes of this sample to look at relationships between attitudes and other factors.

## Behaviors: Cutting School, or Staying and Getting High

The poor school attitudes suggested by the "How important...?" responses just discussed are also apparent in the data for the two student behaviors asked about: cutting classes and being high at school. For each, three questions were asked of all 611 respondents (dropouts as well as students): Did you ever do it? What grade were you in the first time? How often did you do it the last year you were in school?

Both behaviors were extremely common. Virtually all respondents (98.9%) had cut school or skipped classes at some time, and all but three (99.5%) had been high while at school. A little over half had committed each school violation by the time they were in sixth grade (51.7% cut class; 55.0% were high at school). Thus, mean grade at the time of first violation was just over 6 for each behavior (6.2 for cutting class, 6.1 for being high at school). However, younger students began even earlier—four out of five 12–13-year-olds had begun each behavior by sixth grade. As shown in Table 7.4, there were few gender differences in how early these behaviors started among students the same age.

Cutting class was much more frequent behavior for the oldest males than for any other group. The breakdowns in Table 7.4 on page 142 show that almost half of male students age 16–17 cut three or more days a week during the last school year, compared to none of the seven female students this age and about a fourth of younger students. The difference appeared to be correlated with ethnicity; among male students age 16–17, cutting classes three or more days a week was much more common among blacks (43%) and Hispanics (75%) than among whites (25%). Although younger students (age 12–15) cut class less often, they did so frequently enough to present a problem. Some 24% of the males and black females under age 16 reported cutting class at least three days a week. This frequency of cutting was nonexistent (0%) for 16–17-year-old female students and rare (4%) for white females under age 16. Ethnic differences for younger males were minimal. However, the overall size of the problem is indicated by the finding that only 10.3% of the 436 students reported cutting class *less* often than one school day in six during their last school year.

Further, respondent comments to interviewers suggested that *less* cutting often meant fear of punishment, not "attachment to school." These students were still cutting class as often as they felt they could. For example, a 12-year-old answered the question with:

> Not too often--only about once or twice a month to avoid any suspicion.

Some, such as the following 12-year-old, were worried about being held in an after-school detention:

> Only about once a week so I don't get the teach-
> ers' attention. I need to get out of school on
> time each day to start selling my stuff to have my
> own crack.

Others varied their skipping in accordance with other school misbehavior, so as not to make the situation worse, such as the 13-year-old who reported:

> I'd skip about twice a week or more if I could get
> away with it and was good and quiet when I was in
> school classes.

A few linked their cutting to the importance of graduating, like the 15-year-old male who stated:

> I skip about twice a week except when it can get
> me into trouble or thrown out of school. I need to
> get a high school degree to be someone in life.

But others plan to drop out as soon as they are old enough, like the 14-year-old female who said:

> I skip about two or three times a week. I'll drop
> out legally as soon as I get to be 16 years old so
> I skip school now whenever I want to.

But even when these students were in school, chances are very good that they were high on drugs. As Table 7.4 indicates, *most* of these youths said that during their last school year they were high in school *every* day that they attended. This held for two in five older females, three in five students under age 16, and four out of five older males. One 15-year-old reported:

> I do *Bob Marley* [marijuana] on the way to school
> every day, *go-fast*, ya know, *crank* [methamphet-
> amine] on some days, and crack sometimes too.

Altogether, 64.7% of the 436 students said they were high in school every day they went, and 79.1% said they were high more than half the days they went to school. Ethnic differences were minimal, as were age and gender differences among 12–15-year-olds.

Initiation of both school misbehaviors—cutting class and being high at school—is related to age in the same way as initiation into drug/crime involvement. Specifically, the younger the respondent, the earlier the grade at the time of first cutting classes (rho = .33 for the total sample) and being high at school (rho = .37), as well as the younger the age at first crime (rho = .32) and first regular use of marijuana (rho = .35) or alcohol (rho = .47). The direct correlations between grade when first cutting class

**TABLE 7.4**
**School Misbehaviors among Students by Gender and Age***

| | Male | | | Female | |
|---|---|---|---|---|---|
| | 12–13 (N =120) | 14–15 (N = 185) | 16–17 (N = 74) | 14–15 (N = 50) | 16–17 (N = 7) |
| **By sixth grade (% "yes")** | | | | | |
| Cut class | 79.2 | 53.0 | 27.0 | 50.0 | 42.9 |
| High at school | 80.0 | 60.0 | 36.5 | 52.0 | 28.6 |
| **Last school year (% "yes")** | | | | | |
| 3+ cuts/week | 20.8 | 26.5 | 48.6 | 14.0 | 0.0 |
| Always high | 60.0 | 63.8 | 79.7 | 62.0 | 42.9 |
| **Rho with current drug use score:[†]** | | | | | |
| Grade first | | | | | |
| Cut class | –.54 | –.41 | –.22 | –.38 | — |
| High at school | –.55 | –.42 | –.24 | –.52 | — |
| Frequency last year | | | | | |
| Cut class | –.20 | –.20 | — | — | — |
| High at school | +.66 | +.40 | — | +.49 | — |
| **Rho with current crime score:[†]** | | | | | |
| Grade first | | | | | |
| Cut class | –.43 | –.47 | — | –.56 | –.96 |
| High at school | –.40 | –.45 | — | –.57 | –.96 |
| Frequency last year | | | | | |
| Cut class | — | –.20 | — | — | — |
| High at school | +.63 | +.37 | — | +.46 | — |

*"Students" excludes graduates and dropouts.

[†]Rho: Spearman Correlation Coefficient significant at $p < .05$ between the summary score noted and school grade, or days cut last year (1 = no more than 3 days a month through 5 = always), or days high at school last year (1 = no more than 6 days a month through 4 = always).

or being high in school and age at first or first regular drug use or crime are all fairly strong—in the .61 to .68 range for all students, slightly lower than this for 14–17-year-old male students (.45 to .60), and slightly higher for female students (.63 to .78).

But what about the sequencing of first school misbehaviors and early drug/crime involvement? Which came first? To examine this question, "grade at first regular drug use" was estimated by subtracting 5 from "age at first regular drug use" and then calculating how many respondents showed a difference of more than one grade when first regular drug use is compared to first school misbehavior. The results for all 611 respondents came out to "about the same time" in 85% of the cases for first cutting class and 86% of the cases for first being high at school. The few remaining cases were split about evenly between regular drug use first and school misbehavior first. The "about the same time" conclusion is also suggested by a comparison of mean grade or age for these behaviors. Both of the school misbehaviors start at a mean of about grade 6.2, and first regular drug use (almost always—96.7%—marijuana use) began at a mean of age 11.4; a youngster starting first grade at age six would be in grade six by age 11.

The timing is different for regular involvement in criminal activities. As in the case of regular drug use, many respondents began regular crime at about the same time as first skipping classes (54%) or getting high in school (50%). But many more were skipping classes (43%) or getting high in school (48%) *before* they started regular crime. Very few (under 3%) were involved in regular crime prior to these school misbehaviors. Since truancy and in-school drug use are instances of minor delinquency, this finding amounts to the expected sequence of minor delinquency preceding serious degrees of criminal behavior.

The correlation of earlier school misbehaviors and earlier drug/crime initiation suggests that earlier school misbehaviors might also predict greater current drug/crime involvement. This appears to be the case at least for the 12–15-year-olds. As specified in Table 7.4, correlations between initiation grades for the two school misbehaviors and current drug or crime involvement are all in the .38 to .57 range for the three subsamples under age 16. For male students age 16–17, earlier initiation of school misbehaviors has only a weak association with more current drug use and no association with more crime; for their female counterparts, earlier school misbehavior has no relationship to current drug use, although it is strongly related (–.96) to current crime. The probable reason why these relationships are stronger for younger respondents is that, for older respondents, more time has elapsed since their initial school misbehaviors—time during which other factors have also influenced their current levels of drug use and crime.

Finally, Table 7.4 also shows correlations between current school misbehaviors and current drug/crime activity for students. The more serious delinquents did not cut school more often, but—again, at least among respondents under age 16—more serious delinquents were high at school more often. In this instance, the lack of relationship for older youths is likely attributable to the previously discussed tendency for the worst cases—those with both the most school misbehaviors and the most drug/crime involvement in the past year—to be dropouts, who by definition were excluded from the analysis of serious delinquents still in school.

## School Reactions:
## Suspensions/Expulsions

Schools often reacted to these serious delinquents by suspending or even expelling them. Only 11.9% of the total sample (and 15.2% of current students) had *no* suspensions or expulsions. Of the 436 students, 62.8% had at least two and 33.0% had at least three. Mean grade at first suspension/expulsion was 6.5; over a third of the total sample (38.6%) had been suspended or expelled by the time they were in sixth grade. However, as shown in Table 7.5, grade at the first occurrence was much earlier for younger students, as in the case of the school misbehaviors. Also similarly, gender differences are minimal for students of the same age.

Most of the school suspensions and expulsions experienced by this heavily drug- and crime-involved sample had to do with their drug use or criminal behavior. Suspensions/expulsions for smoking, drinking, or use of illicit drugs were reported by four out of five respondents (82.2%); almost half (46.6%) were suspended/expelled for selling drugs, as were over a fourth (26.2%) for other crimes (generally theft or assault). Only four respondents (0.7%) were suspended *only* for misbehaviors unrelated to drug use or crime.

As reported in Table 7.5, suspensions/expulsions for drug use are about equally common among all age groups, but those for dealing and other crimes increase in each age group. Older youths therefore have higher numbers of total suspensions/expulsions. Whereas only 3% of the 12–13-year-old males had five or more suspensions/expulsions on their school records, this was true of 34% of the 16–17-year-old males. Respondents who have since dropped out of school are particularly likely to have multiple suspensions/expulsions, which suggests that high numbers for current students are good predictors of future dropout status.[13]

Grade at first suspension/expulsion is strongly related to age at starting regular drug use (rho = .64) and age at starting regular crime (rho = .65) among current students. These correlations are highly similar to those reported for grade at first cutting class or getting high at school. Thus, it is not surprising that, like earlier school misbehaviors, earlier suspensions are associated with more current drug use and crime. As specified in Table 7.5, this relationship is suggested by correlations for both males and females, and for all three age groups, for both drug use and crime but especially crime (four of the five rhos are in the –.40 to –.55 range). Correla-

---

[13]Ethnic/racial differences are relatively slight. Among 14–17-year-old males, whites had somewhat fewer suspensions/expulsions (rho = –.21); among the youngest boys, blacks had fewer (rho = –.21); for females there was no overall relationship to race. Correlations with family disadvantage give similar results: if there is a relationship, it is certainly not strong (rho = .25 for males age 14–17; rho is not significant at $p < .05$ for younger males or for females).

**TABLE 7.5**
**School Suspensions/Expulsions by Gender and Age**

| | Male | | | Female | |
|---|---|---|---|---|---|
| | 12–13 (N =120) | 14–15 (N = 185) | 16–17 (N = 206) | 14–15 (N = 50) | 16–17 (N = 50) |
| **Percentage** | | | | | |
| Ever | 84.2% | 87.6% | 93.2% | 74.0% | 90.0% |
| For drug use | 78.3% | 82.2% | 86.9% | 74.0% | 80.0% |
| For dealing | 29.2 | 44.3 | 62.6 | 38.0 | 40.0 |
| For other crime | 16.7 | 17.8 | 35.0 | 28.0 | 42.0 |
| Only for non-drug/crime | 0.8 | 0.5 | 0.5 | 0.0 | 2.0 |
| By 6th grade* | 63.3% | 40.5% | 26.2% | 40.0% | 22.0% |
| Student | | | 16.2 | | 28.6 |
| Dropout | | | 32.3 | | 20.9 |
| 3+ times* | 17.5% | 38.9% | 64.6% | 46.0% | 52.0% |
| Student | | | 33.8 | | 42.9 |
| Dropout | | | 83.1 | | 53.5 |
| **Rho with current drug use score:†** | | | | | |
| Grade first | −.48 | −.41 | −.17 | −.25 | — |
| Total number | +.34 | +.40 | +.40 | +.51 | +.25 |
| **Rho with current crime score:†** | | | | | |
| Grade first | −.40 | −.50 | −.24 | −.55 | −.49 |
| Total number | +.37 | +.44 | +.40 | +.53 | +.55 |

*First line includes all 611 respondents, by age group. "Students" are the 74 males and 7 females age 16–17 still in school. "Dropouts" are the 130 males and 43 females age 16–17 who dropped out. The two male graduates are not included as either students or dropouts, for consistency with prior tables.

†Rho: Spearman Correlation Coefficient significant at $p < .05$ between the summary score noted and school grade (if ever suspended/expelled) or total number of suspensions/expulsions (for all respondents, coded 0 = none through 6 = 6+).

tions are even more consistent between total number of suspensions/expulsions and current drug/crime involvement. These findings suggest that serious delinquents still in school are quite likely to come to the attention of school authorities and that it is the drug/crime behavior of these youths that results in disciplinary actions against them.

## Conclusion:
## Serious Delinquents
## Still in School

Overall, these findings indicate that most of the serious delinquents interviewed who were still in school have little if any attachment to school. Few consider high school graduation to be *"very* important," and they assign even less importance to good grades or teachers' opinions of them. They are often absent, and, when they are in school, they are usually high on drugs. Their high rates of suspensions/expulsions suggest that school personnel view them as troublemakers. And indeed many of them are. One of these youths reported:

> You can't be high all day and stay out of trouble with the teachers. Nodding off in class, fighting with kids because they're trying to rip you off or just looking at you strange, trying to sneak off to get *loaded* pisses the teachers off.

Similarly, a member of an honor-student group commented about his drug-using classmates:

> The "druggies" *are* the troublemakers. Why they even bother to come to school is a mystery. They're always high on something; they push you around, they steal, and make school miserable for everyone.

And, finally, an assistant principal offered:

> We tell them, if they are going to use drugs or sell drugs, we don't want them here. *This* is a school, not a crack house or shooting gallery. It is a place to learn. If that's not what a child wants to cooperate with, we'll gladly give them the directions to the front door.

Respondent comments to interviewers frequently suggested that, even in school, the orientation of these youths is toward street concerns. This is perhaps most clearly expressed by the respondent who told us that school isn't so bad—it's "as good a place as any to stay out of too much trouble, get high, and sell dope." For youths under age 16, the legal requirement of school attendance means that street activities during school hours may elicit police response; this becomes a major reason for being in school. Here we see an indication of "social control" in operation, but it is not one reasonably described as "attachment to school." For those old enough to drop out, drug/crime activities occurring in school—resulting in suspensions or even expulsions for drug use, drug sales, and other crimes—are highly likely to be part of the reason for dropping out.

Those serious delinquents who were youngest when they started substance use outside of school were also youngest when first high in school, first cutting classes, and first suspended or expelled. In fact, street drug use and school problems began at roughly the same time for this sample. It is possible that poor school experiences—bad grades, teacher criticisms, etc.—preceded illicit drug use for these youths; for at least a few, this certainly was the case. A 10th-grader remarked in 1987:

> I would get the same crap from every fucking
> teacher. "What's wrong with you?" "Don't you care
> about your future?" "Why don't you study?" "Why
> don't you listen--are you high on something?"
> Maybe getting high is what I should do, I said
> to myself. And when I *did* get high, the fucking
> teachers still gave me the same crap over and
> over again, but at least bein' high they didn't
> bother me.

However, it can be stated that problems in school preceded regular criminal activity by at least a year for many students—e.g., 43% in the case of cutting class. This means that school personnel were aware (by means of attendance records if nothing else) that these soon-to-be serious delinquents were in some way problem students. The school response to these troubled youths, however, was to force them out of school with suspensions and expulsions. These occasions of more time and opportunity for life on the streets may have contributed, in turn, to increased drug use and criminal activities. In any case, it should be recalled in this context that dropout/ student comparisons discussed earlier in this chapter show a clear relationship among more suspensions/expulsions, dropping out, and more serious delinquency.

## POSTSCRIPT

Many of the findings discussed in this chapter are what one might expect in a study of serious delinquents. The majority of these youths are from poor families, and almost all the rest are from working-class backgrounds. Two out of three who are old enough to drop out of school have done so. Almost all who are still enrolled have school attitudes that are poor and attendance records that are worse. They bring their drug use, and sometimes their for-profit crimes, into the schools and are consequently often suspended or expelled. They all either argue with their families or have moved out to live on their own. They have relatively little experience with legal employment.

These findings can be taken as support for both strain theory and social control theory. That is, the general socioeconomic background of these youths suggests the sort of delinquency/class relationship hypothesized by strain theorists, and the troubled or broken relationships with family and school are as predicted by social control theory. However, for both theoretical orientations, the support offered by these findings is at a very general level. More specific examinations turn up both qualifications and contradictions.

Looking first at strain theory, we see the most obvious contradiction in the school findings: dropouts in the sample were clearly more drug and crime involved than youths still enrolled in school. Even more problematically for strain theory, only very weak relationships between drug/crime involvement and degree of family disadvantage were found. Although it is true that very few of the respondents were from middle-class backgrounds, there is a large difference in social status and economic comfort between families on welfare and those headed by men with stable working-class jobs. This difference seems to be sufficiently meaningful that, if social class is important as a factor explaining crime, the correlations between family disadvantage and at least drug/crime history, if not current behaviors, should have been much more impressive than the weak and markedly inconsistent results that were found.

For social control theory, the findings on family interaction cast some doubt on the applicability of this orientation in understanding *serious* delinquency. To begin with, the analysis of early alcohol use suggests that this first step toward delinquency is related to family interaction in an unexpected way. Specifically, youths who first drink with peers on the street, rather than at home, tend to be those who are *less* seriously drug/crime involved, if only because they start substance use at a later age. This can be taken as an instance of "family attachment" that has *undesirable* effects on later drug/crime involvement—a possibility not often entertained by social control theorists. Then, by the time these young drug users have progressed to serious levels of both substance use and criminal behavior, the data suggest that parents are attempting to control such activities—but with little success. More family arguments about drug/crime involvement are associated with more such behaviors; if family were a meaningful source of controls on serious delinquency, these correlations would be negative. Respondent comments suggest that the most vigorous parental efforts to control serious delinquency may be the ones most likely to result in teenagers leaving home to live on their own. Since the data indicate that such youths are more drug/crime involved than their peers still at home, this would be still another instance of parental behavior making serious delinquency worse.

The school findings suggest similar problems. Youth behaviors that logically indicate greater "school attachment," such as better school attendance, may actually stem from street concerns such as avoiding police contact, meeting potential drug customers among other students, or avoiding a detention that would delay arrival at an after-school drug sales job. Further, the data suggest that behaviors of school personnel aimed at controlling troublesome students are likely to backfire by encouraging dropping out, with drug/crime results highly similar to those of teenagers leaving home. This seems particularly disturbing given that school represents an obvious intervention source for serious delinquency. A large number of these youths began cutting class and getting high in school while they were still in elementary school and had not yet engaged in criminal behavior on a regular basis. But even at this early age, most of them were simply "punished" with suspensions. What this means in effect is that schools typically reacted to street behaviors of students by giving them more street time.

What can be concluded from these assorted problems is that many family and school efforts at controlling serious delinquency simply come too late. These youths have been acquiring street values for too long to be reachable by the means that might produce results with a garden-variety delinquent. But to the extent that this is true, it brings one back, full circle, to support for the arguments of control theory. That is, the data of this study indicate clearly the attachment of these youths to street drugs and street crimes rather than to the opinions of parents and teachers. The next chapter suggests that street friends provide still another source of values that make the opinions and criticisms of conventional adults relatively meaningless as sources of social control.

# CHAPTER 8

# "BIRDS OF A FEATHER . . ." BUT WHY?

Although it is generally agreed that delinquents tend to spend time with other delinquents, there is a surprising amount of debate as to why. The various answers to this question have direct implications for explaining why and how delinquency itself originates and persists. Consequently, the initial focus here is on three competing perspectives on delinquent friends. The next section examines the data from the new study concerning peer influences on serious youth drug and crime involvement. Throughout, a special interest is in the degree to which various theories, developed primarily to explain garden-variety delinquency, also apply to serious delinquency.

## PERSPECTIVES AND ISSUES

Social learning theorists imply that delinquent friends are the primary cause of delinquency. They argue that a youngster becomes delinquent by learning attitudes favorable to law violation and then being socially rewarded for delinquent behaviors. Both the learning and the rewards come from the people the youth spends the most time with; for most adolescents, this means friends. Social learning does not have to be deliberate or even conscious. Instead, evidence suggests that for many delinquents it involves "modeling"—imitation of observed behavior (Akers et al. 1979; Conger 1976; Reiss and Rhodes 1964). This modeling effect is doubtless enhanced by the frequently reported tendency for delinquents to see much more delinquency among their friends than nondelinquents do (Elliott and Voss

1974; Figueira-McDonough, Barton, and Sarri 1981; Hindelang 1973; Jessor and Jessor 1977, 1980; Johnson 1979; Kandel, Kessler, and Margulies 1978).

Behavior, in this view, can be much more important than stated opinions or attitudes. For example, Richard E. Johnson, Anastasios C. Marcos, and Stephen J. Bahr (1987) found that attitudes favorable to drug use are less important in explaining why a youth uses drugs than are the drug use behaviors of friends, and Richard Jessor and Shirley L. Jessor (1977) found that youths are involved in delinquent behavior even when they *say* that such behavior is morally wrong. However, attitudes of delinquents are most often found to be conducive to delinquent behavior; evidence shows that delinquents think delinquency is a more common behavior than it is, that they often find rationalizations to "justify" delinquent acts, and even that they approve of delinquent behaviors (Gold 1970; Hindelang 1974; Jessor and Jessor 1980; Matza 1964; Johnson 1979). Akers and his associates (1979) also emphasize the importance of perceived rewards and punishments for delinquent activities in starting and continuing delinquent behavior.

Elements of social learning theory can be traced back to the Chicago school's "social disorganization" perspective. Examples discussed in Chapter 2 include Thrasher's (1927) study of how gangs begin in the ordinary "play groups" of crowded inner-city neighborhoods. Some play groups turn into gangs because they come into conflict with other groups and build a reputation as a gang. But even when this happens, the basis for gang members' relationships remains friendship and common interests. Delinquent youths, in this view, have close-knit, enduring ties similar in closeness to those of a family; they learn values and behaviors from one another in much the same way family members do. Learning delinquency from other delinquents is also stressed in Shaw and McKay's (1942) discussion of the part played in social *disorganization* by the existence of established, *organized* gangs of older youths who teach criminal traditions to younger boys.

In a second view, strain and subcultural perspectives describe the most basic causes of delinquency as resting in the social-class structure of our society, not in the influence of delinquent friends. For example, Cohen (1955) emphasizes the problems faced by poor and working-class boys in dealing with the middle-class standards imposed on them in school. Boys who share this problem interact with one another to develop values that give them social recognition for violating rather than following middle-class adult standards. Thus, the group in essence develops its own delinquent subculture as a solution to a problem that originates in the overall structure of the society. Over time, the shared values of a delinquent subculture cut these boys off from acceptance by not only adults but also nondelinquent peers. Their friendships with other delinquents thus tend to become very close. Delinquent friends, in this view, are not the reason a youth begins delinquency, but they do help determine what kinds of delinquent behaviors will be acted out and they provide social support for the continuation of delinquent behavior in spite of criticism and even punishment.

Still a third view is presented in Hirschi's (1969) version of social control theory, which argues that delinquent peers are essentially irrelevant to why a youth becomes delinquent. Hirschi says that, for normal, conventional youngsters, friends provide the same kind of influence that parents and schools do. That is, friendships are valued relationships that help ensure nondelinquent behavior because youngsters want their friends (as well as family and teachers) to think well of them. The social skills of delinquents, on the other hand, are too inadequate for them to form or sustain friendships, and it is this *lack* of ties to peers that helps inspire delinquency. This kind of explanation has been applied most often to female delinquents (for example, Konopka 1966), but Hirschi argues that it holds for all youth, including lower-class males. Hirschi goes so far as to state that "the idea that delinquents have comparatively warm intimate relations with each other (or with anyone) is a romantic myth" (1969, p. 159).

Studies of garden-variety delinquents by other researchers generally fail to support Hirschi's view of peers as a source of pressure toward conventional behavior, and Hirschi himself concluded that his own findings did not offer strong support for this part of his theory (1969, p. 230). Instead, friends are most often found to be a source of pressure toward delinquency, not conformity. Further, reexaminations of Hirschi's own data (see Elliott, Huizinga, and Ageton 1985; Linden 1978) find that delinquents identify with their friends as much as nondelinquents do; moreover, there are no differences between delinquent and nondelinquent youths in the number and loyalty of their best friends.

Hirschi's view of delinquents as unable to maintain friendships has also been contradicted by a study with more extensive peer-relationship questions and better delinquency measures than Hirschi used. Giordano, Cernkovich, and Pugh (1986) examined differences in (1) intrinsic (self-disclosure, caring, and trust) and extrinsic (useful) rewards and identity support; (2) level of interaction—time spent with friends, longevity of relationships, and peer pressure; and (3) conflict, imbalance, and loyalty in the face of trouble. They found that delinquents are no less likely than nondelinquents to be caring or trusting and no more likely to be jealous or competitive. Delinquents are somewhat more focused on extrinsic rewards, and they have more conflict with friends. But they also care more what their friends think, and they are more likely to believe that their friends would be loyal in a time of trouble.

Recent attempts to integrate learning, strain, and control theories into one model also generally find that association with delinquent peers is a major factor contributing to delinquent behavior. Looking at changes in drug/crime involvement over time, the National Youth Survey researchers found that the *only* factors directly affecting current delinquency were past delinquency and association with delinquent peers (Elliott, Huizinga, and Ageton 1985, pp. 105–118). The superiority of the National Youth Survey data to those of prior delinquency studies makes this finding an important assertion of the role of peer influences in explaining delinquency. However, the same researchers found that peers are a more important factor in explaining minor offenses and marijuana use than they are in accounting for serious crimes and use of pills or cocaine.

Similar questions about serious versus garden-variety delinquency are raised in a study by Fagan, Piper, and Moore (1986). Their sample of violent institutionalized delinquents had much higher rates of delinquency than their comparison samples of inner-city students and dropouts. However, delinquent peers were much more important factors in explaining delinquency among students and dropouts than among violent delinquents. This indicates that, although many youths in inner-city neighborhoods have contact with delinquents, these peer relationships are not the most important factor in determining whether a youth will participate in *violent* offenses or *serious* levels of other criminal behavior. On the other hand, these researchers also found that having friends who had been involved with the juvenile justice system was much more important in explaining delinquency among violent offenders than among students and dropouts. If justice system contacts indicate more serious criminal involvement, this finding suggests that *seriously* delinquent peers are in fact important in explaining crime among *serious* delinquents.

Because the Miami study did not include systematic follow-up interviews, no direct analysis can be undertaken of the question of whether delinquent friends are a cause or a consequence of delinquency—or merely a characteristic that tends to accompany delinquent behavior without being either cause or effect. What can be done, however, is to describe several aspects of the peer relationships of truly serious delinquents at large in the community, with an eye to the implications of these findings for the various competing theories just discussed. Specifically, the next sections present findings on four topics: commission of crime with a partner, people regarded by these youths as their "three best friends," arguments with friends, and relationships with friends who have been incarcerated or in drug treatment. The concluding section is a summary discussion of the implications of these findings for understanding the role of peer relationships in serious youth drug and crime involvement.

## PARTNERS IN CRIME

One aspect of peer relationships among serious delinquents is the question of the extent to which these youths commit crimes as lone offenders or with accomplices. In a recent review of research on crime partners, Albert J. Reiss (1988) indicates that most adolescent offenders have partners, although the typical offender engages in both solo and accomplice crimes. Further, relationships with partners are likely to be short lived, so that active offenders tend to have partnership arrangements with many different individuals. The *most* active criminals thus have the most partnership arrangements, and groups of offenders tend to commit both more serious crimes and higher numbers of offenses than single offenders. Studies based on victim reports to police suggest that solo offenses are somewhat more common among whites than blacks and considerably more common among adults than juveniles.

The Miami findings present the opportunity to examine partnership in relation to both demographic characteristics and offense levels in a fairly unusual kind of sample from which to have partnership data. The great majority of prior research on crime partners has relied on official arrest and victimization statistics, or on samples of offenders processed by the justice system, or on self-report data from only garden-variety delinquents. It may be, for example, that, since the crime patterns of serious delinquents are more like those of adult offenders than like those of other youths, they might also be solo offenders more often than other youths.

In the Miami interviews, questions about partnerships were asked at the same time as questions about how many offenses respondents had committed in the prior 12 months. For each offense type, interviewers asked whether these crimes were "usually" committed with partners and, if so, how many partners. It should be noted that the group activity reflected in the resulting responses is not "gang" behavior. Only 26 respondents (4.3%) had *ever* been gang members, and current membership was very rare (11 youths, which is 1.8% of the sample).

The results show clearly that serious crimes committed by these respondents were highly likely to be group offenses. As reported in Table 8.1, having at least one partner during for-profit major felonies—robbery, burglary, and motor vehicle theft—was reported by almost all youths involved in such offenses (over 95%). Assault, the other major felony asked about, was much more often done by solo offenders, but, still, three out of four youths committing assaults did so *with* partners. Further, partners during assaults were especially common among 14–17-year-old males, who are presumably more dangerous assault offenders than females or 12–13-year-old boys. Having at least one partner during assaults committed in the prior 12 months was reported by 86% of 16–17-year-old males committing assault ($N = 44$) and 94% of their 14–15-year-old counterparts ($N = 17$).

Lesser crimes were only slightly more likely than major felonies to be committed by lone offenders. Partnership was clearly the norm for petty property crimes, including the three most common ones—shoplifting (82% of offenders had partners), stolen goods offenses (94%), and theft from vehicles (87%). Complexity of offense does not seem to be a factor, since nine out of ten youths reported having a partner not only for the relatively complex offenses of confidence games and "bad paper" offenses (illegal

**TABLE 8.1**
**Crime Partners ("Usual" Number during Offenses in the Prior 12 Months)**

| Offense | (N) | Percent with Any Partners | Mean Number of Partners | Max* | Correlations[†] | | | | |
|---|---|---|---|---|---|---|---|---|---|
| | | | | | Age | Male | White | Black | SUM |
| Robbery | (358) | 97% | 1.7 | 3 | -.29 | — | -.10 | — | .60 |
| Assault | (91) | 74 | 0.7 | 1 | — | .46 | — | — | .50 |
| Burglary | (368) | 95 | 2.0 | 3 | -.29 | — | — | — | .70 |
| Motor vehicle theft | (257) | 96 | 1.9 | 3 | -.18 | .14 | — | -.14 | .35 |
| Shoplifting | (567) | 81% | 1.3 | 3 | -.18 | .09 | -.10 | — | .66 |
| Theft from vehicle | (355) | 87 | 1.4 | 3 | -.18 | .18 | — | -.13 | .33 |
| Pickpocketing | (59) | 75 | 1.2 | 2 | -.42 | .42 | — | — | .69 |
| Prostitute's theft | (83) | 64 | 0.9 | 2 | -.21 | — | — | — | .72 |
| Con games | (151) | 95% | 2.5 | 3 | — | .20 | — | — | .53 |
| Bad paper offenses | (185) | 93 | 2.2 | 3 | -.24 | .15 | -.19 | — | .72 |
| Stolen goods offense | (482) | 94 | 1.9 | 3 | -.13 | -.14 | — | — | .79 |
| Property destruction | (176) | 92 | 1.3 | 2 | -.20 | .28 | — | — | .15 |
| Prostitution | (107) | 64% | 0.6 | 1 | -.23 | — | — | — | .63 |
| Summary score[‡] | (611) | 95% | 8.7 | 27 | -.13 | .07 | -.12 | .09 | 1.00 |

*Maximum number coded (so that, e.g., 3 = 3+).

[†]Spearman Correlation Coefficients significant at $p < .05$ with age (12 to 17), being male (1 = male, 0 = female), being white (1 = white, 0 = black or Hispanic), being black (1 = black, 0 = white or Hispanic), and the summary score (see the last line).

[‡]Summary partner score is the simple sum of the number of partners for each of the prior 13 offenses. Range is 0 to 27; median is 7.

use of checks, credit cards, prescriptions) but also for the generally simple offenses of vandalism or other property destruction. The property crime most likely to involve solo offenders was pickpocketing, but partners were still reported by 75% of the 59 pickpockets. Even 64% of the 107 prostitutes normally worked with a partner.

Drug-business offenses by teenagers, of course, are only rarely committed by lone operators. Of the 587 drug-business participants, only 9% reported having no partners. Nonetheless, this offense type is omitted from Table 8.1 because it is not clear what the data mean. Adolescents are almost always at the bottom of drug-business operations, and some respondents made it clear that they were talking about the older dealers who employed them. Other respondents may have been reporting partners in a sense closer to what the term means for the other offenses—peers at relatively the same level, whether as "running partners" or members of the sort of "crew" operation discussed in Chapter 3. However, drug-business offenses are unique in the degree to which they absolutely require a relationship with another offender—if only someone from whom to purchase drugs for resale. The crime types included in Table 8.1, then, are all offenses for which solo operation is entirely possible. This makes the high number of partnership reports reflected in these data all the more meaningful.

As an additional way of looking at the partnership information, especially in relationship to other kinds of variables, a summary score was constructed. An upper limit had been set on each of the partnership items because only a few respondents reported high numbers of partners. As shown in Table 8.1, this maximum is 3 for most offense types (so that 3 actually means 3+); this approach tends to make any potential summary score somewhat more conservative than it would be if the small number of extremely high number-of-partners reports had been kept. The summary score was computed by simply adding the number of partners for each of the 13 specific offense types, a potential 0 to 32 sum; the actual range is 0 to 27 (median = 7). This variable is included as the last line in Table 8.1.[1]

As the prevalence of partnership reports suggests, crime with a partner was the norm for all age groups, both genders, and each ethnicity. However, correlations indicate a fairly consistent tendency toward more partners among younger offenders. Age has a significant negative association with number of partners for 11 of the 13 offense types noted in Table 8.1, and rho is at least .20 for seven of them. This suggests that, as serious delinquents continue crimes through adolescence, they are increasingly confident of their ability to commit offenses without help. However, the inverse implication is that serious delinquency at younger ages is more likely to be peer-supported activity.

---

[1]The last column in the table shows that all 13 items are significantly correlated with the summary score, ten of them moderately to strongly (rho = .50 to .79). Correlations computed separately by age/gender group give highly similar results.

The pattern for gender, in contrast, appears too relatively weak and inconsistent to support the old assumption that female delinquents are significantly less likely than their male counterparts to have relationships with delinquent peers.[2] Rather, it supports the finding of Figueira-McDonough, Barton, and Sarri (1981) that, at least today—perhaps in contrast to earlier decades—peer-group relationships are as important in explaining female as male participation in delinquency.

Correlations also suggest little if any relationship between race and the number of crime partners for particular offense types or for the partnership summary score. This is not consistent with strain or subcultural delinquency theories. That is, in Miami black youths are most likely, and white youths are least likely, to live in neighborhoods with high drug/crime rates. According to strain and subcultural perspectives, this should put black youths at the highest risk, and whites at the lowest risk, of being influenced by existing street subcultures. This assumption has logical consequences for numbers of potential delinquent peers, specifically including the number of potential crime partners. Slightly more support for this view is provided, however, from separate calculations by gender and age group. Race is not related to number of partners among the 12–13-year-old boys, but, among both male and female 14–17-year-olds, whites tend to have fewer partners (rho = −.16 for males, −.22 for females). For males, the correlation with being black, as opposed to white or Hispanic, is lower—.09 ($p <$ .05)—suggesting that it is not so much that blacks had more partners as that whites had fewer.

Finally, relationships between having partners and degree of criminal involvement were examined. Hirschi's version of social control theory implies that the most delinquent of these youths might well be those who tend to commit crimes on their own. Most other theories predict the opposite—that youths who have more friends involved in crime will be more involved in crime themselves. It might be noted that the structure of the data does not necessarily influence the outcome of the analysis. It is true that the partner summary score, as a simple sum of the 13 partnership items, is higher for those involved in more different *types* of crime, but there is no necessary connection between number of types and number of offenses. Neophytes with lower total crimes committed might be the offenders likeliest to do "a few of these" and "a few of those," rather than high numbers of more limited offense types; these same low-total novices might also be the likeliest to want or need the help of friends. It should also be noted that the 0–27 range for the partnership summary score is not a factor either: correlations are nearly identical even when the score is reduced to only three categories formed by trisecting the frequency distribution.

---

[2]Gender is clearly related to number of partners only for assault and pickpocketing offenses: males had more partners (rho > .40). Being male is also correlated with more partners for six other offenses, but rho is .20 or more for only two of them and the overall correlation between being male and the total partnership score is only .07.

The results show rather clearly that more partnership arrangements mean more overall current crime involvement, since the correlation between the two scores is .60, indicating a substantial relationship. Perhaps more tellingly, there is a correlation of .42 between the total partnership score and the current drug involvement score; that is, even this less direct indicator of the peer/delinquency relationship is still clearly significant.[3]

Altogether, the partnership findings suggest the importance of peers in serious delinquency, since crimes committed by these youths were highly likely to be group offenses. This holds for all age groups, both genders, and each ethnicity, but trends in the data suggest that it is especially important for younger offenders and, perhaps, minority youths. Further, doing more crime with peers rather than alone means more overall drug/crime involvement. All of these findings confirm the results of prior research, with the possible exception of the discovery that partnership seems to be even more common among these youths than prior studies might have predicted. Studies cited in Reiss's (1988) review generally find that juveniles have partnership participation rates in the 67–75% range for serious offenses (e.g., robbery and burglary), whereas our results showed rates of 95%. However, prior studies have included a broader range of offenders than our sample of exclusively serious delinquents. Thus, the findings reported here serve as an additional confirmation of the claim made by several researchers that offenders who commit crimes with others have higher crime frequency rates than solo offenders (Erickson 1971; Hindelang 1976).

# "THREE BEST FRIENDS"

Crime partners are not necessarily "friends." Thus, in addition to the partnership questions, we asked a series of eight questions about the people respondents regarded as their "three best friends—guy or girl, relative or not, whatever." Each youth thus used his or her own definition of "best friend." All questions were phrased as "How many of the three . . . ?" and the items concerned (1) length of friendship, (2) two conventional behaviors—school attendance and employment, and (3) five illegal behaviors—cocaine use, heroin use, drug sales, theft with the respondent, and possession of a gun.

---

[3]The correlation between total partnership arrangements and overall current crime involvement is slightly higher for the 12–13-year-old boys (rho = .71) than for the 14–17-year-old males (rho = .57) or females (rho = .59). For the partnership/drug-involvement relationship, correlations are markedly higher for the 12–13-year-old boys (rho = .73) than for the other groups—14–17-year-old males (rho = .42) and 14–17-year-old females (rho = .24, $p < .01$).

## Friends and Partners

One item asked "How many of your three best friends do thefts with you?" This *is* an indicator of crime partners who are "friends," since 97.6% of all respondents had committed some type of petty larceny in the prior 12 months. The most common response was one friend (42.4%), and many reported two or three friends doing thefts with them (34.5%). Only 22.7% of the 611 said *none* of their three best friends did thefts with them. This distribution of answers suggests conclusions very similar to those for the crime partner data: peer participation in the commission of crime is very common. However, these results also suggest that crime is hardly the only basis of respondents' friendships. Doing thefts with more than one best friend was not typical, and doing thefts with all of one's three best friends was reported by only 4.9% of the sample.

## Length of Friendships

The first "three best friends" item asked how many of the three the respondent had known five years earlier. Only 9.2% reported knowing none of the three this long, whereas 72.0% knew at least two for this long. Percentages for all specific age/gender groups are similar, with one exception. Of the 16–17-year-old females, only 37% reported knowing at least two of their three best friends for at least five years. This appears to reflect the high percentage of older girls who were no longer living at home. In leaving family, they also left childhood friends; only 26% of the 38 out on their own knew at least two of their best friends five years before, compared to 67% of the 12 still living at home (chi square $p < .02$). For the rest of the sample, however, this distribution of responses does not support a picture of serious delinquents as having only short-term or recent friendships, as implied in Hirschi's version of social control theory.

Hirschi's theory also implies that longer-term friendships mean less drug/crime involvement. To test this argument, we examined the relationship between how many friends were known five years ago and the respondents' own drug/crime involvement. Again, there was only weak support for Hirschi's position. The most consistent results are for current drug use: respondents who knew more friends five years ago are less drug involved now (rho = −.28 for 12–13-year-old males, −.21 for 14–17-year-old males, and −.41 for 14–17-year-old females). For current crime, all correlations are in the predicted direction but weaker (rho=−.20 for 12–13-year-old males, −.14 for 14–17-year-old males, and not significant for 14–17-year-old females).[4]

---

[4]A further implication of Hirschi's theory is an association between longer-term friendships and fewer delinquent friends. To test this, correlations between "number of three best friends known five years ago" and the other "three best friends" items were examined: how many are

These results constitute rather weak support for the idea that having long-term friendships deters delinquency, but they certainly do *not* show a clear *contradiction* to the hypothesis. One possible interpretation of these findings is that the sort of process Hirschi describes does in fact happen—but so does the opposite process. That is, some youngsters will first get involved in delinquent behaviors and then seek out new peer groups that are more consistent with these activities, whereas other youths learn delinquent values in the same friendship groups they have had since childhood. This interpretation is consistent with findings in the longitudinal research conducted by Kandel (1978) on garden-variety delinquents. She concluded that both processes were occurring, at about equal rates, for both marijuana use and general delinquency. Friends tend to choose each other because of their similarities, but friends also mutually influence each other in developing new behaviors.

## Friends and Behavior Uniformity

The most elementary question about the number of three best friends involved in school/job or drug/crime behaviors is how uniformly a respondent's behaviors match those of his or her friends. Hirschi's version of control theory emphasizes that friends who engage in conventional behaviors exert pressure toward conformity; learning theory and strain theory focus on delinquent friends' exerting pressure toward delinquent behavior. The Miami findings show tendencies toward both kinds of congruity—conformity/conformity and deviance/deviance—but much more inconsistency than one might expect.

---

in school, have a job, use cocaine, sell drugs, use heroin, do thefts with you, and have a gun. The results indicate some possible support for Hirschi's position. None of the correlations are strong and most are not statistically significant, but all seven are in the predicted direction: positive for the two conventional activities (school, job) and negative for the five drug/crime behaviors. The only correlation for the total sample that is greater than .15 is for number of three best friends in school, for which rho = .30. Since number of friends in school is clearly larger for younger respondents (number/age rho = −.57), this item might reflect number of same-age, as opposed to older, friends. If so, this suggests an alternative interpretation: the older the friends, the fewer who are in school and the more delinquent they are. This is still a statement about the relationship of peers to delinquency, but a much weaker one.

Correlations for the same variables among specific gender/age/ethnicity groups showed strong, consistent results for the 12–13-year-old black boys. In this group, the more friends known five years ago, the more friends who were in school (rho = .61) and the fewer friends who used cocaine (rho = −.37), sold drugs (rho = −.38), used heroin (rho = −.31), did theft with the respondent (rho = −.46), or had a gun (rho = −.37). Thus, the more delinquent boys apparently chose new and more delinquent friends. However, no other demographic subsample showed a consistent pattern in the relationship of friends' school/job or drug/crime behaviors and number of friends known five years ago.

For the item on friends in school, 100% of the respondents under age 16 were in school, and almost all reported having at least one best friend who was still enrolled—100% of the 12–15-year-old males and 92% of the 14–15-year-old females. Further, over 75% of both males and females under age 16 reported that at least two of their three best friends were still in school. Among 16–17-year-olds, only 37% of males and 14% of females were students, and only 35% and 18%, respectively, reported that at least two of their three best friends were still in school. For the sample as a whole, the more friends in school, the more likely a respondent was to still be in school (rho = .70).

On the other hand, it should also be noted that respondent/friend school attendance is by no means completely congruent. Only 47% of the 12–13-year-old boys reported that all three of their best friends were still in school, and the corresponding figures are even lower for 14–15-year-old boys (41%) and girls (37%). These best friends who are not in school represent potential models for dropping out, and in Chapter 7 we noted several reasons for believing that dropout rates among present 12–15-year-olds will be high. However, in the present context the most important point is simply that there is clearly some lack of uniformity between respondents and their best friends.[5]

The two drug-use-behavior questions both involved serious drugs; however, although daily use of cocaine was common among the respondents (64.2%), daily use of heroin was rare (4.1%). For both, frequency of the respondent's use is related to number of best friends using: rho = .30 for cocaine; rho = .48 for heroin. The primary reason for the relatively weak correlation for cocaine is that there is very little variation in the responses about friends using cocaine: 94% reported at least two best friends using cocaine. Thus, cocaine use by all three best friends was reported by not only 85% of the 392 daily cocaine users but also 62% of the other 219 respondents. For heroin, on the other hand, having at least one best friend using heroin was reported twice as often among the 265 heroin users (83%) as among the 346 others (42%). Thus, as in the case of the school question, there is significant correspondence between the behaviors of respondents and those of their best friends, but there is also a striking amount of difference.

---

[5]More incongruities appear in the data on friends who have a job. Again, there is an overall agreement (rho = .35) between number of friends employed and respondent's job experience (coded 0 = never, 1 = in past, 2 = job now). However, the correlation is very weak (rho = .20) for the 355 12–15-year-olds, because very few of them had a job when interviewed (under 4%) or had had one in the past (13.5%), although 55% reported having at least one best friend who was employed. Among 16–17-year-olds, the correlation is much stronger (rho = .49). About 16% of older respondents were employed, and 16% reported having at least two best friends who were employed; 43% had no job experience at all, and 40% reported having no best friends with a job.

The same results are apparent for the questions on drug-business involvement. Some 96.1% of all respondents committed at least one such offense in the prior year, and 97.7% reported having at least one best friend who sold drugs. On the other hand, the correlation is not strong (rho = .33) between number of dealer best friends and number of drug-business offenses committed personally. Even though most respondents sold drugs themselves, almost half (46%) reported at least one best friend who was not a dealer.

Gun possession is the most similar of the respondent and friend drug/crime behaviors. Number of best friends having a gun is correlated with carrying a handgun during a crime in the last 12 months (rho = .65). Thus, of the 295 youths who had carried handguns, having at least two best friends with guns was reported by 74%, compared to 13% of the 316 youths who had not carried a handgun. Even here, however, discordances are apparent, since 63% of those who had not personally carried a handgun still reported that at least one best friend had a gun.

This evidence of variation appears to reflect some toleration of differences. That is, these seriously delinquent youths apparently do make some behavioral choices without being coerced by their friends into uniform types and levels of drug/crime involvement. Congruency of deviant activities does exist, probably by both choice of friends and influences from friends. But neither process appears to be so complete as to indicate severe peer pressure. In short, it is not particularly surprising that the extremely drug- and crime-involved respondents were highly likely to have friends engaged in similar activities. What is more surprising is that they also tended to have friends who were more involved or less involved than they were in both deviant and socially approved activities.

Finally, to get a broader picture of the deviance of respondents' three best friends, a total score was computed by adding the number of friends (0 to 3) involved in each of the five drug/crime behaviors (subtotaling 0 to 15) and then subtracting the number of friends involved in each of the two socially approved behaviors (subtotaling 0 to 6). The resulting total scores for the 608 cases with complete data range from –4 through 13, with a median score of 6 (and a mean of 5.9). This "friends' deviance" score is significantly and positively correlated with the scores for current involvement in both crime (rho = .51) and drug use (rho = .52). Separate calculations for the three primary demographic subgroups—12–13-year-old boys and 14–17-year-old males and females—yield correlations nearly identical to these calculations done with the total sample. Correlations of this size suggest very substantial relationships but by no means identical distributions.

Altogether, these findings indicate substantial congruity between the degree of the respondent's own behaviors and the number of best friends engaged in those behaviors. This holds for both deviant and socially approved behaviors, for both specific behavior types and at a summary level, and for all demographic subgroups. At the same time, however, there is entirely too much inconsistency between respondent and friend behaviors to characterize their relationship as one of "uniformity." To some degree, each of the various theories implies that a major peer/ delinquency dynamic is one of peer pressure toward identical behaviors— toward conformity/conformity congruity in the case of Hirschi's version of control theory and toward deviance/deviance congruity in the case of most other delinquency theories. The data reported here indicate too much difference between friend and respondent behaviors to serve as evidence of peer pressures toward uniformity.

Respondent/friend differences, furthermore, suggest that the relationships between serious delinquents and their best friends are based on mutual interests that are broader than shared drug/crime behaviors. When friends' behaviors are extremely closely matched, it is *possible* that the relationship is based primarily (perhaps solely) on a specific shared interest in that behavior. Marked differences between friends' behaviors, on the other hand, suggest the kind of tolerance of differences and broad-spectrum shared interests typical of real friends. This finding supports those theoretical perspectives that describe relationships between delinquents as close, meaningful friendships and contradicts Hirschi's allegation that such relationships are a myth.

## Relative Peer Influence

Strain and subcultural theories argue that delinquency arises from problems in the social-class structure. One expression of such problems is the impact of the overall neighborhood environment. This in turn implies a different degree of influence of best friends for socioeconomically advantaged white youths compared to socioeconomically disadvantaged black youths. The direction of the difference might be hypothesized to be positive or negative. On one hand, if growing up in a bad neighborhood is a primary cause of delinquency, then perhaps the impact of peer pressure from *specific* best friends is more important for youths who became seriously delinquent *without* growing up in such a neighborhood. On the other hand, if a bad neighborhood primarily means more potential delinquent peers and crime partners, then the influence of friends might be *most* important for these youths—leaving the explanation of serious delinquency among more affluent youths completely to other causes, such as bad families or personal psychopathology. No matter which way the difference is hypothesized, however, the prediction implicit in strain theory is that correlations between friend and respondent conformity or deviance will differ by socioeconomic status.

To examine this possibility, a comparison was made between the two demographic subgroups with the most clear-cut socioeconomic differences: whites with family disadvantage scores of 0–4 and blacks with family disadvantage scores of 5–8.[6] This omits four groups: the most

---

[6]Construction of the family disadvantage scores was discussed in Chapter 7.

disadvantaged whites, the least disadvantaged blacks, all Hispanics, and youths living on their own (the last because the "family disadvantage" data apply only to youths still living at home). With controls for age group (12–13 versus 14–17), gender, and this race/disadvantage category, respondent/friend deviance correlations were computed. The results were examined to see whether there was a pattern of differences between the two socioeconomic groups. As shown in Table 8.2, the results do not suggest a strong, consistent pattern, but they don't appear completely random either.

To the extent that different patterns are exhibited, they are only mildly different and they vary by type of behavior. Of the socially approved activities (school and job), there are five comparisons; in two cases the correlations are the same, and in the other three there is a stronger correlation between friend and respondent behaviors among better-off whites than among poorer blacks. This implies that peers are more important as an influence toward conformity for whites from economically comfortable families than for blacks from poor families. This makes sense given

**TABLE 8.2**
**"Relative Peer Pressure" Comparisons: Correlations between Deviance of Respondents and Best Friends by Race plus Socioeconomic Disadvantage\***

| Subsample (N) | SCH | JOB | COC | HER | DLR | GUN |
|---|---|---|---|---|---|---|
| **Male age 12–13** | | | | | | |
| Black + high (48) | † | — | .58 | .37 | .43 | .67 |
| White + low (60) | † | .35 | .35 | — | .58 | .64 |
| **Male age 14–17** | | | | | | |
| Black + high (102) | .58 | .30 | .36 | .34 | — | .46 |
| White + low (96) | .79 | .30 | .33 | .30 | .29 | .73 |
| **Female age 14–17** | | | | | | |
| Black + high (23) | — | — | .50 | .58 | — | — |
| White + low (19) | — | .61 | — | .57 | .40 | .43 |

\* SCH: Friends in SCHool/student = 1, dropout = 0
JOB: Friends with JOB/job now = 2, in past = 1, never = 0
COC: Friends using COCaine/days used it in last 90
HER: Friends using HERoin/days used it in last 90
DLR: Friends who are DeaLeRs/number of drug-business offenses
GUN: Friends who have a GUN/1 = carried handgun, 0 = no
Spearman Correlation Coefficients are those significant at $p < .05$ between the two variables noted above—in each case, "number of three best friends who . . ." and an indicator of the respondent's own current behavior.

†Not applicable, because all 12–13-year-olds are still in school.

that affluence tends to make school success and job opportunities easier and thus more realistic or meaningful as motivators for conventional behavior. This finding also suggests that Hirschi's insistence that peers exert pressure toward conformity may be most applicable to youths from economically comfortable backgrounds.

For the six comparisons on drug use (cocaine and heroin, in the three subsamples), three have correlations that match and three show a stronger correlation between friend and respondent behaviors among more disadvantaged blacks than among better-off whites. Apparently, peers are a greater influence toward the use of especially dangerous drugs for black underclass youths than for affluent whites. This finding recalls the discussion in Chapter 1 of the severity of the crack/crime crisis for inner-city communities. Youths in affluent neighborhoods are also able to get cocaine and heroin, but not from nearly as many possible sources, and they may have to make special efforts. Thus, cocaine and heroin use by affluent youths may often be motivated by highly personal, individual needs or wishes. In neighborhoods with high drug/crime rates, on the other hand, little effort is required to obtain these drugs, and models for their use are much more common.

For the six comparisons on crime (dealing, having a gun), one shows nearly identical correlations but the other five have correlations that are at least .10 stronger among better-off whites than among poorer blacks. Here, the hypothesis suggested is that youths who get involved in serious delinquency without growing up in neighborhoods with high drug/crime rates have a greater need for contacts with specific friends who can help them get started (in drug sales, for example) or who will influence them toward particular illegal behaviors (such as carrying a handgun).

Altogether, these results suggest some support for strain and subcultural emphases on the importance of social class. Respondent and friend school/job and drug/crime behaviors have somewhat different degrees of congruity for disadvantaged black versus more comfortable white youths. The differences are not large, but they are consistent within each behavior type. On the other hand, of the 17 comparisons made, seven show *no* difference. In combination with the relatively small size of the differences that do appear, this implies that, once serious delinquency has begun, social-class differences in peer relationships are of only secondary significance in understanding the processes supporting this behavior.

# ARGUMENTS
# BETWEEN FRIENDS

As noted in the Chapter 7 discussion of arguments within families, the meaning of "arguing" is not always clear. It may indicate lack of agreement about basic values or lack of real commitment to a relationship. On the other hand, *not* arguing may mean broken communication lines or lack of interest in what the other person thinks. In friendships, some disagreements are to be expected. The question is one of whether arguing is related to the level of drug/crime involvement among serious delinquents. If not, then arguing would appear to reflect simply "normal" disagreements among friends; if there is a relationship, drug/crime behaviors may be a source of instability for their friendships.

The questions about arguments with friends were the same as those about arguing with family. The topics were money, school, drugs, respondent's crime, and friends' crime; present-tense phrasing was used ("How often *do* you argue with . . ."); and the answer categories were Often, Sometimes, and Never. However, although arguments with friends were not uncommon, arguing *often* with friends was so rare that these responses were collapsed to form a dichotomy: never versus at least sometimes, coded 0 versus 1. A total score for arguments with friends was then computed by simply adding these codes, for a total of 0 to 5. Both the percentages and the correlations reported below are based on the 607 respondents who answered all questions.

The total score indicates that 36% of the sample reported that they *never* argued with friends about *any* of the five topics (compared to 4% giving such reports about arguments with families, out of 531 respondents living at home). Similarly, very high scores were rare for arguments with friends (under 8% scored 4–5 out of the possible 5), although they were typical for arguments with family (52% scored 8–10 out of the possible 10). That 82% of the 607 respondents had scores of 2 or less indicates few propensities toward arguments with friends among serious delinquents.

Of the five topics, money is the one most frequently argued about with friends. Almost half the sample (49.8%) argued about money, which is twice the percentages arguing about drugs, respondent's crime, or friends' crime (all 23–24%) and ten times more than the reports of arguing about school (4.8%). That almost no one argues with friends about school doubtless reflects the lack of interest in school. A similar finding is reported by Horowitz (1983), who found in her research on gangs that school was rarely a topic of conversation unless a fight occurred or someone graduated.

Arguments with friends have very little relationship to demographic categories. Among blacks and whites age 14–17, the total argument score is not significantly related to either age or gender, and being black is only weakly associated with more total arguments with friends (rho = .20).[7]

Correlations between arguments with friends and drug/crime variables also indicate little if any relationship between (1) arguments over

---

[7]Correlations were also checked between sociodemographic variables and the five specific argument topics. For age and gender, none are even .13 in size. For being black, the four other than school are positive and significant but very weak (rho = .10 to .17).

drugs and the respondent's current overall drug use, (2) arguments over crime (either the respondent's or friends') and the respondent's current overall crime, (3) total arguments with friends (range 0 to 5) and the overall score for either drug or crime involvement, or (4) arguments over drugs or crime and the number of one's three best friends engaged in specific drug use or criminal behaviors. Taken together with the low prevalence of drug/crime arguments in this sample, these results suggest that arguments that do occur between serious delinquents and their friends are not about the appropriateness of drug/crime activities.

Arguing about *money*, however, is significantly related to the drug/crime involvement of both the respondents and their friends. Specifically, correlations between arguments with friends about money (0 = never, 1 = at least sometimes) and the relevant summary scores were as follows:

- .26, overall deviance of three best friends
- .36, total crime partnerships
- .35, respondent's current drug use
- .29, respondent's current crime involvement

The figures are very similar for males (age 12–13 or 14–17) and for females. These results suggest that the drug/crime involvement of serious delinquents *and* their friends causes arguments between them about money. This presumably has some negative consequences for friendships, and it is in fact significantly ($p < .02$)—although only weakly (rho = –.08)—related to knowing fewer best friends five years ago.

# FRIENDS IN TREATMENT
# AND FRIENDS
# INCARCERATED

Immediately following questions about their own drug treatment and incarceration experiences, respondents were asked whether any of their friends had done time in correctional facilities or drug treatment programs (and, if so, how many friends). Of the 598 youths answering both questions, 87.8% reported having at least one friend who had been either incarcerated or in treatment. The much greater prominence of incarceration is indicated by the fact that the median answer (53.5% of the 611 respondents) for treatment is "No—no friends," whereas for incarceration only 17.3% said "No—none" and the median answer was "Yes—two friends."

Number of friends who had been in treatment is related to having more serious levels of drug involvement (rho = .20). However, it is *more* strongly related to being older (rho = .32), and it *most* directly correlates with respondents' having been in treatment themselves (rho = .49). It might be noted that only 14% of this extremely drug-involved sample had been in treatment. Number of friends in treatment is unrelated to gender and, among females and 12–13-year-old boys, unrelated to race. White males age 14–17—the gender/age/ethnicity group most likely to have been in treatment—were slightly more likely than their black and Hispanic counterparts to have friends with drug treatment experience (rho = .23).

Number of friends who had been incarcerated, similarly, has little if any relation to gender (rho < .09) but is strongly related to having been incarcerated and to number of lifetime arrests (rho = .56 for each). The age/friends-incarcerated relationship (rho = .17) is weaker than the age/friends-in-treatment relationship (rho = .32), since 71% of even the 12–13-year-old boys had at least one friend who had been incarcerated (whereas only 24% had a friend who had been in drug treatment). And there is a much stronger relationship between number of friends incarcerated and current crime involvement (rho = .49) than between number of friends in treatment and current drug involvement (rho = .20).[8]

# POSTSCRIPT

The most likely answer to the question of why delinquents end up spending time with other delinquents is that two different processes are both common: some delinquents seek out delinquent friends, whereas others only start delinquent behavior in the first place by learning it from their friends. But this answer still leaves questions—many of them raised most vigorously in Hirschi's version of control theory—about the quality of the relationships involved and the effect of friends on a delinquent's involvement in drug use and crime. These questions are of particular interest given that most prior research on these issues has focused on the overall youth population, whereas serious delinquents may exhibit very different patterns.

---

[8]White, as opposed to black or Hispanic, respondents had fewer friends who had been incarcerated (rho = .28). Reports of two or more friends having been incarcerated were given by 70% of the 358 black and Hispanic respondents but only 44% of the 253 white respondents; figures were very similar with controls for age and gender. The relationship between incarcerated friends and respondent's crime involvement was therefore examined with ethnicity controlled. Results indicate a somewhat weaker relationship for black males (rho = .29) than for the other gender/ethnic groups—specifically, white males (.48), Hispanic males (.55), black females (.42), and white females (.56). This difference suggests that specific friendships—in this case, friends who have been so crime involved as to have been incarcerated—may be more important to inspiring or supporting the criminal behavior of these other groups, whereas for seriously delinquent black males, such friends are less important than other factors—most apparently, being a black male living in an environment of high drug/crime rates.

The findings about the nature of the relationships between serious delinquents and their friends generally contradict Hirschi's theory. These friendships appear to be real, not just short-term, conflict-ridden alliances of convenience centered on shared drug/crime behaviors. Most of the youths interviewed knew at least two of their three best friends for at least five years; many had best friends who were markedly more—or markedly less—drug/crime involved than they were; and frequent arguments concerning drug/crime behaviors were rare. However, arguments with friends about money were fairly common, and they were most typical of respondents with the greatest drug/crime involvement and the most partnership arrangements. This suggests that serious delinquency can cause arguments and thus may lead to the future collapse of friendships. The findings about differences between respondent and friend behaviors also contradict the implications of some delinquent subculture theories, in that these differences are too numerous to permit descriptions of respondent/ friend similarities as evidence of peer *pressures* toward identical drug/ crime behaviors.

Perhaps unexpectedly in a study of serious delinquency, the findings do support Hirschi's emphasis on friends as an influence toward socially approved behavior. Even youths who were so seriously delinquent as to be eligible for this sample were likely to have a good friend involved in such socially approved behaviors as school enrollment or employment. That such friends were most common among the least drug- and crime-involved respondents implies that they may be—as Hirschi argues—an influence toward conventional behavior. More best friends in school or working also meant fewer arguments about money and thus more obvious potential for stable, conflict-free relationships.

The correlations of respondent and best friend socially approved behaviors were at least as strong as those between respondent and best friend drug/crime behaviors. This appears to support findings from the National Youth Survey that the seriousness of delinquency is influenced by attachments to both delinquent peers and conventional people. Specifically, they found that delinquency is most likely to increase over time among youths who are attached only to delinquent peers, less likely for those attached to both delinquent peers and conventional people, still less likely for those unattached to either, and least likely among those attached to only conventional peers and adults (Elliott, Huizinga, and Ageton 1985, pp. 143–145).

However, the correlations between respondent socially approved behaviors and best friend socially approved behaviors tended to be stronger among whites from families with little socioeconomic disadvantage than among blacks from more socioeconomically disadvantaged families. This implies that Hirschi's emphasis on friends as an influence toward conformity might be most applicable to middle-class whites and least appropriate to understanding delinquency in high-crime-rate inner-city neighborhoods. Further, friend/respondent behavior correlations for drug use and crime also vary by socioeconomic status. This finding provides some support for the emphasis of strain theory on the importance of social-class structure as a factor in delinquent behavior, although the size of the differences suggests that the relative influence of social-class differences is not strong.

The best indicator of relationships with delinquent peers is the summary score for the deviance of the respondent's three best friends. This score is central in that it includes (1) both drug use and crime, (2) both drug/crime and socially approved behaviors, and (3)—since it is phrased in terms of "your three best friends"—information about persons in meaningful relationships with the respondent. However, as shown in Table 8.3, this measure is clearly related to other possible indicators of delinquent friends—particularly to involvement in crime with partners rather than alone and to number of friends who have ever been incarcerated. The relationship of all three variables to crime involvement is very similar: the most crime-involved respondents had the most deviant friends, the most friends with incarceration records, and the most crime-partnership arrangements (all rhos in the .49 to .60 range).

Gender was not related to any of the three delinquent/peer variables shown in Table 8.3 at even a rho = .10 level, and age and race were only weakly related—slightly more partners for younger respondents and somewhat more incarcerated friends for black and older youths. Consequently, when the correlations in Table 8.3 were run again with demographic controls, the results were strongly similar for males and females, for blacks and whites, and across the age range of 12 to 17. This is of

**TABLE 8.3**
**Delinquent Friends Summary Correlations**
**for the Total Sample ($N$ = 611)\***

|  | Partners Summary Score | Deviance of 3 Best Friends | Number of Friends Ever Incarcerated |
|---|---|---|---|
| Partners summary score | 1.00 | .48 | .45 |
| Deviance of 3 best friends | .48 | 1.00 | .46 |
| Number of friends ever incarcerated | .45 | .46 | 1.00 |
| **Current overall:** | | | |
| Drug use (last 90 days) | .42 | .52 | .42 |
| Crime (last 12 months) | .60 | .51 | .49 |

\*Spearman Correlation Coefficients significant at $p < .05$.

particular interest because the classic strain and subcultural theories about delinquency were confined to males, and the current youth crime crisis is most often described as a problem of the black underclass. Some of the specific findings can be taken as indirect suggestions that there are gender and race differences in the influence of peers on the *origin* of serious delinquency. However, by the time a youth is involved in a serious level of delinquency, relationships with peers are similar regardless of that youth's background. Chances are very high that he or she will have close friends who are drug/crime involved, who have a record of contact with the criminal justice system, and who serve as partners in a variety of different crimes. Further, the stronger the youth's own drug/crime involvement, the more of these contacts with delinquent peers he or she will have.

# CHAPTER 9

# SUMMARY AND IMPLICATIONS

This book has reported on findings from a street study of serious drug use and crime among adolescents. For this final chapter, two tasks remain. First, since so many specific findings and arguments are discussed in the preceding chapters, a summary and highlights section seems warranted. Second, the implications of this study for policy and research should be discussed, including the AIDS/drugs connection as it relates to serious delinquents and prevention and treatment possibilities for dealing with serious adolescent drug use and crime.

## SUMMARY AND HIGHLIGHTS

The primary focus of this research was the drug use and "serious delinquency" of a sample of Miami youths who were active offenders on the street at the time of interview. *Serious delinquency* was defined as having committed, during the 12 months prior to interview, at least ten FBI "Index" offenses or 100 lesser profit-making crimes. A major rationale for the project was that, for the last 20 years, delinquency research had relied almost exclusively on only two kinds of samples: either representative samples of adolescents in general, or youth enmeshed in the juvenile justice system. Although these investigations have provided important data, neither type of sampling procedure is suitable for describing extremely hard-core adolescent offenders still active on the street. The Miami study was specifically designed to access a segment of that population.

Research subjects were located through multiple starting-point "snowball sampling" techniques in 20 Miami-Dade neighborhoods of varying sociodemographic composition and geographic location. This variation permitted selection of respondents so as to meet preplanned subsample targets for gender, age, and race/ethnicity. Consequently, although the interview neighborhoods included those with Miami-Dade's highest rates of drug use and crime, many were more ordinary working- and middle-class communities.

Between December 1985 and November 1987, a total of 611 youths meeting the selection criteria were contacted and interviewed. Of these, 100 (16.4%) were females, as planned. In addition, 41.4% were whites, 42.2% were blacks, and 16.4% were Hispanics. Although blacks were over-represented in the sample and Hispanics were considerably underrep-resented, this race/ethnic distribution is not unlike that found in other studies of the Miami drug scene (see Inciardi 1986, p. 123; Inciardi and Pottieger 1986; McBride and McCoy 1981; McCoy et al. 1979). These 611 youths had a mean age of 15 years, with nearly equal numbers age 16–17 (42%) and 14–15 (38%), plus 120 boys age 12–13. Although more than two-thirds were still attending school at the time of interview, almost all (88%) had been either suspended or expelled from school at least once, with such disciplinary actions often resulting from drug use or drug sales on school premises. Some 87% were living with a family, rather than with friends or alone.

In addition to these 611 youths systematically interviewed from 1985 through 1987, field contacts continued through late 1991. Rather than planned follow-up interviews, these subsequent contacts were with some 50 adolescent "key informants" located by the senior author. Some of these informants had been interviewed earlier as part of the study, but most were not. The purpose of these contacts was to attain further insights into the patterns and trends of drug use and crime that were suggested by the initial survey data.

## Drugs and Crime

*All* of the youths interviewed had extensive histories of multiple drug use with identifiable patterns of onset and progression. As summarized in Table 9.1, they began drug use at a mean age of 7.6 years with alcohol experimentation, followed by their first alcohol intoxication just over a year later. Experimentation with marijuana began at a mean age of 10.4, fol-lowed within a year by the regular use—i.e., use on three or more days a week—of both marijuana (for 100% of the sample) and alcohol (just over half of the sample). Experimentation with cocaine, speed, heroin, and pre-scription depressants occurred, on average, during the twelfth year, with 93.3% moving on to the regular use of cocaine at a mean age of 13. First use of crack cocaine occurred at a mean age of 13.6, and by age 14 some 85.6% of the sample were regular users of the drug.

The criminal careers of these 611 youths emerged more or less in tandem with their drug-using careers. As shown in Table 9.2, their first crimes occurred at a mean age of 11 years. Over 96% had engaged in drug sales and theft, with mean initiation ages for both offenses of less than 12.

**TABLE 9.1**
**Drug Use Histories (Total Sample, *N* = 611)**

|  | Mean Age at Onset | Percentage Involved |
|---|:---:|:---:|
| **Alcohol** | | |
| First use | 7.6 | 100.0% |
| First high | 8.8 | 99.5 |
| First regular use | 11.0 | 53.7 |
| **Marijuana** | | |
| First use | 10.4 | 100.0% |
| First regular use | 11.4 | 100.0 |
| **Cocaine** | | |
| First use | 12.3 | 99.2% |
| First regular use | 13.0 | 93.3 |
| **Heroin** | | |
| First use | 12.8 | 56.5% |
| First regular use | 12.7 | 16.2 |
| **Prescription depressants** | | |
| First use | 12.6 | 75.8% |
| First regular use | 13.2 | 44.7 |
| **Speed** | | |
| First use | 12.7 | 59.9% |
| First regular use | 13.6 | 14.9 |
| **Crack** | | |
| First use | 13.6 | 95.7% |
| First regular use | 14.0 | 85.6 |

Almost two-thirds had participated in a robbery, and 89% of the females had engaged in prostitution; these offenses first occurred at a mean age of less than 13. In addition, 90% had histories of arrest and almost half had been incarcerated, but only 13.4% had ever been in any substance abuse treatment.

Polydrug use—most often marijuana plus cocaine plus a depressant—characterized the current drug use of these youths (i.e., use during the 90 days prior to interview). Marijuana was used daily (*every* day) by 82% of the sample; 64% used some form of cocaine daily; and 91% used at

**TABLE 9.2**
**Crime and Criminal Justice Histories (Total Sample, *N* = 611)**

|  | Mean Age at First Occurrence | Percentage Involved |
|---|---|---|
| Crime (any type) | 11.0 | 100.0% |
| Drug sale |  |  |
|    Marijuana | 11.5 | 94.9% |
|    Other drug | 12.5 | 89.7 |
| Theft | 11.7 | 98.5% |
| Prostitution | 12.6 | 19.5 |
| Robbery | 12.9 | 64.5 |
| Arrest | 12.1 | 90.0% |
| Arrest resulting in adjudication | 12.8 | 74.1 |
| Incarceration | 13.5 | 45.5% |
| Drug/alcohol treatment | 14.2 | 13.4 |

least one coca product (powder cocaine, crack cocaine, or coca paste) three or more times a week. By contrast, even weekly use was rare for speed (5%) and hallucinogens and/or inhalants (2%). Only 7% used heroin at least twice a week, although *some* heroin use was fairly common (42%), as was regular alcohol use (47%) and at-least-weekly use of prescription depressants (46%). Of the seven drug types studied, respondents used an average of 4.6 different types in the prior 90 days, and they used an average of 2.6 types *regularly* during this time.

Table 9.3 permits a number of insights into the criminal activity of these youths. The criminal involvement tallied here is substantial. These 611 youths reported committing some 429,136 crimes during the 12 months prior to interview—an average of 702 offenses per subject. Although this figure might seem astronomical, analysis by offense type indicates that the majority of these crimes are clustered into what are generally considered "less serious" offenses. Most notably, some 60% are "drug business" offenses—primarily retail sales of small quantities but also manufacture (typically the small-scale production of crack), transportation (usually helping to move drug consignments within the city), and lesser involvements such as "steering" customers to dealers or being a lookout for a crack house. In addition, 10% of the total offenses involve prostitution or pimping, 12% are incidents of shoplifting, and 11% are stolen goods offenses (selling, trading, or buying to resell). Thus, 92.8% of the 429,136 offenses entail only four crime types: drug business, vice, shoplifting, and dealing in stolen property.

**TABLE 9.3**
**Crime in the 12 Months Prior to Interview (Total Sample, $N = 611$)**

|  | Total Number Committed | Percentage of Total Offenses | Percentage of Sample Involved |
|---|---|---|---|
| **Major felonies** | 18,477 | 4.3% | 78.1% |
| Robberies | 6,269 | 1.5% | 59.1% |
| Assaults | 721 | 0.2 | 14.9 |
| Burglaries | 10,070 | 2.3 | 60.2 |
| Motor vehicle thefts | 1,417 | 0.3 | 42.1 |
| **Property crimes** | 109,538 | 25.5% | 98.2% |
| Shoplifting | 49,582 | 11.6% | 93.3% |
| Theft from vehicle | 2,720 | 0.6 | 58.3 |
| Pickpocketing | 552 | 0.1 | 9.7 |
| Prostitute's thefts | 3,005 | 0.7 | 13.6 |
| Other larcenies | 949 | 0.2 | 3.8 |
| Confidence games | 925 | 0.2% | 24.7% |
| Bad paper | 3,635 | 0.8 | 30.3 |
| Stolen goods offenses | 47,572 | 11.1 | 80.5 |
| Property destruction | 383 | <0.1 | 28.8 |
| Other | 215 | <0.1 | 0.7 |
| **Vice offenses** | 43,962 | 10.2% | 26.8% |
| Prostitution | 38,044 | 8.9% | 17.5% |
| Procuring | 5,918 | 1.3 | 20.1 |
| **Drug business** | 257,159 | 59.9% | 96.1% |
| **Grand total** | 429,136 | 100.0% | 100.0% |

   This does not mean, however, that these youths were not serious offenders. The sheer volume of their criminal acts suggests that they were. In addition, they were responsible for some 18,477 major felonies. Among these were 10,070 burglaries and 6,269 robberies. The majority of the robberies were purse snatches, but a significant number were armed robberies in homes, at shops, and on the street. In fact, 88% of the sample reported carrying weapons most or all of the time, and 48% specifically reported having a handgun with them while committing the crimes discussed above.
   The involvement of these adolescents in drug use and crime is noteworthy in at least three different respects. First, these youths represent a major problem for law enforcement, school authorities, and social services now—and show every probability of continuing to do so as they age

into legal adulthood. Second, the precocity and severity of this involvement far exceed those reported for previous samples of "serious delinquents," even those located by such well-designed studies as the National Youth Survey and the Midwest metropolitan-area study (e.g., Cernkovich, Giordano, and Pugh 1985). This graphically demonstrates both the inability of random-sample surveys to access truly serious delinquents and the need to study such offenders with street-research techniques. Third and finally, the initiation ages for these youths are markedly younger than those reported by adult heroin users in the same geographic area ten years earlier, and the significance of drug-business offenses in the teenage phase of their careers is also much greater (see Inciardi 1979). This suggests that a major change has occurred in street drug/crime patterns, apparently attributable to the rise of crack cocaine as the preeminent street drug of preference.

## The Crack Business

Preliminary analyses of the first interviews completed showed unexpectedly high rates for use of crack, at that time a very recently popular drug. Of the 200 youths interviewed by July 1986, 93% had used crack. This finding motivated the design of a supplementary crack-data instrument that was used during the final 254 interviews, from October 1986 through November 1987. Differences between this subsample and the total 611 cases already described were minimal, because they were recruited in the same manner and were drawn from the same locales. However, the additional data collected provided the opportunity to examine the role of crack in more detail, including not only crack use and acquisition but also the involvement of these adolescents in crack distribution.

Only 50 of the 254 youths in the subsample (19.7%) had no participation in marketing crack. Twenty youths (7.9%) had "minor" involvement, in that they sold the drug only to their friends, worked for dealers as lookouts and spotters, or steered customers to one of Miami-Dade's many crack houses. Most (138 or 54.3%) were crack "dealers," involved directly in retail sales of crack. Finally, 46 subjects (18.1%) were designated as "dealer+," since they not only sold the drug but also manufactured, smuggled, or wholesaled it.

This four-category indicator for crack-business involvement was clearly related to use of not only crack but also other drugs. The greater a youth's participation in the crack business, the more likely was the "daily" or at least "regular" use of marijuana, alcohol, and prescription depressants. Especially pronounced differences were apparent with crack use, with the percentage using the drug *daily* ranging from 2% of those with no crack-business involvement to 87% of those in the dealer+ group. Further, even though almost all dealers often received crack as partial payment for their dealing, they nonetheless spent a median of over $2,000 to purchase crack in the prior 90 days.

Degree of crack-market participation was also related to earlier and greater general crime involvement, *including violent crime*. The more involved a youth was in crack distribution, the earlier he or she first committed a crime and was first arrested, convicted, and incarcerated, and the more likely his or her current involvement in a range of crimes against persons and property. This specifically includes violence—robberies and assaults. More crack-market participation was associated with both greater likelihood of committing violent crime and a larger number of violent crimes per offender.

This analysis suggests that crack use and consequent crack-market participation have criminogenic effects not previously observed among adolescent drug users. Crack is cocaine that is (1) so cheap that teenagers can *start* using it with the money from their allowances, (2) so widely available that, in cities, 12-year-olds have no problem finding it, and (3) so powerful and short acting a euphoric drug that it is both rapidly addicting and unlimited in its potential financial requirements. As a result, adolescents can find themselves entangled in the kind of classic addictive drug cycle originally described only for adult heroin users: dealing finances use, use encourages more use, and more use requires more profit-making crimes of all sorts to support an ever-growing addictive use pattern. Until the 1980s this cycle was simply not seen among adolescents, for two reasons. First, they did not commonly use addictive drugs with potentially high financial obligations (i.e., heroin and cocaine). Second, adults severely limited the involvement of adolescents in drug-marketing networks. The advent of crack changed both of these factors, with highly criminogenic consequences for street kids.

## Implications for Delinquency Theory

The primary purpose of this study was *description* of drug use and crime among serious delinquents still active on the street. Delinquency theory was used to supply concepts and implicit hypotheses for this effort, but theory testing—let alone construction of an integrated model—is beyond the scope of this book. Because this kind of sample has not been studied in many years, the focus has been on very basic descriptions—frequencies and first-order relationships—of very basic variables. Nonetheless, the findings from this study necessarily have some implications for delinquency theory.

To begin with, this study confirms some common assertions from a variety of theoretical orientations. One is strain theory's insistence on the negative association between social class and serious delinquency: the sample actually located when interviewers went to the streets of Miami to find serious delinquents turned out to be almost entirely (over 95%) lower- and working-class in background. A second confirmation is the primacy of peers as an influence toward youth crime, compared to the effect of family and school social controls working against it. Expressed in terms of correlations, drug/crime levels were related to peer variables at about a rho = .50 level, compared to the .20 to .35 range for family and school variables. Third, however, this study found that family and school ties had an obvious dampening effect on youth crime, even in this sample of *serious* delinquents. Youths living on their own, and school dropouts, were significantly more drug/crime involved than their age peers still living at home or still enrolled in school. A fourth area of confirmation is the concept of delinquency as a progressive involvement. Comparisons of initiation ages showed clear patterns of progression, going from minor delinquency such as truancy to specifically criminal offenses and from use of alcohol and marijuana to entanglement with more addictive and expensive substances. Fifth and finally, as implied by the variety of theoretical orientations included in this listing, this study affirms the need for an integrated perspective on delinquency—one that takes into account social class *and* deviant peers *and* family/school constraints *and* the logic of progressive career development.

On the other hand, findings from this study also imply some major limitations on traditional delinquency theory as applied to *serious* delinquency. The most obvious of these problems is the inadequate attention given to the role of drug use as a causal factor in the development of adolescent criminal involvement. The only consideration given to drug use in traditional delinquency theories is inclusion as just another type of delinquent behavior. This study suggests, in contrast, that, at least for serious delinquents and at least since the mid-1980s, drug use is much more than this. In this sample, drug sales were a very common first criminal offense, which is not surprising since more than casual illicit drug use *requires* some contact with the drug market. Thus, use of illicit drugs and other illegal behaviors not only first appear at more or less the same time in the histories of these serious delinquents, but regular drug use tends to *precede* regular profit-making crime. Further, the criminogenic consequences of crack-market participation, as discussed above, add still further pressure toward commitment to a drugs/crime lifestyle.

A second limitation of traditional delinquency theory suggested by this study has to do with the sociodemographic characteristics of serious delinquents. The findings from this study show surprisingly little variation by gender, except for the prominence of prostitution in female crime patterns. This finding stands in sharp contrast to decades of delinquency theory and research suggesting that serious delinquency is a male phenomenon. Similarly, the findings reported here show minimal variation by race/ethnicity, contradicting the implications of prior theory and research that black males are likely to be the *most* serious of serious delinquents.

If sociodemographic background does make a difference among serious delinquents, it is most likely to be at the entry point. That is, gender and social class tend to present sociocultural situations—rules, expectations, social enforcement efforts—that result in different entry routes into serious delinquency for males versus females and for youths from poor versus better-off families. Several findings in the preceding chapters suggest, for example, that family and school social control factors may be more important among females and among males from more comfortable (even if working-class) socioeconomic backgrounds, whereas neighborhood-level ecological factors are more important for males and for children brought up in areas with high rates of poverty, street crime, and availability of illegal drugs. Once youths from these varied backgrounds are enmeshed in street life, however, differences in current drug/crime behavior become minimal. This suggests that the single most important factor keeping them in street life is street life itself—drug use, fast money, peers with like interests, and the excitement of crime and other risks. Better understanding of this situation requires both theoretical and research attention to a variety of serious delinquents, not just the ones who end up in the justice system and not just those arrested for assault.

Third, a major limitation of the social control perspective in particular suggested by this study is its failure to consider that control efforts by schools and families can backfire. The serious delinquents interviewed for this study who were still living at home usually reported that their families argued with them about their drug use, their crime, and their friends' crime. Similarly, most of these youths (88%) had been expelled or suspended by their schools, disciplinary actions typically motivated by an effort to control drug use or drug sales on school premises. Both kinds of pressure, however, appear likely to result in youths' avoiding the arguments not by getting back in line—they are too street involved for that—but by getting out of the situation. And, as previously noted, youths who leave home or drop out of school have even higher levels of drug use and crime than their age peers still at home or in school.

# The AIDS/Drugs Connection[1]

The risks of illegal drug use have been well documented. In addition to the potential for overdose (Chitwood 1985; Inciardi et al. 1978; Platt 1986, pp. 85–87), the street-drug subcultures and black markets are distinguished by high rates of assault, robbery, and homicide as both users and dealers are the continuous victims of their peers and rivals (Agar 1973; Goldstein 1986; McBride 1981). Perhaps most characteristic is the progressive risk of arrest,

---

ments of this analysis were drawn from Inciardi (1989) and Inciardi et al. (1991).

conviction, and incarceration as the result of both possession and sale of illegal substances on the one hand and participation in income-generating crimes to support a drug habit on the other (Inciardi 1979; Nurco, Kinlock, and Hanlon 1990).

Since the onset of the 1980s there has been the added risk of HIV infection and AIDS among injecting drug users. Although the nature and extent of AIDS-related risk behaviors have been well documented among adult populations of drug users (Galea, Lewis, and Baker 1988; Turner, Miller, and Moses 1989), little has been written about HIV risk behaviors of seriously delinquent youths.

## HIV and AIDS

Human immunodeficiency virus type-1 (HIV-1) is a sexually transmitted and blood-borne microorganism that infects and, in most persons, gradually destroys the body's immune system response. HIV infection can have myriad manifestations, ranging from subclinical abnormalities with no apparent symptoms, to only mildly debilitating indications, to a variety of life-threatening conditions caused by progressive destruction of the immune system, the brain, or both. AIDS (acquired immunodeficiency syndrome) is a severe manifestation of infection with HIV (Kaslow and Francis 1989).

HIV is transmitted when virus particles or infected cells gain direct access to the bloodstream. This can occur during all forms of sexual intercourse that involve the transmission of body fluids, as well as in oral/genital intercourse with an infected partner. There are three other major routes of transmission: (1) intravenous (IV) drug users can be infected from sharing needles and other drug-taking paraphernalia; (2) the virus can be passed to unborn or newborn children by infected mothers; and (3) individuals can be contaminated through transfusions from an infected blood supply (National Academy of Sciences 1986).

Thus, the "high risk" groups for HIV and AIDS include homosexual and bisexual men, intravenous drug users, recipients of blood products, the sexual partners of these three groups, and children born to infected mothers. As of September 30, 1991, there were a total of 195,718 known cases in the United States (Centers for Disease Control 1991). Some 192,406 AIDS cases involved adults and adolescents (age 13 and above); of these, 59% had been infected through male homosexual/bisexual contact, 22% through IV drug use, 7% through IV drug use *and/or* male homosexual/bisexual contact, 6% through heterosexual contact, 3% through the receipt of infected blood products, and the remaining cases from undetermined exposure. Of the 3,312 reported pediatric cases (under age 13), 84% had been infected through a mother with or at risk for HIV infection, 14% through the receipt of infected blood products, and the balance from undetermined exposure.

Although reported cases of AIDS among adolescents are rare (0.4% of total AIDS cases), there is growing evidence that the potential for HIV infection in this age group is increasing. Analyses of blood samples from more than one million teenagers (aged <20 years) applying for military service found HIV seropositivity prevalence rates of 0.34 per 1,000, or approximately 1 out of every 3,000 applicants (Burke et al. 1990). This large database indicated that HIV seropositivity rates were related to age, sex, race/ethnicity, and two characteristics of the subject's home area: prevalence of active AIDS cases and population density. Nonwhite adolescents living in urban settings with a high incidence of active AIDS cases were especially prone to HIV infection. Several urban centers, including Miami, New York, Baltimore, and the District of Columbia, recorded cumulative prevalence rates exceeding 1 per 1,000 (Burke et al. 1990; *Miami Herald*, October 12, 1989, p. 10A). Black youths appear to be at the highest risk for HIV infection, since they account for 35% of all overt adolescent AIDS cases (Hopkins 1987). Moreover, the military-applicants study found that adolescent black females are four times more likely than adolescent white males to be HIV positive.

Further, some 20% of persons with AIDS were in the age 20–29 range at the time of diagnosis (Centers for Disease Control 1991). The often long incubation period between HIV infection and the appearance of AIDS suggests that many young adults with AIDS were infected during adolescence.

Transmission of HIV among adolescents parallels that among adults; primary sources are injecting drug use and related behaviors and unprotected sexual activities with infected and multiple sex partners. National studies report that 70% of teens have had at least one heterosexual experience by age 19 (National Center for Health Statistics 1991; Shafer 1988), 17% of males and 6% of females have had at least one homosexual experience (Remafedi 1987; Shafer 1988), and almost 20% of high school seniors had used illegal drugs—although rarely by injection—during the 30 days prior to being questioned (*Alcoholism and Drug Abuse Week*, February 14, 1990, pp. 1–2; *New York Times*, February 14, 1990, p. A16; *Substance Abuse Report*, March 1, 1990, pp. 1–3).

The introduction of crack cocaine among adolescent drug users, particularly in the inner cities, may be a contributing factor to the transmission of HIV infection. The drug use survey reports cited above indicate that crack use is concentrated among non-college-bound youths and is more prevalent among those high school seniors living in urban areas. The use of crack is often associated with higher levels of sexual activity, most notably through "sex for drugs" exchanges (Forney and Holloway 1990; Inciardi 1989, 1991). It has been reported that 51% of black adolescent crack users who combine crack use with sexual activity have histories of sexually transmitted diseases, as opposed to 32% of those who do not combine these behaviors (Fullilove et al. 1990). In addition, the link between drug use and prostitution is well known (Goldstein 1979; James 1976; Silbert and Pines 1982), and the relationship of IV drug use and multiple sex partners to HIV transmission has been documented among adults (Castro et al. 1988; Selik, Castro, and Pappaioanou 1988), although not as yet among adolescents.

With respect to this population of serious delinquents, the data on prostitution, IV drug use, and sex-for-crack exchanges suggest that a significant proportion of these 611 Miami youths were engaging in behaviors that put them at risk for HIV infection and AIDS. This is especially significant given the extent of AIDS and HIV infection in the Miami/Dade County area. As of September 30, 1991, for example, a total of 5,848 diagnosed AIDS cases had been reported to the Centers for Disease Control (1991). Only three other cities in the United States had a greater number of known cases (New York, Los Angeles, and San Francisco). Furthermore, Miami's rate of newly reported AIDS cases per 100,000 population as of late 1991 was 91.4 (almost a doubling of the previous year's rate), ranking second in the nation (after San Francisco, with 129.1). And, finally, studies in the Miami community have found that, of injecting drug users recruited from the street, as many as 26% of the men and 37% of the women were HIV positive (Chitwood et al. 1992).

## Prostitution

Male as well as female respondents were asked how many acts of prostitution they had committed during the 12 months prior to interview. Of the 511 males, only 20 (4.9%) reported even one such act, and the median for this group was only 6.5 acts (mean = 26). However, this prostitution entailed male homosexual contact, the HIV risk behavior that accounts for the great majority of known AIDS cases. All 20 male prostitutes—or at least the 15 with more than one or two prostitution offenses (range = 5 to 200)— were consequently running a significant risk of HIV infection. Further, eight of those 20 male prostitutes were current intravenous drug users and another six had tried IV drug use in the past.

Not surprisingly, female prostitution was considerably more common: of the 100 seriously delinquent girls interviewed, 87 reported a median of 200 acts of prostitution (mean = 431) in the prior 12 months. This greater range of prostitution involvement among female respondents suggested that more detailed analysis might be useful with this group. Thus, female prostitution was examined as a four-category variable based on major breaks in the prostitution frequency distributions: none (13% of female respondents), 3–75 acts (13%), 100–325 (53%), and 420 or more (21%).

Greater prostitution on this four-category scale was associated with use of alcohol, marijuana, and cocaine at significantly earlier ages (rho = −.27 to −.37) and with significantly greater current usage levels for these drugs plus heroin and prescription depressants (rho = .25 to .45). By the time of interview, the norm for drug use among the frequent prostitutes

(100+ offenses) was regular alcohol, daily marijuana, daily cocaine (most often crack), pills at least once or twice a week, and some use of heroin. Heroin use, furthermore, included intravenous use for 42% of these 74 prostitutes. The female prostitutes thus exhibited the same high degree of association between prostitution and IV drug use seen for the male prostitutes. In fact, only those female adolescents currently engaged in prostitution had ever injected drugs.

Prior studies suggest that the causal linkages between drug use and prostitution are multiple. Most notably: (1) drug use can make prostitution psychologically easier; (2) use of highly deviant drugs (such as cocaine or heroin) can give a woman a street reputation as a prostitute whether she is one or not; (3) prostitution and use of highly deviant drugs tend to be equally rare or prevalent in any given geographic area, so that the girl who grows up seeing heroin and cocaine everywhere will find prostitution to be equally commonplace; and (4) it is often easier, more lucrative, and more reliable for women to finance drug use through prostitution than through drug dealing, which remains a primarily male province and has become increasingly violent in recent years (Goldstein 1979, 1985; Inciardi 1986, pp. 156–169; James 1976; Silbert and Pines 1982).

The multiplicity of these theoretical linkages, reflected in the consistency of the empirical linkages discussed above, suggests that female delinquents engaged in particularly early and heavy drug use are highly likely to become engaged in prostitution. This, in turn, suggests that such drug involvement may itself be an HIV risk behavior (albeit indirect), since it has such a strong relationship to prostitution and thus to multiple sex partners in locales with typically high rates of IV drug use. These risks are compounded for cocaine-using prostitutes by the strong addictiveness of cocaine and the notoriously extreme tendency of cocaine addicts to neglect food, sleep, and other essential requirements for good general health, thus increasing susceptibility to all types of infections, including HIV/AIDS.

## Intravenous (IV) Drug Use

During the 90-day period prior to interview, 23% of the 611 respondents—a primarily cocaine/marijuana/alcohol-involved sample—had used heroin or speed intravenously. Most IV use was only occasional: median number of days used (during the last 90 days) was two for injecting speed (49 youths) and five for IV heroin use (129 youths, of whom 35 also injected speed). Other indicators, however, suggest the potential for a larger problem. Most directly, a full 40% of these 611 adolescents had at some time at least experimented with IV use of heroin (34%) or speed (25%). Thus, over half of those who had ever tried IV use of these drugs (58% of 245) were still engaged in at least occasional IV drug use. A few of this very young group had even progressed to addictive frequency levels: 24 youths (3.9% of the 611 total) used IV heroin every day in the prior 90 days.

An additional indicator of potential IV drug use problems in this sample stems from the fact that most heroin addicts progress to daily IV use only after an initial period of using heroin by other routes of administration—most commonly snorting and then "skin popping" (subcutaneous rather than intravenous injection). Of the 611 adolescents interviewed, 49% had experimented with such use and 31% had engaged in it during the 90 days prior to interview. Altogether, then, 56% of all respondents had at least tried heroin in some form.

In some groups, furthermore, current IV drug use was surprisingly prevalent—notably females (47% of the 49 black females and 29% of the 51 white females, for 38% of the total 100) and black males (36% of the 209 respondents). Among white males, in contrast, current IV drug use was relatively uncommon (6% of 202). Altogether, 69% of the IV users were black, 20% were white, and 12% were Hispanic.

Prostitution was also more common among the IV drug users. All 38 female IV drug users had engaged in prostitution during the prior 12 months, with 89% of them doing so on 100 or more occasions; of the 62 females not involved in IV use, 21% engaged in no prostitution during that time and considerably fewer (65%) engaged in it 100 or more times. Among males, only 3.0% of non-IV users committed any prostitution, compared to 7.6% of the IV users.

## Sex-for-Crack Exchanges

In the supplementary data-collection instrument focusing exclusively on crack cocaine (discussed in Chapter 6), a specific question on "sex for crack" exchanges was included as one in a series of items on how crack was obtained during the 12 months prior to interview. Of the 254 subjects on which these data were collected, some 15% ($N = 38$) were female; of these, a total of 27 had engaged in the trading of sex for crack. These 27 girls ranged in age from 14 to 17, with a mean of 15.6 years. Some 33% were white/non-Hispanic, and the balance were black.

Despite their youthful ages, these 27 adolescents had relatively long careers in substance abuse. Their first drug use was alcohol at a mean age of 6.1 years, with 93% progressing to regular drinking (3 or more times a week) by a mean age of 9 years. Marijuana use began at a mean of 9 (for 100%), followed by cocaine at 11.2 (100%), heroin at 11.4 (74%), prescription depressants at age 12.4 (100%), and crack at age 13.1 (100%). As such, all of these youths were well into their drug-using careers before trying crack, and in all instances the regular use of cocaine had preceded any experimentation with crack.

In terms of "current" drug use (use during the prior 90 days), *all* reported the use of marijuana, cocaine, and crack; 92% used alcohol; 85% used prescription depressants; and 51% used heroin. Importantly, 92% ($N = 25$) were using crack cocaine on a daily basis (*every* day).

Not only had these 27 adolescent females initiated their drug-using careers at an early age, but their criminal activities had also begun while they were very young. For example, involvement in crime typically began at a mean age of 9.9 years with marijuana sales, followed by theft at age 10, prostitution at age 10.6, and robbery at age 11.9. Whereas *all* of these youths had engaged in drug sales, theft, and prostitution, and 78% had committed at least one robbery (typically a purse snatching), less than half of the sample had committed as many as 10 robberies and only 22% had ever participated in an armed robbery. The overwhelming majority of these young women (93%) had contacts with the criminal justice system, also at an extremely young age (a mean age of 10.2 at first arrest). None, however, had ever been in treatment for drug or alcohol abuse.

The total criminal involvement of these respondents during the 12 months prior to interview was considerable. They reported an annual total of 43,732 offenses, which is an average of 1,620 offenses per subject, or 4.4 per day. Prostitution accounted for some 43.6% of the offenses, reflecting an average of 706 tricks per subject, or 1.9 per day.

Since this research was originally designed as a general study of drug use and crime among serious delinquents, more detailed measures of sex-for-crack exchanges were not included. However, these data, combined with subsequent observations and interviews conducted by the senior author in and around crack houses during 1988 through early 1991, suggest a number of interesting considerations about the sex-for-crack phenomenon.

*First*, it was found that both sex-for-crack exchanges *and* prostitution for money to purchase crack were typical within this population and that the frequency of sex-for-crack exchanges varied considerably. Of these 27 girls, for example, 11 had traded sex for crack on fewer than six occasions during the year prior to interview, but they had nevertheless engaged in a total of 6,850 acts of prostitution. By contrast, there were many who traded sex for crack on hundreds of occasions. Or, as one 14-year-old crack addict put it during early 1989:

> There are days when it seems like all I do is put out and do crack. One weekend it seemed like I had my legs spread the whole time. I was in a *get-off* house on Miami Beach, in a back room, and I bet I had 40–50 customers. Sometimes I didn't even have time to clean up between *johns*, not that I cared anyway.

*Second*, a number of subjects had conceptual problems regarding what constituted a "sex for crack" exchange and what constituted "prostitution." Although all of these girls had little difficulty in estimating the relative number of men with whom they had had sex (for money, drugs, food, or gifts) during the 12 months prior to interview, many did not view a sex-for-crack exchange as "prostitution." Moreover, for some the nature and variety of exchanges were such that they found estimations difficult. For example, as one 16-year-old, who remarked that she had serviced no fewer than 5,000 men and boys in the past six years, explained in late 1988:

> Sure, there be times when a man say "Here, girl, you can have this [crack] if you be nice to me for a few minutes." That kind is easy to count. But how 'bout when the man offers you a big amount of stuff to take on all his friends? What is that? One? Two? Three? Ten? Twenty tricks? Then there's times when for a nickel [$5] you unzip a guy's pants an' do him real quick an' then ya run next door and get some crack for it. What do ya call that? And how 'bout when you do a guy or a couple boys for just a taste of their stuff?

*Third*, significant numbers of the sex-for-crack exchanges within this population involved oral sex. Whereas sexual intercourse was the typical pattern for several females, particularly those who engaged in sex/crack trades in dwellings rather than crack houses, for the majority oral sex was the most common practice. In this regard, one 17-year-old offered the following comment:

> Let's face it--most of it has to be quick and dirty, cheap sex. Mostly blow jobs. Let's face it --what do you expect for a few hits on a crack pipe? Romance? Tenderness? Sensuality? Soft lights and music? Sexy undergarments? A good lay? Fuck no, man! All you want to do is get 'em up and get 'em off as quick as you can, and we both know what that is.

Or, similarly, a 16-year-old remarked:

> . . . but ya gotta remember where you are. In the house [crack house] there's usually a few people around and a lotta guys just don't want to be droppin' their pants. But they don't seem to have much qualms about a quick blow job, when people can see them, so long as they can keep their pants up. . . . And then there are others that a blow job is the only thing they really want, maybe because they can't get it at home or somethin' else, or if you're in a car or a doorway or some place like that there's not much more ya can do.

*Fourth*, although many sex-for-crack exchanges appear to involve casual, on-the-spot arrangements, there are crack houses in which sex is provided by "house girls" and sometimes "house boys." In exchange for room and board (typically just a mattress and junk-food snacks), cigarettes, wine, and crack provided by the crack-house owner, house girls and boys provide any manner of sex, in public or private, as often as requested, to crack-house customers. Some of these house boys and girls have been observed to be in their early teens (Inciardi 1991).

*Fifth*, those Miami adolescents who engage in exchanges of sex for crack tend to be more deeply enmeshed in drug-using and criminal careers than those who do not. In the special crack-data subsample, 11 of the 38 females had never traded drugs for sex (although they did admit to some 2,800 acts of prostitution during the 12 months prior to interview). In comparison to the 27 who had reported sex-for-crack trades: fewer had dropped out of school (27% vs. 37%) or been expelled/suspended (19% vs. 100%); they began drug use at a later mean age (alcohol, 11.9 vs. 6.1; marijuana, 12.5 vs. 9; cocaine, 13.8 vs. 11.2; crack, 14 vs. 13.1); fewer had ever used heroin (9% vs. 74%) or were current users of heroin (9% vs. 51%); none were daily users of crack (as opposed to 92% of those who exchanged sex for crack); their first drug sale occurred at a later mean age (13.8 vs. 9.9), as did their first theft (10.8 vs. 10) and first prostitution (13.1 vs. 10.6); and fewer had ever participated in robberies (9% vs. 78%) or had arrest histories (9% vs. 93%). In terms of current criminality, those who engaged in sex for crack participated in almost four times the number of crimes per offender during the year prior to interview. These contrasts suggest that sex-for-crack exchanges are more characteristic of those adolescents with longer histories and more intense current involvement in both drug use and crime.

*Sixth*—and perhaps most importantly from a public health point of view—it appears that the potential risk for infection with HIV within this population is significant. The 27 female adolescents involved in sex-for-crack exchanges had engaged in some 19,055 acts of prostitution during the 12 months prior to interview. Moreover, they had been prostitutes an average of 5 years. If their sexual behaviors are similar to those of other drug users studied in Miami and elsewhere (McCoy et al. 1989; Snyder and Myers 1989), it is unlikely that the use of condoms was common. In fact, a 14-year-old "house girl" commented to the senior author during a crack-house interview in 1990:

```
Condoms, in here? I never see no rubbers, no con-
doms. If a man givin' you crack for brains [oral
sex] an' you say "rubber," he laugh, or he beat
you, you know, slap you around a little, or he
call the rat [crack-house proprietor] who then
slap you around too. . . . When you be givin' him
brains or just sexin' him, he want his dick in my
mouth or pussy, not in no rubber balloon.
```

In addition, ethnographic observations and interviews suggested that many of these girls' sex partners were intravenous cocaine and/or heroin users. And too, more than half of these females were current heroin users. These factors, combined with the observation that many of these youths had blisters and lesions on their lips and/or tongues,[2] place those who exchange sex for crack at multiple risk for HIV infection. Moreover, the volatile combination of multiple sex partners with IV drug use within this population may help explain the higher prevalence rate of HIV infection among inner-city juveniles.

## POLICY IMPLICATIONS

What should be done with juvenile offenders—particularly those who are as profoundly involved in drug use and crime as the hundreds contacted in this Miami street study? Quite clearly, these serious delinquents will not automatically grow out of their law-breaking activities, as most youths who commit "deviant" acts tend to do. These adolescents are already well entrenched in a culture and lifestyle that include a profusion of illicit drug-taking and drug-seeking behaviors. Moreover, they are heavily involved in a range of additional economic, violent, and other predatory crimes less directly associated with their acquisition of drugs. It appears that, for many, there may be no turning back from the criminal way of life. As one of these youths said to the senior author not too long ago during an interview in the attic of a North Miami crack house:

> In many ways you can say that I'm pretty close to
> the end of the line, maybe even *past* the end of
> the line. I'm 16 years old and I'm strung out on a
> couple of different drugs. I've turned at least a
> thousand tricks; I've been raped so many times
> I've lost count--starting off with my father when
> I was 7 and ending off with a priest when I was
> 15, with an assortment of other chickenshits, ass-
> holes, and scumbags in between; I've stolen every-
> thing there is to steal; I've cut up a lot of
> people, a few pretty badly; I've been arrested 19
> times and been fucked over by the system--and I
> mean really fucked over, I mean literally fucked
> by a cop, a correction officer, and fucked again
> by my lawyer; I've done time in three different
> counties. And to add insult to injury I'm probably
> HIV-positive, which means I'm gonna fucking die.
> What are you gonna do with me? Hand me over to
> some social worker? Tell me to clean up my act?
> Put me in a convent? Put me back in jail so I can

---

[2]Blisters or open sores on the lips and tongue are characteristic of many chronic crack smokers—the result of the constant intense heat of the crack pipe.

> be fucked over, or just fucked, by somebody else
> all over again? How about college? Can you send me
> to college? Or you can get me a job, maybe some-
> thing really good like making fries at Burger
> King? Give me a break and just leave me a-fucking-
> lone.

Similarly, a 17-year-old male respondent indicated:

> This *is* the end of the line, and there *is* no turn-
> ing back. Come back in 10 years and I'll be 10
> years older, and probably doing a 10- or 20-year
> stretch in the state penitentiary, or maybe I'll
> fool you and just be dead.

In retrospect, it would not be surprising if the majority of the sampled subjects are as cynical and negative about their lives and futures as these two youths. Most have experienced prolonged involvement in criminal social networks, even though the oldest in the sample was just under age 18 when contacted; almost all began using alcohol and other drugs as children; most started their criminal careers at very early ages and have increased their involvement over time—not only the numbers and types of offenses but their seriousness as well. Moreover, each new age cohort seems to start both drug use and crime earlier and earlier.

The problem is made worse by the fact that these hard-core delinquents have few external supports that might be marshaled to assist them in making some sort of a transition on their own. For example:

1. They have either dropped out of school or attended so infrequently that their educational skills are extremely limited. Few are qualified for anything but menial jobs that pay "chump change," as they themselves put it.
2. Although some have working mothers and fathers, most do not have much of a family support system. It is unlikely that many would be able to find employment through family networks and contacts. Moreover, among the oldest in the sample, many have already moved out of the parental home.

Within such a context, what are the possibilities?

## County-Based Intervention Strategies

In many U.S. urban jurisdictions in which juvenile delinquency and youth crime are viewed as problematic, "serious delinquency" is invariably interpreted as "a juvenile gang problem." Although this is certainly the case in many locales, it is *not* necessarily so in the greater Miami-Dade metropolitan area, where fewer than 5% of the 611 street youths sampled had ever been involved with gangs. Yet, as in many other municipalities, the Miami approach has been gang oriented. For example, from 1987 through 1990, the Metro-Dade Police Department, the Dade County School Board, and other criminal justice agencies and community groups worked together to implement a number of initiatives aimed at reducing the frequency and severity of delinquent activities. The efforts of participating agencies included: (1) a multi-agency police task force that attended special events where gangs were likely to gather, (2) a computer database and "clearinghouse" that provided law enforcement with information on gang members and activities, (3) specialized gang-oriented training for police, (4) facilitation of community-level responses designed to provide youths with alternatives to gang membership, and (5) legislative proposals for dealing with juvenile criminal activity (Stokes and Silbert 1990).

In late 1988 the Dade-Miami Criminal Justice Council found that there were seven prevention/intervention programs in the county, almost half of which were operating without funds of any kind (Stokes and Silbert 1990). In fact, throughout the 1980s much of what was occurring in Dade County regarding the youth crime problem was a series of committees and recommendations, but little else. For example:

- A 1984 community task force on gangs recommended a public information and education campaign, family involvement/intervention strategies, recreational activities, and educational programs.
- A 1985 Dade County Grand Jury Report on Youth Gangs recommended that educational, recreational, and vocational programs be introduced to address the growing gang problem.
- A 1985 issue paper published by Metro-Dade County identified a number of needed gang programs, including training/employment, dropout prevention, counseling, and recreational programs.
- A 1987 report published by the Florida House of Representatives emphasized the need for a comprehensive gang prevention and intervention program in the South Florida area.
- A 1988 Grand Jury Report recommended the development of gang prevention and intervention efforts aimed at predelinquent and delinquent youth.
- A 1988 Survey of Police Departments and Social Service Agencies conducted by the Metro-Dade Department of Justice Assistance revealed widespread agreement over the need for improved planning and coordination and direct services programs aimed at youth gang prevention/intervention (Stokes and Silbert 1990).
- In 1990 the City of Miami established a Youth Task Force (another unfunded program) to establish goals and recommendations for dealing with the juvenile crime problem.

The recommendations of all of these "committees," "task forces," "grand juries," and "reports" were essentially the same: increased employment opportunities and job training for youth; special skills proficiency classes; counseling and treatment to assist youths and their families in acquiring skills that promote healthy lifestyles, drug-free behavior, self-esteem, and social and environmental responsibility; outreach to identify "youths in trouble"; recreational and cultural activities that provide positive alternatives to gang/criminal involvement; and prevention education and leadership involvement.

Not surprisingly, few of these objectives were actually implemented. What happened in Miami is not unusual. Although task-force recommendations are always well intended, the necessary staff and resources to make them operational are usually unavailable. Thus, the question remains: what *are* the alternatives for dealing with hard-core "serious delinquents"? Several options can be addressed, including *diversion/nonintervention*, *"get tough" approaches, Scared Straight programs, shock incarceration, nurturing*, and *compulsory treatment*.

## The Diversion/ Nonintervention Strategy

The policy implication of labeling theory—leave delinquents alone and they will grow out of it—seems inappropriate. This might work for "garden-variety" delinquents, but diversion into day treatment, community service, or restitution programs so that young offenders will avoid being placed in institutions and labeled as "criminals" is insufficient for the hard-core cases. Most are already too far entrenched in a criminal lifestyle. With no educational or job skills, all that is available for these youths is the minimum-wage sector. Such jobs pay barely enough to survive, so that they do not permit acquisition of the skills for additional options. This is a hard road, even for adults who are strongly oriented toward law-abiding citizenship. An adolescent long immersed in street life would simply never maintain the required motivation to live this way. For the same reason, job-training or drug programs alone would never be sufficient.

## The "Get Tough" Strategy

It has long been argued that prolonged jail sentences are the answer. This could be accomplished by processing "serious delinquents" through adult courts (which is permissible under state "waiver of jurisdiction" statutes) or by holding "amenability hearings" in juvenile court and finding youths with long criminal records *nonamenable*. This means that they could be sentenced as adults and held for as long as the law permits. One of the more vocal proponents of this approach over the years has been Ernest van den Haag, professor of jurisprudence and public policy at Fordham University. Van den Haag would have everyone over the age of 13 dealt with by the adult criminal courts. "The first offense is on the house," he argues, since probation is typically the most serious consequence for delinquent acts and is intended to discourage further lawbreaking. But he further states:

> A second conviction, at any rate, demonstrates that the first did not discourage the offender. Punishment for young second offenders should be harsh enough to deter them and their peers from pursuing criminal careers. For second offenses, youth should be a reason for severity rather than a ground for leniency. (Kramer 1988, p. 227)

Although this approach would keep delinquent youths off the streets for a while, it would likely accomplish little else for the serious delinquents studied here. These youths were, on average, only 11 years old at the time of their first crime, and by the time of their second conviction they were at a mean age of 14 years. Thus, the severe sentence van den Haag recommends would likely occur too far into a youth's criminal career to serve as an effective deterrent to further crime. (And this, of course, assumes that severity of punishment does actually serve as a deterrent at all.)

Harsh reformatory and prison sentences would likely do no more than turn "serious delinquents" into "serious adult criminals." If the American system of criminal justice initiates the high costs of jail and penitentiary confinement at age 14, it will be paying for institutional space for these offenders for the rest of their lives (unless they kill one another off before that by AIDS or AK-47s). In this regard, Ira M. Schwartz's study of Florida training schools reported a 60% recidivism rate within *one year* of release (Schwartz 1989, p. 51). In addition, 60% of the youths released from an adult prison were recommitted within four years—a greater percentage than for adult offenders.

## The "Scared Straight" Strategy

In 1976 a Juvenile Awareness Project was established at New Jersey's Rahway State Prison by a group of inmates known as the Lifers Group. The purpose of the project was to enlighten youths about the consequences of involvement in crime and to present the most negative aspects of prison life. It relied extensively—almost exclusively—on scare tactics, starting from the moment the participating youths walked through the prison gates. They were harassed by correction officers who served as guides for a brief tour of the prison, and then they were escorted to the prison auditorium where the members of the Lifers Group verbally assaulted them. Explicit street language was used; prison rapes, assaults, and killings were described in grisly detail. Rapes and assaults were even threatened, and in general the youths were confronted physically, verbally, and psychologically (Finckenauer 1982, 1984, pp. 85–86). A documentary film entitled *Scared Straight* was produced and shown on national television in 1979 and again in 1987. The film won an Academy Award and became a model for similar programs in other states (Kramer 1988, p. 256). Would a Scared Straight program work for the serious delinquents studied in Miami? Probably not. Given how enmeshed they are in the street cultures of drugs and crime, it is unlikely that most of them could be scared by much of anything. Moreover, it is debatable that a taste of prison for one afternoon would be enough to spoil *any* delinquent's appetite for crime, let alone a *serious* delinquent's. In fact, Scared Straight and similar programs have proven to be generally ineffective with all types of youths. The teenagers are impressed with the presentation, but they leave with the attitude "Not me, I can beat it" (Kramer 1988, p. 256).

## The Shock
## Incarceration Strategy

Among the more recent innovations in the correctional field is what some jurisdictions refer to as "shock incarceration" and others call "boot camp." This is a three- to six-month regimen of military drill, physical exercise, drug treatment, hard labor, and academic work in return for having one's sentence shortened considerably. Inmates spend 16-hour days, with two-mile runs, calisthenics, and orders shouted in their faces as daily staples. Like Marine Corps trainees, they wear military fatigues, rise before dawn to march in platoon formation, and adhere to spit-shine discipline. The idea is to "shock" budding felons out of careers in crime by imposing large amounts of rigor and order in what appear to be chaotic and otherwise purposeless lives (Inciardi 1990b, p. 595).

Since 1984, boot-camp correctional programs have been established in almost half the states, and additional jurisdictions are considering them. Yet the reviews are mixed. Some observers argue that the approach teaches discipline and self-esteem, whereas others are not convinced (MacKenzie, Layton, and Souryal 1991). For truly serious delinquents, it seems doubtful that marching and chanting can overcome the behavioral patterns and value orientations that result in criminal careers.

## The Humanitarian/
## Nurturing Strategy

It can be argued that what is needed is some sort of humane program that treats its participants with respect and provides opportunities for change. One of the few such programs put into place became known in Miami as "Gelber's folly" or "the great Miami experiment." This intensive effort was orchestrated by Judge Seymour Gelber of Florida's Eleventh Judicial Circuit and was based on the belief of many social workers that, under ideal conditions and circumstances, every delinquent child can be saved. The Miami experiment tested that concept. As Judge Gelber himself described it:

> Take a handful of recently convicted hard-core delinquents, who all have long rap sheets and don't give a damn about society. Sentence them to the harshest punishment in the juvenile system, namely, putting them on the next bus to the state reformatory. Meanwhile, obtain the best street-wise counselor; have him pull these young toughs off the bus. Tell them that not only are they free, but also that every need of theirs and their families will be attended to in the coming year. Jobs, schooling, counseling, housing, and clothing will be provided through the auspices of a Master Counselor. (Gelber 1988, p. xiii)

Judge Gelber's "master counselor" was one Cornelius Foster, a former liquor store holdup specialist from Miami's Liberty City. Foster was no stranger to the criminal justice process, having done five years' hard time in Florida's Raiford State Prison. And Foster had lots of help, for, as Judge Gelber put it:

> Throw in a college-trained supervisor who follows the book and knows all the bureaucratic ropes to assist Master counselor Foster. Add an idealistic judge who will open doors, guaranteeing everything they are entitled to, and more. (Gelber 1988, p. xiii)

Gelber added that, by mixing these ingredients with recalcitrant, selfish, unyielding, unappreciative clients, the hypothesis for a great social experiment was created. That is, by providing the highest-quality staff, available 24 hours a day and seven days a week, without limitations on time or cost, and utilizing every worthwhile resource in the community—cajoling, directing, and nurturing—the end product should be once-alienated youths who had made remarkable progress toward becoming accepted and contributing members of society.

At the end of a two-year period, the findings suggested that Judge Gelber's Miami experiment had been a failure. Two of the six youths had not gotten into further trouble with the law, three had been arrested on new criminal charges and were serving multiyear sentences at Florida's Apalachicola Youthful Offender Institution, and one was nowhere to be found.

In retrospect, was the experiment indeed a failure? Much was learned from it, especially about the operations of the local criminal justice system and the human service delivery network. Perhaps most importantly, the project made it clear that, no matter what the resources, any attempt to salvage youths who had rejected community values would be slow, drawn out, and uncertain.

## The Compulsory
## Treatment Strategy

The argument can easily be made that, for the most part, the "crime problem" and the "drug problem" are one and the same. After all, look at the Drug Use Forecasting (DUF) data. The DUF program was established by the National Institute of Justice to measure the prevalence of drug use among those arrested for serious crimes (Office of National Drug Control Policy 1990). Since 1986 the initiative has provided for urine testing on samples of arrestees in selected major cities across the United States to determine recent drug use. Urine specimens are collected anonymously and voluntarily; the tests detect the use of ten different drugs, including cocaine, marijuana, PCP, methamphetamine, and heroin. The DUF data have consistently demonstrated that drug use is pervasive among both adults and juveniles coming to the attention of the criminal justice system (U.S. Department of Justice 1991c). At the same time, *recent research has demonstrated not only that drug-abuse treatment works but that coerced treatment works best* (Hubbard et al. 1989; Platt, Kaplan, and McKim 1990). Although logic would dictate that voluntary treatment should have more beneficial effects than mandatory treatment, the opposite appears to be the case. The key variable most related to success in treatment is "length of stay in treatment," and those who are forced into treatment remain longer than those who volunteer (Leukefeld and Tims 1988). By remaining longer, they benefit more.

There are some very important reasons why compulsory treatment efforts should be utilized for serious delinquents. *"Serious delinquents" are not in need of rehabilitation. What they need is "habilitation" or "capacitation."* "Rehabilitation" involves a process of renovation and repair and a returning to a useful and constructive place in society; it implies the restoration of something or someone damaged to a prior good condition. The serious delinquents in the Miami study—and for that matter the majority of chronic offenders who clog the nation's courts, jails, and correctional systems—were never in good condition in the first place. Most, disenfranchised socially, educationally, economically, and psychologically since birth, never developed the self-esteem, maturity, and value system necessary for effectively coping with contemporary society. As such, it is a process of capacitation or habilitation that is required.

The most appropriate setting for the compulsory capacitation of serious delinquents is the therapeutic community—in the prison setting for those offenders who represent a threat, in the community setting for those who do not. The therapeutic community (better known as the "TC" by practitioners in the drug field) is unquestionably the most appropriate forum for drug-abuse treatment in correctional settings because of the many aspects of the prison environment that make habilitation difficult. Not surprisingly, the availability of drugs in reformatories, jails, detention centers, and prisons is a pervasive problem. In addition, there is the violence associated with inmate gangs, often formed along racial lines for the purposes of establishing and maintaining status, "turf," and unofficial control over sectors of the institution for distributing contraband and providing "protection" for other inmates (Bowker 1980; Fleisher 1989; Johnson 1987). Finally, there is the prison subculture, a system of norms and values that, among other things, holds that "people in treatment are faggots," as one Delaware inmate put it in 1988 (Inciardi 1992, p. 277).

In contrast, the therapeutic community is a total treatment environment isolated from the rest of the institutional population—separated from the drugs, the violence, and the norms and values that militate against treatment and habilitation. The primary clinical staff of the TC are typically former substance abusers/offenders ("recovering addicts") who themselves have been clients in therapeutic communities. The treatment perspective of the TC is that drug abuse is a disorder of the whole person; that is, the problem is the *person* and not the drug, and addiction is a *symptom* and not the essence of the disorder. In the TC's view of recovery, the primary goal is to change the negative patterns of behaving, thinking, and feeling that predispose drug use and crime. The end result is a responsible drug-free and crime-free lifestyle (De Leon and Ziegenfuss 1986; Yablonsky 1989).

Recovery through the TC process depends on positive and negative pressures to change, and this is brought about through a self-help process in which relationships of mutual responsibility are built among all residents in the program. As the noted TC researcher Dr. George De Leon (1985) once described it:

> The essential dynamic in the TC is mutual self-help. Thus, the day-to-day activities are conducted by the residents themselves. In their jobs, groups, meetings, recreation, personal, and social time, it is residents who continually transmit to each other the main messages and expectations of the community.

In addition to individual and group counseling, the TC process includes a system of explicit rewards that reinforce the value of earned achievement. As such, privileges are *earned*. Also, TCs have their own specific rules and regulations that guide the behavior of residents and the management of their facilities. Their purposes are to maintain the safety and health of the community and to train and teach residents through the use of discipline. TC rules and regulations are numerous, the most conspicuous of which are total prohibitions against violence, theft, and drug use. Violation of these cardinal rules typically results in immediate expulsion from a TC.

Therapeutic communities have been in existence for decades, and their successes have been well documented (De Leon 1990). Yet few exist in either institutional or community-based settings, and an even smaller number have been designed for juveniles. The juvenile TC is probably the only viable alternative for seriously delinquent youth. Although the operation of a therapeutic community is costly, averaging $65/day per client, it is an extremely cost-effective approach when one considers the nature and extent of street crime by drug-involved serious delinquents.

# POSTSCRIPT

The data from this study of serious delinquents in Miami suggest that these young criminal offenders have received very little help from community agencies. Only a small proportion of this extremely drug-involved group have ever been in treatment for substance abuse. The high expulsion/suspension rates for these adolescents suggest that their schools responded to student drug-related behaviors only with punitive measures; the high dropout rates suggest even less success by schools with serious delinquents than with inner-city adolescents generally. The justice system seems to be equally unsupportive. Almost all of these juveniles had been arrested at least once, and most had been arrested during the 12-month period prior to interview. A mean of 702 offenses per youth in the prior 12 months, however, implies that intervention attempts resulting from those arrests were either not undertaken or obviously unsuccessful.

It is disconcerting that such a substantial number of these drug-using adolescents are potential AIDS victims. That they cannot be frightened off the street by information about their risk for *eventual* HIV infection is suggested by their cocaine use and street crimes, which put them at risk *now, daily,* for death by overdose or assault. The possibility that adolescents may be HIV infected for years before becoming symptomatic for AIDS increases the potential for contagion.

Education aimed at adolescents about the risks for HIV infection can be only part of the solution, since knowledge alone does not necessarily alter high-risk behaviors (Turner, Miller, and Moses 1989). Conventional AIDS education efforts, furthermore, do not seem likely to succeed among adolescents whose lives are so extremely unconventional. Rather, it would appear that strenuous *outreach* prevention/intervention programs are needed to work with street populations of adolescents, including prostitutes, other seriously drug- and crime-involved youths, and runaways (the latter being particularly likely to join the ranks of young street criminals). Culturally specific programs sensitive to the problems of this special population are needed to break into the interrelated complex of their HIV-risk behaviors.

The data in this study suggest that drug treatment, especially treatment for cocaine dependence, must be a central component of these efforts. Unfortunately, however, drug treatment for adolescents and treatment of cocaine dependence are the two most problematically underdeveloped aspects of the American drug treatment enterprise. Further, few AIDS outreach programs have been initiated with adolescent delinquents—a result, perhaps, of these youths' general inaccessibility, their reputation for being

violence prone, and/or the unwillingness of many researchers and clini-
cians to deal with the special federal regulations involving the use of mi-
nors as research subjects.

For those youths who are not, as yet, "serious delinquents," the
need is for delinquency prevention programs. The difficulty, however, is
where to focus attention and resources, since serious delinquents begin as
garden-variety delinquents, who are not clustered in any one type of community or group. They can be found in middle-class, working-class, and
underclass communities. They are black, white, Hispanic, and Asian. They
are both male and female. There is no accurate way of predicting *who* will
become delinquent. There should be no attempt to pick out individual
youths for preventive strategies; it never has worked in the past.

A logical focus for prevention would be the community rather than
the individual, but with the school as the locus of the effort. The school is in
every community, and in some it is the only existing community-wide
institution. Moreover, its suitability for delinquency prevention efforts has
been well recognized (Gottfredson 1986; Greenwood 1985; Kingsley 1989).
What may not be recognized, however, as this study of serious delinquents
has demonstrated, is that schools all too often "give up" too quickly on the
"troublemakers"—the budding delinquents who are in the most need of
intervention and support.

As a concluding note, there is the matter of future research needs.
When initiated in 1985, this was the first street study of nongang delinquents to be conducted in some two decades. Since then, as described in
Chapter 2, considerably more delinquency research has been conducted in
high-crime-rate neighborhoods and more research attention has been paid
to serious drug involvement among adolescents. This new work, however,
still has not entailed research on the type of sample discussed here: (1)
*serious* delinquents who are (2) *at large* in the community and (3) are *not
gang* members. This continuing lack of research is a problem for at least
three reasons.

First, the generalizations possible from this one study are necessarily limited. Miami was a good site in the late 1980s for street research on
the relationship of drug use to serious delinquency, since the crack phenomenon had hit there especially hard especially early. Nonetheless, as
detailed throughout this book, Miami has its own specific characteristics,
resulting in unknown limitations on how far researchers can generalize
beyond this one sample. This project suggests some of the dimensions of
the youth crime problem today in Miami, along with reasons for thinking
that the issues and characteristics entailed are similar in many other cities.
Only street research on serious nongang delinquents in other cities can
support or counter this supposition.

A second reason why further research of this type is needed is that
there are so many reasons to think serious delinquency will continue as a
major urban problem. Use of crack and other drugs has fallen off among
youngsters from economically comfortable family backgrounds who stay

in school and appear headed toward becoming contributing members of society. No such decline has been seen in the DUF data or in other studies of people enmeshed in street life, be they adult criminals or serious delinquents. There continues to be growth in the number of youth subjected to the economic strains that have always, everywhere, been associated with high rates of serious crime. Crisis conditions persist in the criminal justice system, and drug treatment programs are inundated—particularly with cases of cocaine addiction, for which treatment remains problematic. Deep street-culture involvement now brings with it the risk of death from AIDS. And yet there are severe shortages in both the financial resources and the practical experience necessary to successfully prevent serious delinquency or intervene in its progression. Street research on serious delinquents is *not a sufficient answer, but it is an absolutely necessary part of the solution*. Detailed, up-to-date information about the behavior in question is required for successful prevention and intervention.

Third and finally, street research on serious nongang delinquents is necessary for delinquency researchers and theorists to get back in touch with their subject matter. Earlier chapters of this book demonstrated that the old classic theories provide many helpful concepts and perspectives for understanding serious delinquency as it appears on the street today. At the same time, however, those same theories are absolutely silent about other aspects of the problem.

A particularly obvious example is the role of drug use in the initiation and continuation of serious youth crime. Twenty years ago, cheap cocaine did not exist and cocaine use by adolescents was virtually unheard of. Today preadolescents use it and teenagers sell it, sometimes right on the street corner. This new fact of street life can have enormous consequences for a young delinquent's future life—and potential early death. Similarly, the classic theories of *serious* delinquency describe it as *gang* delinquency, focusing on gang dynamics and ghetto environments for their explanations. The Miami study, in contrast, indicates that serious delinquency today *also* entails crime among youths from more ordinary working-class neighborhoods who have never been gang members. The more recent classic theories have been developed on the basis of random-sample research on students, seeking to explain garden-variety delinquency. But the Miami study adds to the evidence that different processes are sometimes involved in garden-variety than in serious delinquency.

All of these contrasts and contradictions show that serious delinquency today is not even well described, let alone explained, by street studies from the 1930s through 1965, or by 1970s and 1980s random-sample surveys of the conventional youth population. The only way of improving this situation is for future delinquency research to recognize the importance of serious delinquency among nongang members and to put field studies back into their methodological arsenal, along *with* studies of garden-variety and institutionalized delinquents.

# Glossary

**addiction:** a drug use behavior pattern entailing (1) chronic repeated use of a particular drug, which leads (through **physical dependence** or **psychological dependence**) to (2) compulsion to use again, such that the user—now the addict—cannot stop using even after (3) the drug use produces severe or repeated adverse consequences, physically, psychologically, or socially.

**control theory:** a delinquency explanation focusing on the personal and social factors that tend to *prevent* delinquency. In Hirschi's (1969) version, these factors are: (1) attachments to other people; (2) commitment to conformity through investments of time, energy, past achievements, reputation, etc.; (3) involvement in conventional activities; and (4) belief in the legitimacy of conventional values.

**correlation:** a measure of the degree of relationship between two variables, ranging from –1.000 to +1.000 (representing completely negative to completely positive correlations); a correlation near .00, whether positive or negative, means the variables are not related at all; see **rho.**

**deviance syndrome:** a general behavioral pattern of deviant, rebellious, and socially problematic activities; one theoretical explanation for the consistent general association between drug use and crime among adolescents.

**differential association:** in **social learning theory,** different degrees of interaction, for particular individuals, with groups having favorable versus unfavorable attitudes toward conformity.

**differential social reinforcement:** in **social learning theory,** different degrees of social rewards and costs (e.g., verbal expression of approval or disapproval) as a consequence of particular behaviors.

**felony:** generally, a crime punishable by death or incarceration in a state or federal prison; compare **misdemeanor.**

**garden-variety delinquency:** minor law violations, status offenses, and other misbehaviors that are extremely common during adolescence.

**incidence:** in studies of social (and medical) problem rates, the number of *occurrences* of a particular problem (such as crime) during a specific time (compare **prevalence**).

**Index offenses:** in the *Uniform Crime Reports,* the **Part I offenses:** the most serious crimes against both persons (homicide, forcible rape, aggravated assault, and robbery) and property (burglary, motor vehicle theft, arson, and larceny).

**juveniles:** persons below the legal age of adulthood, most commonly age 18.

**labeling theory:** a deviance explanation arguing that being labeled deviant can cause further deviant behavior by affecting the person's self-concept; thus, societal reactions are more important in defining deviance than are rule-breaking behaviors themselves.

**mean:** a measure of central tendency; specifically, an arithmetic average, computed by finding the sum of a set of numbers and then dividing by the number of individual numbers in the set; compare **median.**

**median:** a measure of central tendency; specifically, the middle number when a set of numbers are put into numerical order; compare **mean.**

**misdemeanor:** a crime for which the maximum punishment is incarceration for less than a year in a local jail; compare **felony.**

**National Youth Survey:** a 1977–1984 study of drug use, crime, and mental health among American youths. The 1,725 respondents were interviewed once a year from 1977 through 1981 and a sixth time in 1984 concerning their behaviors during the prior 12 months. Because the sample was representative of the total 11–17-year-old population, its findings for 1976 can be generalized to American youth as a whole. For analysis, the National Youth Survey defined "serious delinquency" as having committed, in the previous year, at least three serious offenses (felony assault, robbery, motor vehicle theft, burglary, or a $50+ theft). For details, see, e.g., Elliott, Huizinga, and Ageton 1985 or Elliott, Huizinga, and Menard 1989.

**Part I offenses:** in the *Uniform Crime Reports,* the most serious crime categories, used to construct the national Crime Index; see **Index offenses.**

**Part II offenses:** in the *Uniform Crime Reports,* lesser crimes against persons or property (assaults not involving weapons or injury, forgery, fraud, embezzlement, stolen goods offenses, and vandalism) and **public order offenses.**

**physical (drug) dependence:** a state in which a drug has been used in sufficient quantity over sufficient time that the user's body has changed to accommodate the presence of the drug and now requires that presence to function normally; especially common with repeated use of central nervous system depressants but also possible for marijuana and stimulants, including cocaine.

**polydrug use:** use of multiple psychoactive substances, including use at levels such that the effects of one drug necessarily modify the effects of another.

**prevalence:** in studies of social (and medical) problem rates, the number of *persons* involved in a particular problem (such as crime) during a specific time (compare **incidence**).

**psychological (drug) dependence:** a craving for the pleasurable mental effects of a drug and a strong preference for those effects over a normal state of consciousness.

**problem drug use:** drug use resulting in severe or repeated adverse consequences: social conflicts, behavioral failures, emotional or other psychological difficulties, or physical impairment.

**public order offenses:** violations of laws designed to protect general public safety and moral standards (as opposed to property or persons), including laws concerning alcohol and other drugs, prostitution, gambling, possession of weapons, and a wide range of minor nuisance behaviors such as loitering and disorderly conduct.

**purposive sample:** a sample in which members are deliberately selected according to previously defined characteristics, generally (and only appropriately) when a **random sample** cannot be drawn because the population of interest cannot be completely identified in advance.

**random sample:** a sample in which every potential member has an equal chance of being included, which means that findings from a correctly drawn random sample can be used to make accurate generalizations about the much larger total population from which the sample was drawn (compare **purposive sample**).

**rho:** the Spearman (rank-order) Correlation Coefficient.

**self-report:** a method of gathering information about people's behavior, especially illegal behavior, by asking them to report their own past activities; most often contrasted to studies of official data such as arrest rates or drug treatment entries.

**serious delinquents:** youths under the age of 18 involved in major and/or chronic criminal behavior.

**social disorganization:** a breakdown in the ability of families, schools, and other community-based groups and organizations to control deviant behavior.

**social learning theory**, a deviance explanation emphasizing the ways in which deviance is learned in the process of interacting with other people, just as conformity is, through **differential association** and **differential social reinforcement.**

**status offenses:** behaviors that have been made illegal because they violate the standards of behavior expected of **juveniles,** such as running away, being truant, staying out late, drinking, engaging in sexual behavior, and disobeying parents.

**strain theory:** a delinquency explanation asserting that delinquency results from frustrated needs and wants; most often used to explain lower-class delinquency, with the argument that the social-class position of youngsters in poverty areas makes it difficult for them to achieve economic success.

**tolerance (to drugs):** the need, as the body adjusts to a drug, for more of the drug in order to get the same effect.

**underclass:** people with little chance to ever escape poverty; most often the urban poor locked out of the normal occupational structure of American society by low educational levels, low numbers of jobs available in city locations, and few if any role models or job-location contacts for successful employment.

*Uniform Crime Reports (UCR):* a nationwide compilation of crime and arrest data from local police departments, prepared every year by the Federal Bureau of Investigation (FBI).

**withdrawal rebound:** the experience, for an addict who stops drug use suddenly, of not just no further psychic drug effects but the opposite psychic effects: agitation for depressants, severe depression for stimulants.

# REFERENCES

Agar, Michael H. 1973. *Ripping and Running: A Formal Ethnography of Urban Heroin Addicts*. New York: Seminar Press.

Akers, Ronald L. 1977. *Deviant Behavior: A Social Learning Approach*. Belmont, CA: Wadsworth.

Akers, Ronald L., and John K. Cochran. 1985. "Adolescent Marijuana Use: A Test of Three Theories of Deviant Behavior." *Deviant Behavior* 6:323–46.

Akers, Ronald L., Marvin D. Krohn, Lonn Lanza-Kaduce, and Marcia Radosevich. 1979. "Social Learning and Deviant Behavior: A Specific Test of a General Theory." *American Sociological Review* 44:636–55.

Akerstrom, Malin. 1985. *Crooks and Squares*. New Brunswick, NJ: Transaction Books.

Almeida, M. 1978. "Contrabución al Estudio de la Historia Natural de la Dependencia a la Pasta Basica de Cocaina." *Revista de Neuro-Psiquiatria* 41:44–45.

Amsel, Zili, Wallace Mandell, Lynda Matthias, Carol Mason, and Irit Hocherman. 1976. "Reliability and Validity of Self-Reported Illegal Activities and Drug Use Collected from Narcotic Addicts." *International Journal of the Addictions* 11:325–36.

Anglin, M. Douglas, and George Speckart. 1986. "Narcotics Use, Property Crime, and Dealing: Structural Dynamics across the Addiction Career." *Journal of Quantitative Criminology* 2:355–75.

Arif, A., ed. 1987. *Adverse Health Consequences of Cocaine Abuse*. Geneva: World Health Organization.

Austin, Gregory A., and Dan J. Lettieri, eds. 1976. *Drugs and Crime*. Rockville, MD: National Institute on Drug Abuse.

Bachman, Jerald G., Patrick M. O'Malley, and Jerome Johnston. 1978. *Adolescence to Adulthood: Change and Stability in the Lives of Young Men. Youth in Transition, Volume VI*. Ann Arbor: University of Michigan Press.

Baldwin, John. 1979. "Ecological and Areal Studies in Great Britain and the United States." Pp. 29–66 in *Crime and Justice: An Annual Review of Research*, Vol. 1, edited by N. Morris and M. Tonry. Chicago: University of Chicago Press.

Ball, John C. 1967. "The Reliability and Validity of Interview Data Obtained from 59 Narcotic Drug Addicts." *American Journal of Sociology* 72:650–54.

Ball, John C., Lawrence Rosen, John A. Flueck, and David N. Nurco. 1981. "The Criminality of Heroin Addicts: When Addicted and When Off Opiates." Pp. 39–65 in *The Drugs-Crime Connection*, edited by J. A. Inciardi. Beverly Hills, CA: Sage.

Bernard, Godwin. 1983. "An Economic Analysis of the Illicit Drug Market." *International Journal of the Addictions* 18:681–700.

Beschner, George M. 1985. "The Problem of Adolescent Drug Abuse: An Introduction to Intervention Strategies." Pp. 1–12 in *Treatment Services for Adolescent Substance Abusers*, edited by A. S. Friedman and G. M. Beschner. Rockville, MD: National Institute on Drug Abuse.

Binderman, Murray B., Dennis Wepman, and Ronald B. Newman. 1975. "A Portrait of 'The Life.'" *Urban Life* 4:213–25.

Blumstein, Alfred, Jacqueline Cohen, Jeffrey A. Roth, and Christy A. Visher, eds. 1986. *Criminal Careers and "Career Criminals,"* Vol. 1. Washington, DC: National Academy Press.

Bondavalli, Bonnie J., and Bruno Bondavalli. 1981. "Spanish-Speaking People and the North American Criminal Justice System." Pp. 49–69 in *Race, Crime, and Criminal Justice*, edited by R. L. McNeely and C. E. Pope. Beverly Hills, CA: Sage.

Bonito, Arthur J., David N. Nurco, and John W. Shaffer. 1976. "The Veridicality of Addicts' Self-Reports in Social Research." *International Journal of the Addictions* 11:719–24.

Bookin-Weiner, Hedy, and Ruth Horowitz. 1983. "The End of the Youth Gang: Fad or Fact?" *Criminology* 21:585–602.

Bowker, Lee H. 1977. *Drug Use among American Women, Old and Young: Sexual Oppression and Other Themes*. San Francisco: R and E Associates.

Bowker, Lee H. 1980. *Prison Victimization*. New York: Elsevier.

Boyer, Debra, and Jennifer James. 1982. "Easy Money: Adolescent Involvement in Prostitution." Pp. 73–97 in *Justice for Young Women: Close-up on Critical Issues*, edited by S. Davidson. Tucson: New Directions for Young Women.

Braucht, G. Nicholas. 1980. "Psychosocial Research on Teenage Drinking: Past and Future." Pp. 109–43 in *Drugs and the Youth Culture*, edited by F. R. Scarpitti and S. K. Datesman. Beverly Hills, CA: Sage.

Brownfield, David. 1986. "Social Class and Violent Behavior." *Criminology* 24: 421–38.

Brunswick, Ann F., and Peter Messeri. 1985. "Timing of First Drug Treatment: A Longitudinal Study of Urban Black Youth." *Contemporary Drug Problems* 12:401–18.

Burgess, Robert L., and Ronald L. Akers. 1966. "A Differential Association-Reinforcement Theory of Criminal Behavior." *Social Problems* 14:128–47.

Burke, D. S., J. F. Brundage, M. Goldenbaum, L. I. Gardner, M. Peterson, R. Visintine, R. R. Redfield, and the Walter Reed Retrovirus Research Group. 1990. "Human Immunodeficiency Virus Infections in Teenagers: Seroprevalence among Applicants for U.S. Military Service." *Journal of the American Medical Association* 263:2074–77.

Bursik, Robert J., Jr. 1988. "Social Disorganization and Theories of Crime and Delinquency: Problems and Prospects." *Criminology* 26:519–51.

Canter, Rachelle J. 1982. "Sex Difference in Self-Report Delinquency." *Criminology* 20:373–93.

Carpenter, Cheryl, Barry Glassner, Bruce D. Johnson, and Julia Loughlin. 1988. *Kids, Drugs, and Crime*. Lexington, MA: Lexington Books.

Carroll, Kathleen M., Daniel S. Keller, Lisa R. Fenton, and Frank Gawin. 1987. "Psychotherapy for Cocaine Abusers." Pp. 75–105 in *The Cocaine Crisis*, edited by D. F. Allen. New York: Plenum.

Castro, K. G., S. Lieb, H. W. Jaffe, J. P. Narkunal, C. H. Calisher, T. J. Bush, J. W. Witte, and the Belle Glade Field Study Group. 1988. "Transmission of HIV in Belle Glade, Florida: Lessons for Other Communities in the United States." *Science* 239:193–97.

Centers for Disease Control. 1991. *HIV/AIDS Surveillance*. October.

Cernkovich, Stephen A., Peggy C. Giordano, and Meredith D. Pugh. 1985. "Chronic Offenders: The Missing Cases in Self-Report Delinquency Research." *Journal of Criminal Law and Criminology* 76:705–32.

Chaiken, Jan M., and Marcia R. Chaiken. 1982. *Varieties of Criminal Behavior*. Santa Monica, CA: Rand Corporation.

Chaiken, Marcia R., and Bruce D. Johnson. 1988. "Characteristics of Different Types of Drug-Involved Offenders." *National Institute of Justice, Issues and Practices*, February (NCJ 108560).

Chein, Isidor, Donald L. Gerard, Robert S. Lee, and Eva Rosenfeld. 1964. *The Road to H: Narcotics, Delinquency, and Social Policy*. New York: Basic Books.

Chitwood, Dale D. 1985. "Patterns and Consequences of Cocaine Use." Pp. 111–29 in *Cocaine Use in America: Epidemiologic and Clinical Perspectives*, edited by N. J. Kozel and E. H. Adams. Rockville, MD: National Institute on Drug Abuse.

Chitwood, Dale D., James A. Inciardi, Duane C. McBride, Clyde B. McCoy, H. Virginia McCoy, and Edward J. Trapido. 1992. *A Community Approach to AIDS Intervention: Exploring the Miami Outreach Project for Injecting Drug Users and Other High Risk Groups*. Westport, CT: Greenwood Press.

Cimons, Marlene. 1989. "More Children Being Placed in Care Outside Their Families, Report Says." *Los Angeles Times*, as reprinted in the *Philadelphia Inquirer*, Dec. 12:11–A.

Clayton, Richard R. 1981. "The Delinquency and Drug Use Relationship among Adolescents: A Critical Review." Pp. 82–103 in *Drug Abuse and the American Adolescent*, edited by D. J. Lettieri and J. P. Ludford. Rockville, MD: National Institute on Drug Abuse.

Clayton, Richard R., and Harwin L. Voss. 1981. *Young Men and Drugs in Manhattan: A Causal Analysis*. Rockville, MD: National Institute on Drug Abuse.

Cloward, Richard A., and Lloyd E. Ohlin. 1960. *Delinquency and Opportunity: A Theory of Delinquent Gangs*. New York: Free Press.

Cohen, Albert K. 1955. *Delinquent Boys: The Culture of the Gang*. New York: Free Press.

Cohen, Sidney. 1985. *The Substance Abuse Problems, Vol. 2: New Issues for the 1980s*. New York: Haworth Press.

Cohen, Sidney. 1987. "Causes of the Cocaine Outbreak." Pp. 3–9 in *Cocaine: A Clinician's Handbook*, edited by A. M. Washton and Mark S. Gold. New York: Guilford.

Cohen, Sidney. 1988. *The Chemical Brain: The Neurochemistry of Addictive Disorders*. Irvine, CA: CareInstitute.

Collins, James J., Robert L. Hubbard, and J. Valley Rachal. 1985. "Expensive Drug Use and Illegal Income: A Test of Explanatory Hypotheses." *Criminology* 23:743–64.

Colvin, Mark, and John Pauly. 1983. "A Critique of Criminology: Toward an Integrated Structural-Marxist Theory of Delinquency Production." *American Journal of Sociology* 89:513–51.

Conger, Rand. 1976. "Social Control and Social Learning Models of Delinquent Behavior: A Synthesis." *Criminology* 14:17–40.

Cook, Philip J., and John H. Laub. 1986. "The (Surprising) Stability of Youth Crime Rates." *Journal of Quantitative Criminology* 2:265–77.

Cox, Thomas J., and Bill Longwell. 1974. "Reliability of Interview Data Concerning Current Heroin Use from Heroin Addicts on Methadone." *International Journal of the Addictions* 9:161–65.

Cusson, Maurice. 1983. *Why Delinquency?* (translated by D. R. Crelinsten). Toronto: University of Toronto Press.

Dade County. N.d. *Children in Need: A Social Crisis*. Report prepared by the Dept. of Human Resources and the Dept. of Youth and Family Development. Metropolitan Dade County, Florida.

Dade County Grand Jury. 1985. Dade Youth Gangs. Final Report of the Grand Jury, May 14.

Dade County Grand Jury. 1988. Dade Youth Gangs—1988. Final Report of the Grand Jury, May 11.

De Leon, George. 1985. "The Therapeutic Community: Status and Evolution." *International Journal of the Addictions* 20:823–44.

De Leon, George. 1990. "Treatment Strategies." Pp. 115–38 in *Handbook of Drug Control in the United States*, edited by James A. Inciardi. Westport, CT: Greenwood Press.

De Leon, George, and James T. Ziegenfuss. 1986. *Therapeutic Communities for the Addictions*. Springfield, IL: Charles C Thomas.

Dembo, Richard, Dean V. Babst, William Burgos, and James Schmeidler. 1981. "Survival Orientation and the Drug Use Experiences of a Sample of Inner City Junior High School Youths." *International Journal of the Addictions* 16(6):1031–47.

Dembo, Richard, Max Dertke, Lawrence La Voie, Scott Borders, Mark Washburn, and James Schmeidler. 1987. "Physical Abuse, Sexual Victimization and Illicit Drug Use: A Structural Analysis among High Risk Adolescents." *Journal of Adolescence* 10:13–33.

Dembo, Richard, Gary Grandon, Lawrence La Voie, James Schmeidler, and William Burgos. 1986. "Parents and Drugs Revisited: Some Further Evidence in Support of Social Learning Theory." *Criminology* 24:85–104.

Dembo, Richard, and David Shern. 1982. "Relative Deviance and the Process(es) of Drug Involvement among Inner-City Youth." *International Journal of the Addictions* 17:1373–99.

Dembo, Richard, Mark Washburn, Eric D. Wish, Horatio Yeung, Alan Getreu, Estrellita Berry, and William R. Blount. 1987. "Heavy Marijuana Use and Crime among Youths Entering a Juvenile Detention Center." *Journal of Psychoactive Drugs* 19:47–56.

Dembo, Richard, Linda Williams, Werner Wothke, James Schmeidler, Alan Getreu, Estrellita Berry, Eric D. Wish, and Candice Christensen. 1990. "The Relationship between Cocaine Use, Drug Sales and Other Delinquency among a Cohort of High Risk Youths over Time." Pp. 112–35 in *Drugs and Violence: Causes, Correlates, and Consequences*, edited by M. De La Rosa, E. Y. Lambert, and B. Gropper. Rockville, MD: National Institute on Drug Abuse.

Donovan, John E., and Richard Jessor. 1983. "Problem Drinking and the Dimension of Involvement with Drugs: A Guttman Scalogram Analysis of Adolescent Drug Use." *American Journal of Public Health* 73:543–52.

Donovan, John E., and Richard Jessor. 1985. "Structures of Problem Behavior in Adolescence and Young Adulthood." *Journal of Consulting and Clinical Psychology* 53:890–904.

Drug Enforcement Administration. 1989. *Crack/Cocaine Overview 1989.* Washington, DC: U.S. Department of Justice.

Dunford, Franklin W., and Delbert S. Elliott. 1984. "Identifying Career Offenders Using Self-Reported Data." *Journal of Research in Crime and Delinquency* 21:57–86.

Duster, Troy. 1987. "Crime, Youth Unemployment, and the Black Urban Underclass." *Crime & Delinquency* 33(2):300–16.

Earls, C. M., and H. David. 1989. "Male and Female Prostitution: A Review." *Annals of Sex Research* 2:5–28.

Eddy, Paul, Hugo Sabogal, and Sara Walden. 1988. *The Cocaine Wars.* New York: W. W. Norton.

Edelbrock, Craig. 1980. "Running Away from Home: Incidence and Correlates among Children and Youth Referred for Mental Health Services." *Journal of Family Issues* 1:210–28.

Elliott, Delbert S., and A. Rex Ageton. 1976. "The Relationship between Drug Use and Crime among Adolescents." Pp. 297–321 in *Drug Use and Crime: Report to the Panel on Drug Use and Criminal Behavior*, edited by Research Triangle Institute. Springfield, VA: National Technical Information Service.

Elliott, Delbert S., and David Huizinga. 1983. "Social Class and Delinquent Behavior in a National Youth Panel." *Criminology* 21:149–77.

Elliott, Delbert S., and David Huizinga. 1984. "The Relationship between Delinquent Behavior and ADM Problem Behaviors." Paper presented at the ADAMHA/OJJDP "State of the Art" Research Conference on Juvenile Offenders with Serious Alcohol, Drug Abuse and Mental Health Problems. Bethesda, MD, April 17–18.

Elliott, Delbert S., David Huizinga, and Suzanne S. Ageton. 1985. *Explaining Delinquency and Drug Use.* Beverly Hills, CA: Sage.

Elliott, Delbert S., David Huizinga, and Scott Menard. 1989. *Multiple Problem Youth: Delinquency, Substance Use, and Mental Health Problems.* New York: Springer-Verlag.

Elliott, Delbert S., and Harwin L. Voss. 1974. *Delinquency and Dropouts.* Lexington, MA: Lexington Books.

English, Clifford, and Joyce Stephens. 1975. "On Being Excluded: An Analysis of Elderly and Adolescent Street Hustlers." *Urban Life* 4:201–12.

Erickson, Maynard. 1971. "The Group Context of Delinquent Behavior." *Social Problems* 19:114–29.

Erickson, Patricia G., Edward M. Adlaf, Glenn F. Murray, and Reginald G. Smart. 1987. *The Steel Drug: Cocaine in Perspective.* Lexington, MA: Lexington Books.

Estroff, Todd Wilk.•1987. "Medical and Biological Consequences of Cocaine Abuse." Pp. 23–32 in *Cocaine: A Clinician's Handbook*, edited by A. M. Washton and Mark S. Gold. New York: Guilford.

Extein, Irl, and Charles A. Dackis. 1987. "Brain Mechanisms in Cocaine Dependency." Pp. 73–84 in *Cocaine: A Clinician's Handbook*, edited by A. M. Washton and Mark S. Gold. New York: Guilford.

Fagan, Jeffrey. 1989. "The Social Organization of Drug Use and Drug Dealing among Urban Gangs." *Criminology* 27:633–69.

Fagan, Jeffrey, Karen V. Hansen, and Michael Jang. 1983. "Profiles of Chronically Violent Juvenile Offenders: An Empirical Test of an Integrated Theory of Violent Delinquency." Pp. 91–119 in *Evaluating Juvenile Justice*, edited by J. R. Kleugel. Beverly Hills, CA: Sage.

Fagan, Jeffrey, and Edward Pabon. 1990. "Contributions of Delinquency and Substance Use to School Dropout among Inner City Youths." *Youth and Society* 21:306–54.

Fagan, Jeffrey, Elizabeth Piper, and Melinda Moore. 1986. "Violent Delinquents and Urban Youths." *Criminology* 24:439–71.

Fagan, Jeffrey, Joseph G. Weis, and Yu-Teh Cheng. 1990. "Delinquency and Substance Use among Inner-City Students." *Journal of Drug Issues* 20:351–402.

Fagan, Jeffrey, and Sandra Wexler. 1987. "Family Origins of Violent Delinquents." *Criminology* 25:643–69.

Federal Bureau of Investigation. 1989. *Uniform Crime Reports: Crime in the United States—1988.* Washington, DC: FBI.

Federal Bureau of Investigation. 1991. *Uniform Crime Reports: Crime in the United States—1990.* Washington, DC: FBI.

Feldman, Harvey W. 1968. "Ideological Supports to Becoming and Remaining a Heroin Addict." *Journal of Health and Social Behavior* 9:131–39.

Feldman, Harvey W. 1977. "A Neighborhood History of Drug Switching." Pp. 249–78 in *Street Ethnography*, edited by R. S. Weppner. Beverly Hills, CA: Sage.

Ferrence, Roberta G., and Paul C. Whitehead. 1980. "Sex Differences in Psychoactive Drug Use: Recent Epidemiology." Pp. 125–201 in *Research Advances in Alcohol and Drug Problems, Vol. 5: Alcohol and Drug Problems in Women*, edited by O. J. Kalant. New York: Plenum.

Figueira-McDonough, Josephina, William H. Barton, and Rosemary C. Sarri. 1981. "Normal Deviance: Gender Similarities in Adolescent Subcultures." Pp. 17–45 in *Comparing Female and Male Offenders*, edited by M. Q. Warren. Beverly Hills, CA: Sage.

Finckenauer, James O. 1982. *Scared Straight! and the Panacea Phenomenon.* Englewood Cliffs, NJ: Prentice-Hall.

Finckenauer, James O. 1984. *Juvenile Delinquency and Corrections: The Gap between Theory and Practice.* Orlando: Academic Press.

Fleisher, Mark S. 1989. *Warehousing Violence.* Newbury Park, CA: Sage.

Forer, Lois G. 1988. "Bring Back the Orphanage: An Answer for Today's Abused Children." *Washington Monthly*, April:17–22.

Forney, Mary Ann, and T. Holloway. 1990. "Crack, Syphilis and AIDS: The Triple Threat to Rural Georgia." *Georgia Academy of Family Physicians Journal* 12:5–6.

Fullilove, Robert E., Mindy Thompson Fullilove, Benjamin P. Bowser, and Shirley A. Gross. 1990. "Risk of Sexually Transmitted Disease among Black Adolescent Crack Users in Oakland and San Francisco, Calif." *Journal of the American Medical Association* 263:851–55.

Galea, Robert P., Benjamin F. Lewis, and Lori A. Baker, eds. 1988. *AIDS and IV Drug Abusers: Current Perspectives.* Owings Mills, MD: National Health Publishing.

Gandossy, Robert P., Jay R. Williams, Jo Cohen, and Henrick J. Harwood. 1980. *Drugs and Crime: A Survey and Analysis of the Literature.* Washington, DC: National Institute of Justice.

Gans, Herbert J. 1962. *The Urban Villagers: Group and Class in the Life of Italian Americans.* New York: Free Press.

Garbarino, James. 1989. "The Incidence and Prevalence of Child Maltreatment." Pp. 219–61 in *Family Violence,* edited by L. Ohlin and M. Tonry. Chicago: University of Chicago Press.

Gelber, Seymour. 1988. *Hard-Core Delinquents: Reaching Out through the Miami Experiment.* Tuscaloosa: University of Alabama Press.

Gibbs, Jewelle Taylor, ed. 1988. *Young, Black and Male in America: An Endangered Species.* New York: Auburn House.

Giordano, Peggy C., Stephen A. Cernkovich, and Meredith D. Pugh. 1986. "Friendship and Delinquency." *American Journal of Sociology* 91:1170–1202.

Gold, Martin. 1966. "Undetected Delinquent Behavior." *Journal of Research in Crime and Delinquency* 3:27–46.

Gold, Martin. 1970. *Delinquent Behavior in an American City.* Pacific Grove, CA: Brooks/Cole.

Gold, Martin, and David J. Reimer. 1975. "Changing Patterns of Delinquent Behavior among Americans 13 through 16 Years Old: 1967–1972." *Crime and Delinquency Literature* 7:483–517.

Goldman, Fred. 1981. "Drug Abuse, Crime, and Economics: The Dismal Limits of Social Choice." Pp. 155–81 in *The Drugs-Crime Connection,* edited by J. A. Inciardi. Beverly Hills, CA: Sage.

Goldstein, Paul J. 1979. *Prostitution and Drugs.* Lexington, MA: Lexington Books.

Goldstein, Paul J. 1981. "Getting Over: Economic Alternatives to Predatory Crime among Street Drug Users." Pp. 67–84 in *The Drugs-Crime Connection,* edited by J. A. Inciardi. Beverly Hills, CA: Sage.

Goldstein, Paul J. 1985. "The Drugs/Violence Nexus: A Tripartite Conceptual Framework." *Journal of Drug Issues* 15:493–506.

Goldstein, Paul J. 1986. "Homicide Behavior Related to Drug Traffic." *Bulletin of the New York Academy of Medicine* 62:509–16.

Goodman, Howard. 1989. "Teens Adrift in the Justice System." *Philadelphia Inquirer,* Dec. 31:1, 7B.

Gottfredson, Denise C. 1986. "An Empirical Test of School-Based Environmental and Individual Interventions to Reduce the Risk of Delinquent Behavior." *Criminology* 24:705–31.

Gould, Leroy C., Andrew L. Walker, Lansing E. Crane, and Charles W. Lidz. 1974. *Connections: Notes from the Heroin World.* New Haven, CT: Yale University Press.

Green, Judith. 1979. "Overview of Adolescent Drug Use." Pp. 17–44 in *Youth Drug Abuse: Problems, Issues, and Treatment,* edited by G. M. Beschner and A. S. Friedman. Lexington, MA: Lexington Books.

Greenberg, Stephanie W., and Freda Adler. 1974. "Crime and Addiction: An Empirical Analysis of the Literature, 1920–1973." *Contemporary Drug Problems* 3:221–70.

Greenwood, Peter. 1985. *The Juvenile Rehabilitation Reader*. Santa Monica, CA: Rand Corporation.

Grinspoon, Lester, and James B. Bakalar. 1985. *Cocaine: A Drug and Its Social Evolution*, rev. ed. New York: Basic Books.

Gugliotta, Guy, and Jeff Leen. 1989. *Kings of Cocaine*. New York: Simon and Schuster.

Hagedorn, John M. 1988. *People and Folks: Gangs, Crime and the Underclass in a Rustbelt City*. Chicago: Lake View Press.

Hamparian, Donna M., Linda K. Estep, Susan M. Muntean, Ramon R. Priestino, Robert G. Swisher, Paul L. Wallace, and Joseph L. White. 1982. *Youth in Adult Courts: Between Two Worlds*. Washington, DC: National Institute for Juvenile Justice and Delinquency Prevention.

Hamparian, Donna M., Richard L. Schuster, Simon Dinitz, and John P. Conrad. 1978. *The Violent Few: A Study of Dangerous Juvenile Offenders*. Lexington, MA: Lexington Books.

Hanson, Bill, George Beschner, James M. Walters, and Elliott Bovelle, eds. 1985. *Life with Heroin: Voices from the Inner City*. Lexington, MA: Lexington Books.

Hartstone, Eliot, and Karen V. Hansen. 1984. "The Violent Juvenile Offender: An Empirical Portrait." Pp. 83–112 in *Violent Juvenile Offenders: An Anthology*, edited by R. A. Mathias, P. DeMuro, and R. S. Allinson. San Francisco: National Council on Crime and Delinquency.

Hendin, Herbert, Ann Pollinger, Richard Ullman, and Arthur C. Carr. 1981. *Adolescent Marijuana Abusers and Their Families*. Rockville, MD: National Institute on Drug Abuse.

Hewlett, Sylvia Ann. 1986. *A Lesser Life*. New York: William Morrow.

Hindelang, Michael J. 1973. "Causes of Delinquency: A Partial Replication and Extention." *Social Problems* 20:471–87.

Hindelang, Michael J. 1974. "Moral Evaluations of Illegal Behaviors." *Social Problems* 21:370–85.

Hindelang, Michael J. 1976. "With a Little Help from Their Friends: Group Participation in Reported Delinquent Behaviour." *British Journal of Criminology* 16:109–25.

Hindelang, Michael J., Travis Hirschi, and Joseph G. Weis. 1981. *Measuring Delinquency*. Beverly Hills, CA: Sage.

Hirschi, Travis. 1969. *Causes of Delinquency*. Berkeley: University of California Press.

Hirschi, Travis, and Michael J. Hindelang. 1977. "Intelligence and Delinquency: A Revisionist Review." *American Sociological Review* 42:571–87.

Hopkins, D. R. 1987. "AIDS in Minority Populations in the United States." *Public Health Reports* 102:677–81.

Horowitz, Ruth. 1983. *Honor and the American Dream: Culture and Identity in a Chicano Community*. New Brunswick, NJ: Rutgers University Press.

Hotaling, Gerald T., and Murray A. Strauss, with Alan J. Lincoln. 1989. "Intrafamily Violence, and Crime and Violence outside the Family." Pp. 315–75 in *Family Violence*, edited by L. Ohlin and M. Tonry. Chicago: University of Chicago Press.

Hubbard, Robert L., Mary Ellen Marsden, J. Valley Rachal, Henrick J. Harwood, Elizabeth R. Cavanaugh, and Harold M. Ginzburg. 1989. *Drug Abuse*

*Treatment: A National Study of Effectiveness*. Chapel Hill: University of North Carolina Press.

Huizinga, David, and Delbert S. Elliott. 1986. "Reassessing the Reliability and Validity of Self-Report Delinquency Measures." *Journal of Quantitative Criminology* 2:293–327.

Inciardi, James A. 1979. "Heroin Use and Street Crime." *Crime & Delinquency* 25:335–46.

Inciardi, James A. 1986. *The War on Drugs: Heroin, Cocaine, Crime, and Public Policy*. Palo Alto, CA: Mayfield.

Inciardi, James A. 1987. "Beyond Cocaine: Basuco, Crack, and Other Coca Products." *Contemporary Drug Problems* 14:461–92.

Inciardi, James A. 1989. "Trading Sex for Crack among Juvenile Drug Users: A Research Note." *Contemporary Drug Problems* 16:689–700.

Inciardi, James A. 1990a. "The Crack-Violence Connection within a Population of Hardcore Adolescent Offenders." Pp. 92–111 in *Drugs and Violence: Causes, Correlates, and Consequences*, edited by M. De La Rosa, E. Y. Lambert, and B. Gropper. Rockville, MD: National Institute on Drug Abuse.

Inciardi, James A. 1990b. *Criminal Justice*. San Diego: Harcourt Brace Jovanovich.

Inciardi, James A. 1991. "Kingrats, Chicken Heads, Slow Necks, Freaks, and Blood Suckers: A Glimpse at the Miami Sex for Crack Market." Paper presented at the Annual Meeting of the Society for Applied Anthropology, Charleston, SC, March 13–17.

Inciardi, James A. 1992. *The War on Drugs II: The Continuing Epic of Heroin, Cocaine, Crack, Crime, AIDS, and Public Policy*. Mountain View, CA: Mayfield.

Inciardi, James A., and Duane C. McBride. 1989. "Legalization: A High-Risk Alternative in the War on Drugs." *American Behavioral Scientist* 32:259–89.

Inciardi, James A., Duane C. McBride, Anne E. Pottieger, Brian R. Russe, and Harvey A. Siegal. 1978. *Legal and Illicit Drug Use: Acute Reactions of Emergency Room Populations*. New York: Praeger.

Inciardi, James A., and Anne E. Pottieger. 1986. "Drug Use and Crime among Two Cohorts of Women Narcotics Users: An Empirical Assessment." *Journal of Drug Issues* 16:91–106.

Inciardi, James A., Anne E. Pottieger, Mary Ann Forney, Dale D. Chitwood, and Duane C. McBride. 1991. "Prostitution, IV Drug Use, and Sex-for-Crack Exchanges among Serious Delinquents: Risks for HIV Infection." *Criminology* 29:301–15.

Inciardi, James A., and Brian R. Russe. 1977. "Professional Thieves and Drugs." *International Journal of the Addictions* 12:1087–95.

Innes, Christopher A. 1988. "Drug Use and Crime: State Prison Inmate Survey, 1986." Bureau of Justice Statistics Special Report, July (NCJ-111940).

Institute of Medicine, National Academy of Science. 1982. *Marijuana and Health*. Washington, DC: National Academy Press.

James, Jennifer. 1976. "Prostitution and Addiction: An Interdisciplinary Approach." *Addictive Diseases* 2:601–18.

Jensen, Gary F., and David Brownfield. 1983. "Parents and Drugs: Specifying the Consequences of Attachment." *Criminology* 21:543–54.

Jeri, F. Raul. 1984. "Coca-Paste Smoking in Some Latin American Countries: A Severe and Unabated Form of Addiction." *Bulletin on Narcotics* (April–June): 15–31.

Jessor, Richard, and Shirley L. Jessor. 1977. *Problem Behavior and Psychosocial Development: A Longitudinal Study of Youth*. New York: Academic Press.

Jessor, Richard, and Shirley L. Jessor. 1980. "A Social-Psychological Framework for Studying Drug Use." Pp. 102–09 in *Theories on Drug Abuse*, edited by D. J. Lettieri, M. Sayers, and H. W. Pearson. Rockville, MD: National Institute on Drug Abuse.

Joe, Delbert, and Norman Robinson. 1980. "Chinatown's Immigrant Gangs: The New Young Warrior Class." *Criminology* 18:337–45.

Joe, Tom. 1987. "Economic Inequality: The Picture in Black and White." *Crime & Delinquency* 33(2):287–99.

Johnson, Bruce D. 1973. *Marihuana Users and Drug Subcultures*. New York: Wiley.

Johnson, Bruce D. 1980. "Toward a Theory of Drug Subcultures." Pp. 110–19 in *Theories on Drug Abuse*, edited by D. J. Lettieri, M. Sayers, and H. W. Pearson. Rockville, MD: National Institute on Drug Abuse.

Johnson, Bruce D., Paul J. Goldstein, Edward Preble, James Schmeidler, Douglas S. Lipton, Barry Spunt, and Thomas Miller. 1985. *Taking Care of Business: The Economics of Crime by Heroin Abusers*. Lexington, MA: Lexington Books.

Johnson, Richard E. 1979. *Juvenile Delinquency and Its Origins: An Integrated Theoretical Approach*. New York: Cambridge University Press.

Johnson, Richard E. 1980. "Social Class and Delinquent Behavior: A New Test." *Criminology* 18:86–93.

Johnson, Richard E. 1986. "Family Structure and Delinquency: General Patterns and Gender Differences." *Criminology* 24:65–84.

Johnson, Richard E., Anastasios C. Marcos, and Stephen J. Bahr. 1987. "The Role of Peers in the Complex Etiology of Adolescent Drug Use." *Criminology* 25:323–40.

Johnson, Robert. 1987. *Hard Time: Understanding and Reforming the Prison*. Pacific Grove, CA: Brooks/Cole.

Johnston, Lloyd D., Patrick M. O'Malley, and Jerald G. Bachman. 1987. *National Trends in Drug Use and Related Factors among American High School Students and Young Adults, 1975–1986*. Rockville, MD: National Institute on Drug Abuse.

Johnston, Lloyd D., Patrick M. O'Malley, and Leslie K. Eveland. 1978. "Drugs and Delinquency: A Search for Causal Connections." Pp. 137–56 in *Longitudinal Research on Drug Use*, edited by D. B. Kandel. Washington, DC: Hemisphere.

Kandel, Denise B. 1975. "Reaching the Hard-to-Reach: Illicit Drug Use among High School Absentees." *Addictive Diseases* 1:465–80.

Kandel, Denise B. 1978. "Homophily, Selection, and Socialization in Adolescent Friendships." *American Journal of Sociology* 84:427–36.

Kandel, Denise B. 1980. "Drug and Drinking Behavior among Youth." Pp. 235–85 in *Annual Review of Sociology*, Vol. 6, edited by A. Inkeles, N. J. Smelser, and R. H. Turner. Palo Alto, CA: Annual Reviews.

Kandel, Denise B. 1981. "Drug Use by Youth: An Overview." Pp. 1–24 in *Drug Abuse and the American Adolescent*, edited by D. J. Lettieri and J. P. Ludford. Rockville, MD: National Institute on Drug Abuse.

Kandel, Denise B. 1988. "Issues of Sequencing of Adolescent Drug Use and Other Problem Behaviors." *Drugs & Society* 3:55–76.

Kandel, Denise B., Ronald C. Kessler, and Rebecca Z. Margulies. 1978. "Anteced-
ents of Adolescent Initiation into Stages of Drug Use: A Developmental
Analysis." Pp. 73–99 in *Longitudinal Research on Drug Use*, edited by D. B.
Kandel. Washington, DC: Hemisphere.

Kandel, Denise B., Ora Simcha-Fagan, and Mark Davies. 1986. "Risk Factors for
Delinquency and Illicit Drug Use from Adolescence to Young Adulthood." *Journal of Drug Issues* 16:67–90.

Kandel, Denise B., and Kazuo Yamaguchi. 1987. "Job Mobility and Drug Use: An
Event History Analysis." *American Journal of Sociology* 92:836–78.

Kaslow, Richard A., and Donald P. Francis, eds. 1989. *The Epidemiology of AIDS:
Expression, Occurrence, and Control of Human Immunodeficiency Virus Type 1
Infection.* New York: Oxford University Press.

Katz, Jack. 1988. *Seductions of Crime.* New York: Basic Books.

Kelly, Delos H. 1982. *Creating School Failure, Youth Crime and Deviance.* Los Angeles:
Trident Shop.

Kingsley, Ronald. 1989. "A Peer Connection Program: An In-School Resource for
High-Risk, Delinquency-Prone Students." *Juvenile and Family Court Journal*
40:20–29.

Klein, Dorie. 1973. "The Etiology of Female Crime: A Review of the Literature."
Reprinted from *Issues in Criminology* 8, No 2:3–30 as pp. 70–105 in *Women,
Crime, and Justice*, edited by S. K. Datesman and F. R. Scarpitti. New York:
Oxford University Press, 1980.

Klein, Malcolm W. 1971. *Street Gangs and Street Workers.* Englewood Cliffs, NJ:
Prentice-Hall.

Komarovsky, Mirra. 1962. *Blue-Collar Marriage.* New York: Vintage.

Konopka, Gisela. 1966. *The Adolescent Girl in Conflict.* Englewood Cliffs, NJ:
Prentice-Hall.

Kramer, Rita. 1988. *At a Tender Age: Violent Youth and Juvenile Justice.* New York:
Henry Holt.

Kruttschnitt, Candace, Linda Heath, and David A. Ward. 1986. "Family Violence,
Television Viewing Habits, and Other Adolescent Experiences Related to
Violent Criminal Behavior." *Criminology* 24:235–67.

Kufeldt, Kathleen, and Margaret Nimmo. 1987. "Youth on the Street: Abuse and
Neglect in the Eighties." *Child Abuse & Neglect* 11:531–43.

Kvaraceus, William C. 1966. *Anxious Youth: Dynamics of Delinquency.* Columbus,
OH: C. E. Merrill.

LaGrange, Randy L., and Helene Raskin White. 1985. "Age Differences in Delinquency: A Test of Theory." *Criminology* 23:19–45.

Laub, John H., and Michael Hindelang. 1981. *Juvenile Criminal Behavior in Urban,
Suburban and Rural Areas.* Washington, DC: Office of Juvenile Justice and
Delinquency Prevention.

Leukefeld, Carl G., and Frank M. Tims, eds. 1988. *Compulsory Treatment of Drug
Abuse: Research and Clinical Practice.* Rockville, MD: National Institute on
Drug Abuse.

Linden, Rick. 1978. "Myths of Middle Class Delinquency: A Test of the Generaliz-
ability of Social Control Theory." *Youth & Society* 9:407–32.

Lindquist, John H. 1988. *Misdemeanor Crime: Trivial Criminal Pursuit.* Newbury
Park, CA: Sage.

Lingeman, Richard R. 1974. *Drugs from A to Z*, rev. ed. New York: McGraw-Hill.

Lipkin, Richard. 1991. "Kentucky's Other Grass." *Insight*, July 1:12–19.

Liska, Allen E., and Mark D. Reed. 1985. "Ties to Conventional Institutions and Delinquency: Estimating Reciprocal Effects." *American Sociological Review* 50:547–60.

Lyerly, Robert Richard, and James K. Skipper, Jr. 1981. "Differential Rates of Rural-Urban Delinquency: A Social Control Approach." *Criminology* 19:385–99.

MacKenzie, Doris Layton, and Claire C. Souryal. 1991. "Boot Camp Survey." *Corrections Today*, October: 90–96.

Mandel, Jerry, and Harvey W. Feldman. 1986. "The Social History of Teenage Drug Use." Pp. 19–42 in *Teen Drug Use*, edited by G. Beschner and A. S. Friedman. Lexington, MA: Lexington Books.

Mann, Coramae Richey. 1984. *Female Crime and Delinquency*. University, AL: University of Alabama Press.

Massey, James L., and Marvin D. Krohn. 1986. "A Longitudinal Examination of an Integrated Social Process Model of Deviant Behavior." *Social Forces* 65: 106–34.

Matsueda, Ross L. 1982. "Testing Control Theory and Differential Association: A Causal Modeling Approach." *American Sociological Review* 47:489–504.

Matsueda, Ross L., and Karen Heimer. 1987. "Race, Family Structure, and Delinquency: A Test of Differential Association and Social Control Theories." *American Sociological Review* 52:826–40.

Matza, David. 1964. *Delinquency and Drift*. New York: Wiley.

McBride, Duane C. 1981. "Drugs and Violence." Pp. 105–23 in *The Drugs-Crime Connection*, edited by J. A. Inciardi. Beverly Hills, CA: Sage.

McBride, Duane C., and Clyde B. McCoy. 1981. "Crime and Drug-Using Behavior: An Areal Analysis." *Criminology* 19:281–302.

McBride, Duane C., and Clyde B. McCoy. 1982. "Crime and Drugs: The Issues and Literature." *Journal of Drug Issues* 12:137–52.

McCarthy, Belinda R., and J. David Hirschel. 1984. "Race, Sex and Drug Abuse in the 'New' South." *Journal of Drug Issues* 14:579–92.

McCoy, Clyde B., Duane C. McBride, Brian R. Russe, J. Bryan Page, and Richard R. Clayton. 1979. "Youth Opiate Use." Pp. 353–75 in *Youth Drug Abuse: Problems, Issues, and Treatment*, edited by G. M. Beschner and A. S. Friedman. Lexington, MA: Lexington Books.

McCoy, H. Virginia, Edward J. Trapido, James A. Inciardi, Dale D. Chitwood, and Duane C. McBride. 1989. "Sexual Activities of IV Drug Users with Multiple Sex Partners." Fifth International Conference on AIDS, Montreal, June 4–9.

McGlothlin, William H., M. Douglas Anglin, and Bruce D. Wilson. 1978. "Narcotic Addiction and Crime." *Criminology* 16(3):293–315.

Merton, Robert K. 1938. "Social Structure and Anomie." *American Sociological Review* 3:672–82.

Mieczkowski, Thomas. 1986. "Geeking Up and Throwing Down: Heroin Street Life in Detroit." *Criminology* 24:645–66.

Mikuriya, Tod H., and Michael R. Aldrich. 1988. "Cannabis 1988: Old Drug, New Dangers—The Potency Question." *Journal of Psychoactive Drugs* 20:47–55.

Miller, Judith Droitcour. 1981. "Epidemiology of Drug Use among Adolescents." Pp. 25–38 in *Drug Abuse and the American Adolescent*, edited by D. J.

Lettieri and J. P. Ludford. Rockville, MD: National Institute on Drug Abuse.

Miller, Walter B. 1958. "Lower Class Culture as a Generating Milieu of Gang Delinquency." *Journal of Social Issues* 14(3):5–19.

Miller, Walter B. 1975. *Violence by Youth Gangs and Youth Groups as a Crime Problem in Major American Cities*. Washington, DC: U.S. Dept. of Justice, National Institute for Juvenile Justice and Delinquency Prevention.

Moore, Joan W. 1978. *Home Boys: Gangs, Drugs, and Prison in the Barrios of Los Angeles*. Philadelphia: Temple University Press.

Morningstar, Patricia J., and Dale D. Chitwood. 1987. "How Women and Men Get Cocaine: Sex-Role Stereotypes and Acquisition Patterns." *Journal of Psychoactive Drugs* 19:135–42.

National Academy of Sciences. 1986. *Mobilizing against AIDS: The Unfinished Story of a Virus*. Cambridge, MA: Harvard University Press.

National Center for Health Statistics. 1991. "Premarital Sexual Experience among Adolescent Women—United States, 1970–1988." *Morbidity and Mortality Weekly Report* 39(January 4):929–32.

National Commission on Marihuana and Drug Abuse. 1973. *Drug Use in America: Problem in Perspective. Second Report of the National Commission on Marihuana and Drug Abuse*. Washington, DC: U.S. Government Printing Office.

National Institute on Drug Abuse. 1990. *Annual Data, 1989: Data from the Drug Abuse Warning Network (DAWN)*. Rockville, MD: National Institute on Drug Abuse.

Nelson, Jack E., Helen Wallenstein Pearson, Mollie Sayers, and Thomas J. Glynn. 1982. *Guide to Drug Abuse Research Terminology*. Rockville, MD: National Institute on Drug Abuse.

Newcomb, Michael D., and Peter M. Bentler. 1988. *Consequences of Adolescent Drug Use: Impact on the Lives of Young Adults*. Newbury Park, CA: Sage.

Nurco, David N. 1979. "Etiological Aspects of Drug Abuse." Pp. 315–24 in *Handbook on Drug Abuse*, edited by R. L. DuPont, A. Goldstein, J. A. O'Donnell, and B. Brown. Rockville, MD: National Institute on Drug Abuse.

Nurco, David N., Timothy W. Kinlock, and Thomas E. Hanlon. 1990. "The Drugs-Crime Connection." Pp. 71–90 in *Handbook of Drug Control in the United States*, edited by J. A. Inciardi. Westport, CT: Greenwood Press.

Nye, F. Ivan. 1958. *Family Relationships and Delinquent Behavior*. New York: Wiley.

Nye, F. Ivan. 1980. "A Theoretical Perspective on Running Away." *Journal of Family Issues* 1:274–99.

Nye, F. Ivan, and Craig Edelbrock. 1980. "Introduction: Some Social Characteristics of Runaways." *Journal of Family Issues* 1:147–50.

O'Donnell, John A., Harwin L. Voss, Richard R. Clayton, Gerald T. Slatin, and Robin G. W. Room. 1976. *Young Men and Drugs—A Nationwide Survey*. Rockville, MD: National Institute on Drug Abuse.

Office of National Drug Control Policy. 1990. *Leading Drug Indicators: ONDCP White Paper*. Washington, DC: Office of National Drug Control Policy.

Osgood, D. Wayne, Lloyd D. Johnston, Patrick M. O'Malley, and Jerald G. Bachman. 1988. "The Generality of Deviance in Late Adolescence and Early Adulthood." *American Sociological Review* 53:81–93.

Osgood, D. Wayne, Patrick M. O'Malley, Jerald G. Bachman, and Lloyd D. Johnston. 1989. "Time Trends and Age Trends in Arrests and Self-Reported Illegal Behavior." *Criminology* 27:389–417.

Page, J. Bryan. 1980. "The Children of Exile: Relationships between the Accultura-tion Process and Drug Use among Cuban Youth." *Youth & Society* 11: 431–47.

Petersilia, Joan, Peter W. Greenwood, and Marvin Lavin. 1978. *Criminal Careers of Habitual Felons*. Washington, DC: National Institute of Law Enforcement and Criminal Justice.

Platt, Jerome J. 1986. *Heroin Addiction: Theory, Research, and Treatment*, 2nd ed. Malabar, FL: Robert E. Krieger.

Platt, Jerome J., Charles D. Kaplan, and Patricia J. McKim, eds. 1990. *The Effective-ness of Drug Abuse Treatment*. Malabar, FL: Robert E. Krieger.

Pope, Carl E., and R. L. McNeely. 1981. "Race, Crime, and Criminal Justice: An Overview." Pp. 9–27 in *Race, Crime, and Criminal Justice*, edited by R. L. McNeely and C. E. Pope. Beverly Hills, CA: Sage.

Pope, Lisa. 1989. "The Toll at Bridge House: Juvenile Justice in a Jam." [Wilmington, DE] *Sunday News Journal*, Nov. 19:A1, 19

Preble, Edward, and John J. Casey, Jr. 1969. "Taking Care of Business: The Heroin User's Life on the Street." *International Journal of the Addictions* 4:1–24.

Rankin, Joseph H. 1983. "The Family Context of Delinquency." *Social Problems* 30:466–79.

Reiss, Albert J., Jr. 1988. "Co-offending and Criminal Careers." Pp. 117–70 in *Crime and Justice*, Vol. 10, edited by M. Tonry and N. Morris. Chicago: Univer-sity of Chicago Press.

Reiss, Albert J., Jr., and A. Lewis Rhodes. 1964. "An Empirical Test of Differential Association Theory." *Journal of Research in Crime and Delinquency* 1:5–18.

Reiss, Albert J., Jr., and Michael Tonry, eds. 1986. *Communities and Crime*. Chicago: University of Chicago Press.

Remafedi, G. 1987. "Homosexual Youth: A Challenge to Contemporary Society." *Journal of the American Medical Association* 258:222–25.

Research Triangle Institute, eds. 1976. *Drug Use and Crime: Report of the Panel on Drug Use and Criminal Behavior*. Springfield, VA: National Technical Infor-mation Service.

Robins, Lee N. 1966. *Deviant Children Grown Up*. Baltimore: Williams and Wilkins.

Rosen, Lawrence. 1985. "Family and Delinquency: Structure or Function?" *Crimi-nology* 23:553–73.

Rosen, Lawrence, and Kathleen Neilson. 1982. "Broken Homes and Delinquency." Pp. 126–35 in *Contemporary Criminology*, edited by L. Savitz and N. Johnston. New York: Wiley.

Rosenbaum, Marsha. 1981. *Women on Heroin*. New Brunswick, NJ: Rutgers Univer-sity Press.

Rutter, Michael, and Henri Giller. 1984. *Juvenile Delinquency: Trends and Perspectives*. New York: Guilford.

Sampson, Robert J. 1986. "Crime in Cities: The Effects of Formal and Informal Social Control." Pp. 271–311 in *Communities and Crime*, edited by A. J. Reiss, Jr., and M. Tonry. Chicago: University of Chicago Press.

Schafer, Walter E., and Kenneth Polk. 1967. "Delinquency and the Schools." Pp. 222–77 in *Task Force Report: Juvenile Delinquency and Youth Crime. Task Force on Juvenile Delinquency, President's Commission on Law Enforcement and Administration of Justice*. Washington, DC: U.S. Government Printing Office.

Schuster, Richard L. 1981. "Black and White Violent Delinquents: A Longitudinal Cohort Study." Pp. 109–25 in *Race, Crime, and Criminal Justice*, edited by R. L. McNeely and C. E. Pope. Beverly Hills, CA: Sage.

Schwartz, Ira M. 1989. *(In)Justice for Juveniles—Rethinking the Best Interests of the Child*. Lexington, MA.: D. C. Heath.

Schwartz, R. H., P. Gruenwald, and M. Klitzner. 1988. "Effects on Short-Term Memory in Cannabis-Dependent Adolescents." *American Journal of Diseases of Children* 142:404.

Selik, R. M., K. G. Castro, and M. Pappaioanou. 1988. "Distribution of AIDS Cases, by Racial/Ethnic Group and Exposure Category, United States, June 1, 1981–July 4, 1988." *Morbidity and Mortality Weekly Report* 37:1–10.

Sellin, Thorsten, and Marvin E. Wolfgang. 1964. *The Measurement of Delinquency*. New York: Wiley.

Shafer, Mary-Ann. 1988. "High Risk Behavior during Adolescence." Pp. 329–34 in *AIDS in Children, Adolescents, and Heterosexual Adults*, edited by R. F. Schinaze and A. J. Nahmias. New York: Elsevier.

Shapiro, Don. 1985. "Many Doorways: A Comprehensive Approach to Intervention and Treatment of Youthful Drug Users." Pp. 164–77 in *Treatment Services for Adolescent Substance Abusers*, edited by A. S. Friedman and G. M. Beschner. Rockville, MD: National Institute on Drug Abuse.

Shaw, Clifford R., and Henry D. McKay. 1942. *Juvenile Delinquency and Urban Areas*. Chicago: University of Chicago Press.

Shoemaker, Donald J. 1984. *Theories of Delinquency*. New York: Oxford University Press.

Shoemaker, Donald J. 1988. "The Duality of Juvenile Justice in the United States: History, Trends, and Prospects." *Sociological Spectrum* 8:1–17.

Short, James F., Jr., and F. Ivan Nye. 1958. "Extent of Unrecorded Juvenile Delinquency: Tentative Conclusions." *Journal of Criminal Law and Criminology* 49:296–302.

Short, James F., Jr., and Fred L. Strodtbeck. 1965. *Group Process and Gang Delinquency*. Chicago: University of Chicago Press.

Sidel, Ruth. 1986. *Women and Children Last*. New York: Viking Penguin.

Silbert, Mimi H., and Ayala M. Pines. 1982. "Entrance into Prostitution." *Youth and Society* 13:471–500.

Simcha-Fagan, Ora, and Joseph E. Schwartz. 1986. "Neighborhood and Delinquency: An Assessment of Contextual Effects." *Criminology* 24:667–703.

Single, Eric, and Denise B. Kandel. 1978. "The Role of Buying and Selling in Illicit Drug Use." Pp. 118–28 in *Drugs, Crime, and Politics*, edited by A. Trebach. New York: Praeger.

Smart, Carol. 1976. *Women, Crime and Criminology: A Feminist Critique*. London: Routledge & Kegan Paul.

Smith, David E. 1986. "Cocaine-Alcohol Abuse: Epidemiological, Diagnostic and Treatment Considerations." *Journal of Psychoactive Drugs* 18:117–29.

Snyder, F., and M. Myers. 1989. "Risk-Taking Behaviors of Intravenous Drug Users." Fifth International Conference on AIDS, Montreal, June 4–9.

Sorrells, James M., Jr. 1977. "Kids Who Kill." *Crime & Delinquency* 23:312–20.

Sorrells, James M., Jr. 1980. "What Can Be Done about Juvenile Homicide?" *Crime and Delinquency* 26:152–61.

Stark, Rodney. 1987. "Deviant Places: A Theory of the Ecology of Crime." *Criminology* 25:893–909.

Steinhart, David. 1988. "California Public Opinion Poll: Public Attitudes on Youth Crime." National Council on Crime and Delinquency: NCCD Focus, December.

Stephens, Richard. 1972. "The Truthfulness of Addict Respondents in Research Projects." *International Journal of the Addictions* 7:549–58.

Stephens, Richard C. 1985. "The Sociocultural View of Heroin Use: Toward a Role-Theoretic Model." *Journal of Drug Issues* 15:433–46.

Stephens, Richard C. 1987. *Mind-Altering Drugs: Use, Abuse, and Treatment*. Newbury Park, CA: Sage.

Stokes, William M., and Jeffrey M. Silbert. 1990. "The Juvenile Delinquency and Gang Prevention 'Plan' for the Eleventh Judicial Circuit." Dade-Miami Criminal Justice Council, unpublished.

Strasburg, Paul A. 1978. *Violent Delinquents*. New York: Monarch.

Strasburg, Paul A. 1984. "Recent National Trends in Serious Juvenile Crime." Pp. 5–30 in *Violent Juvenile Offenders: An Anthology*, edited by R. A. Mathias, P. DeMuro, and R. S. Allinson. San Francisco: National Council on Crime and Delinquency.

Sutherland, Edwin H. 1939. *Principles of Criminology*, 3rd ed. Philadelphia: Lippincott.

Sutter, Alan G. 1966. "The World of the Righteous Dope Fiend." *Issues in Criminology* 2:177–222.

Sutter, Alan G. 1969. "Worlds of Drug Use on the Street Scene." Pp. 802–29 in *Delinquency, Crime, and Social Process*, edited by D. R. Cressey and D. A. Ward. New York: Harper & Row.

Suttles, Gerald D. 1968. *The Social Order of the Slum: Ethnicity and Territory in the Inner City*. Chicago: University of Chicago Press.

Thomas, W. I. 1923. *The Unadjusted Girl*. New York: Harper & Row.

Thompson, Elaine Adams, Kathleen Smith-DiJulio, and Tom Matthews. 1982. "Social Control Theory: Evaluating a Model for the Study of Adolescent Alcohol and Drug Use." *Youth and Society* 13:303–26.

Thornberry, Terence P. 1987. "Toward an Interactional Theory of Delinquency." *Criminology* 25:863–87.

Thornberry, Terence P., and Margaret Farnworth. 1982. "Social Correlates of Criminal Involvement: Further Evidence on the Relationship between Social Status and Criminal Behavior." *American Sociological Review* 47:505–18.

Thornberry, Terence P., Melanie Moore, and R. L. Christenson. 1985. "The Effect of Dropping Out of High School on Subsequent Criminal Behavior." *Criminology* 23:3–18.

Thrasher, Frederick M. 1927. *The Gang: A Study of 1,313 Gangs in Chicago*, 2nd rev. ed. Chicago: University of Chicago Press.

Turner, Charles F., Heather G. Miller, and Lincoln E. Moses, eds. 1989. *AIDS: Sexual Behavior and Intravenous Drug Use*. Washington, DC: National Academy Press.

U.S. Bureau of the Census. 1989. *The Black Population in the United States: March 1988*. Washington, DC: Current Population Reports, Series P-20, No. 442.

U.S. Department of Justice. 1991a. *Prisoners in 1990*. Washington, DC: Bureau of Justice Statistics Bulletin.

U.S. Department of Justice. 1991b. *Jail Inmates, 1990.* Washington, DC: Bureau of Justice Statistics Bulletin.

U.S. Department of Justice. 1991c. *Drug Use Forecasting—1990.* Washington, DC: National Institute of Justice.

University of Michigan. 1991. News and Information Services Release. January 24.

Van Voorhis, Patricia, Francis T. Cullen, Richard A. Mathers, and Connie Chenoweth Garner. 1988. "The Impact of Family Structure and Quality on Delinquency: A Comparative Assessment of Structural and Functional Factors." *Criminology* 26:235–62.

Waldorf, Dan. 1973. *Careers in Dope.* Englewood Cliffs, NJ: Prentice-Hall.

Washton, Arnold M. 1987. "Cocaine: Drug Epidemic of the '80's." Pp. 45–63 in *The Cocaine Crisis,* edited by D. F. Allen. New York: Plenum.

Watters, John K., Craig Reinarman, and Jeffrey Fagan. 1985. "Causality, Context, and Contingency: Relationships between Drug Abuse and Delinquency." *Contemporary Drug Problems* 12:351–73.

Weisberg, D. Kelly. 1985. *Children of the Night: A Study of Adolescent Prostitution.* Lexington, MA: Lexington Books.

Weiss, Roger D., and Steven M. Mirin. 1987. *Cocaine.* Washington, DC: American Psychiatric Press.

Weissman, James C. 1978. "Understanding the Drugs and Crime Connection: A Systematic Examination of Drugs and Crime Relationships." *Journal of Psychedelic Drugs* 10:171–92.

Weithorn, Lois A. 1988. "Mental Hospitalization of Troublesome Youth: An Analysis of Skyrocketing Admission Rates." *Stanford Law Review* 40(3):773–838.

Weitzel, Susan L., and William R. Blount. 1982. "Incarcerated Female Felons and Substance Abuse." *Journal of Drug Issues* 12:259–73.

Wells, L. Edward, and Joseph H. Rankin. 1986. "The Broken Homes Model of Delinquency: Analytic Issues." *Journal of Research in Crime and Delinquency* 23:68–93.

White, Helene Raskin. 1990. "The Drug Use-Delinquency Connection in Adolescence." Pp. 215–56 in *Drugs, Crime and the Criminal Justice System,* edited by R. Weisheit. Cincinnati: Anderson.

White, Helene Raskin, and Erich W. LaBouvie. 1989. "Towards the Assessment of Adolescent Problem Drinking." *Journal of Studies on Alcohol* 50:30–37.

White, Helene Raskin, Robert J. Pandina, and Randy L. LaGrange. 1987. "Longitudinal Predictors of Serious Substance Use and Delinquency." *Criminology* 25:715–40.

Whyte, William Foote. 1943. *Street Corner Society: The Social Structure of an Italian Slum.* Chicago: University of Chicago Press.

Wiatrowski, Michael D., David B. Griswold, and Mary K. Roberts. 1981. "Social Control Theory and Delinquency." *American Sociological Review* 46:525–41.

Williams, Terry M. 1989. *The Cocaine Kids: The Inside Story of a Teenage Drug Ring.* Reading, MA: Addison-Wesley.

Williams, Terry M., and William Kornblum. 1985. *Growing Up Poor.* Lexington, MA: Lexington Books.

Wilson, William Julius. 1987. *The Truly Disadvantaged: The Inner City, the Underclass, and Public Policy.* Chicago: University of Chicago Press.

Wish, Eric D. 1987. "Drug Use Forecasting: New York 1984 to 1986." National Institute of Justice, Research in Action, February.

Wolfgang, Marvin E., Robert M. Figlio, and Thorsten Sellin. 1972. *Delinquency in a Birth Cohort*. Chicago: University of Chicago Press.

Wolfgang, Marvin E., Terence P. Thornberry, and Robert M. Figlio. 1987. *From Boy to Man, From Delinquency to Crime*. Chicago: University of Chicago Press.

Wu, Tzu-Chin, Donald P. Tashkin, Behnam Djahed, and Jed E. Rose. 1988. "Pulmonary Hazards of Smoking Marijuana as Compared with Tobacco." *New England Journal of Medicine* 318(Feb. 11):347–51.

Yablonsky, Lewis. 1989. *The Therapeutic Community: A Successful Approach for Treating Substance Abusers*. New York: Gardner Press.

Zimring, Franklin E. 1977. "The Serious Juvenile Offender: Notes on an Unknown Quantity." Pp.15–31 in *The Serious Juvenile Offender, Proceedings of a National Symposium*. Washington, DC: Office of Juvenile Justice and Delinquency Prevention.

Zinberg, Norman E. 1984. *Drug, Set, and Setting: The Basis for Controlled Intoxicant Use*. New Haven, CT: Yale University Press.

# AUTHOR INDEX

# SUBJECT INDEX

Abuse (*see* Child abuse and neglect; Youth drug abuse)
Academic performance, 37
Accomplice crimes, 153–58
Addiction, 38–41, 197, 201
Age of offender:
  crime histories and, 8
  current criminality and, 92
  current drug use and, 81
  drug histories and, 75, 77–78
AIDS, 81
  drugs and, 180–89
  HIV and, 181–83
  intravenous drug use and, 181
  risk of, 198
Alcohol use, 41, 75
  adult attitude toward, 134–36
  family disadvantage and, 136
Amenability hearings, 192
Amphetamine use, 41, 75
Anomie, 14
Arguments:
  family, 131–34
  friends and, 165–67
Assault, 54–55
Attitudes toward school, 138–39

Bad paper offenses, 154–55
Balks, interview, 67
Behaviorism, 19
Behaviors in school, 140–43
Behavior uniformity, friends and, 160–63
Birth cohort studies, 20–21, 22, 23, 25, 42
Boot-camp correctional programs, 194

California Youth Authority, 7
Capacitation, 196

Chicago school, 11–13, 14, 19, 151
Child abuse and neglect, 9
Child welfare, crisis in, 8–10
Chipping, 40
Chronic serious delinquents, 5, 21, 23, 37
Cocaine potency, 41
Cocaine sales, 41
Cocaine use, 7, 29, 30, 31, 40, 41, 42, 43, 74, 75–77, 79, 161
  cost of, 42–43
Coca paste, 74
Coerced drug-abuse treatment, 196
Columbus arrest study, 2, 24, 62
Common-cause deviance syndrome theory, 32–34, 37
Compulsory treatment strategy, 196–98
Confidentiality, 64, 65
Conformity, 19
Control theory, 19, 34, 118, 137, 138, 148, 152, 157, 201
  variables in, 124–25
Conventional life, lack of ties to, 118–125
Corner boys, 14
Correlation, 69–70, 201
County-based intervention strategies, 190–92
Crack-business involvement, 98–104
Crack potency, 41
Crack sales, 41, 100–2, 110–12
Crack use, 1, 7, 40, 41, 42–43, 75–77, 79, 97–116, 178
  AIDS and, 182
  sex exchange and, 185–89
Crime (*see also* Youth crime)
  drugs and, 28–49, 173–77
  paying for drugs with, 41–43